Endpapers:
Obaharok led them like a giant.
He cut in and out of the lines, yelling,
running here and there,
seeming to be in as many as four places at once.
It was a wonder the man could cover
so much ground so quickly.

Headlines in newspapers around the world told the story of Wyn Sargent's banishment from New Guinea. Scandalous lies were printed. She was accused of marrying a cannibal chief for the purpose of studying primitive sexual practices.

In truth, the American photo-journalist had incensed Indonesian officials by her outspoken views and by gathering evidence—including photographs—of their brutality toward the Dani tribesmen.

People of the Valley is the true story of Wyn Sargent's sojourn in the Baliem Valley—how she set off with her Indonesian interpreter-companion Sjam to photograph, study, and write about the culture and character of the Dani.

As she moved from village to village, the striking character of these remarkable people began to emerge. At first, she was simply intrigued with these almost-naked people who smeared their bodies and hair with pig fat to make themselves look beautiful; whose men and women lived separately in small bamboo-and-grass huts; whose ancestors' ghosts (who inhabited sacred stones and caves) were integrated into their daily lives; who cut off their fingers and ears to mourn the dead. War was the "recreation" and they lived in constant fear of walking through another chieftain's jurisdiction.

But as Wyn Sargent administered to their needs, she began to develop a special affection for these remote tribesmen. She also discovered that the Indonesian police (who were

(continued on back flap)

PEOPLE OF THE VALLEY

Random House   New York

PEOPLE
OF THE
VALLEY

Wyn Sargent

Photographs by the author.

Library of Congress Cataloging in Publication Data
Sargent, Wyn.
People of the valley.
1. Dani (New Guinea people) I. Title.
DU744.S27   919.5'1   74-9069
ISBN 0-394-49386-9

Manufactured in the United States of America
Design by Lilly Kolker
9 8 7 6 5 4 3 2
First Edition

This book is written for Kelion and Kolo,
for Walek and Obaharok,
and for all the people who followed them.
The people call themselves the Dani,
a people whom I love
and was forced to leave.

PREFACE

I guess one of the most painful experiences in my life has been the writing of this book. I loved the Dani people I was writing about and I'd been forced to leave them.

I would never have written parts of this book if I had not had the corroboration of my Indonesian interpreter, Sjamsuarni Sjam. Sjam, too, has learned about sorrow and suffering and the fear of political imprisonment by her own government. During the months of writing this piece, Sjam fled from city to city in an effort to hide from Indonesian Intelligence. They wanted to question her concerning our discoveries in the Baliem Valley. It must have been awful for her.

There were times during these last months when I wished for more hours in the day and the physical stamina to go with them. Often I was overwhelmed with fatigue at the end of the day, but still left with the urgency to write and finish the manuscript at the moment.

It was interesting to me that many events taking place in the Baliem Valley nearly canceled others. In the writing of them I had to work hard to maintain balance and separate things. The people, for example, were real people with great minds and imaginations, and their boundaries became limitless. Their personalities tried to seep, sometimes into chapters where they should not have been.

I have written the real picture of how it was when I was there, the things I saw and thought and learned. I have not put down anything I did not see or do.

The memory of the Valley that remains for me is an obsessing one. It is early morning. I remember walking away from the

Valley like a stiff mechanical person, the blood pounding in my temples. There was a sick, salty taste in my mouth and a hard knot in my stomach. I remember hearing the crying and screaming that followed me.

I thought that, perhaps, with the writing of this book my personal sorrow might slip away and somehow lay the ghost.

But it hasn't.

I have let the story unfold as it happened.

CONTENTS

PEOPLE OF THE VALLEY

Two Warriors DRAWINGS BY KELION

CHAPTER ONE

Kelion

(1)

The Indonesian President was stocking-footed. I supposed his feet hurt. He had spent the entire morning walking around Disneyland.

"You really should see West Irian," said President Suharto, rubbing his feet together. "The people are very primitive there and they need help, badly."

It was May 31, 1970. My son, Jmy, and I were in the presidential suite of the Hotel Disneyland in Anaheim, California. We were there to discuss, with the visiting Suhartos, the progress of the Sargent-Dyak Fund, Inc., a corporation of which I was president.

While I was writing about the arts, traditions and customs of the primitive Dyak headhunters in Central Borneo, Indonesia, in 1968, I had been appalled by the poverty, disease and shocking mortality rate existing among the natives. In an effort to alleviate their sufferings, I established the Sargent-Dyak Fund, Inc., in 1969 for the purpose of providing the Dyaks with medicine, agricultural supplies, livestock and educational materials. Madame Suharto had agreed to be the Honorary Recipient of the endeavor. Three years later the Sargent-Dyak Fund, Inc., had successfully been placed on location in Central Borneo and was administrated by the Indonesian government, and I had finished writing the final pages of the Dyak headhunter manuscript.

Now, in 1972, my thoughts turned back to President Suharto's suggestion that West Irian in New Guinea was a potential area for another cultural study. But I began to feel uneasy about making another trip into the jungle. I felt that *something* would go wrong this time. That uneasiness reached a new height when I learned that West Irian was a cannibal kingdom.

I talked it over with some of my friends. They advised me to "play my hunches," forget the trip and stay home. As the days passed, however, and nothing happened, I began to feel that my fears were foolish and unfounded. I set my heels against worry and decided to go.

I wrote the Indonesian consulate in San Francisco requesting a visa for three months, the longest time allowed before renewal was necessary. I enclosed a check to cover the visa fee.

Ten days later the visa arrived. It was identical in nature to the one issued me in 1968 to research the headhunters in Borneo. However, the consulate had written on the visa; "Valid fifteen days." An accompanying letter stated, moreover, that special police permission would be required to enter the West Irian territory. That permission could be obtained only in Jakarta.

Now all I needed was an interpreter. I remembered Sjamsuarni Sjam, my good friend in Indonesia. She was the interpreter who had steered me around Borneo on and off for three years.

Sjam is ten years younger than I am. By her nature she's a woman of action. That action comes in packages of variety. Sjam is boisterous, compassionate, shy, very dear, always intelligent, sometimes complicated, and once in a while she's an entertaining screwball who can contribute all kinds of gaiety to a usually dull crowd.

I knew I wouldn't have to sandbag Sjam into going to West Irian. If she could arrange her tourism business to be taken care of, she would go. Even if she couldn't, it was likely she'd toss everything out the window and go anyhow.

I put in a long-distance call to Jakarta, reached Sjam, and told her what I was up to. The idea of living with cannibals shocked her a little, but she said she'd go. She said it in nearly a manner of wonder at herself.

I scheduled departure for October 1, 1972, just one month away. Meanwhile, both of us did what research we could. There wasn't much material available. I read the missionary classic, *Cannibal Valley*, written by Russell Hitt, and *Gardens of War*, by Robert Gardner and Karl Heider. The titles of these books suggested that I'd do well to stay home. I also studied the accounts written by a few naturalists in old *National Geographic Magazines*.

Sjam mailed me a map of West Irian. There were little dotted lines drifting around over the paper which made no sense whatsoever. There were large unmapped sections with no names and not even dots, and those areas looked far from welcoming anyone to enter them.

Sjam's research turned up some interesting information. She wrote to say that she'd found an air service from Jakarta to the capital city of West Irian, Jayapura. From there, small missionary planes and the domestic airline, Merpati, were available to drop down into the several "cities" in the country. Wamena was listed among those cities. It was located at the southern end of something called the Grand Baliem Valley. From Wamena, travel would be done entirely by foot through the jungleland.

A jungle was no stranger to us. The years of tramping around Borneo together had provided Sjam and me with many experiences in jungle living. And we'd learned a few sharp lessons about surviving in such a place. We knew exactly what clothes we needed to take and what supplies we'd find most useful.

The purpose of our little expedition was to photograph and record a culture and write an account about the people called the Dani in the Baliem Valley. Our personal belongings had to be minimal because we wanted to be able to move around easily.

I pulled the three small aluminum suitcases from their storage place in the closet. They were the same cases I had used in Borneo. There was a small dent in one of them. They were still filled with sponge rubber, the kind that is used for packing camera equipment against breakage.

The photographic equipment went into the cases first. Three cameras, an electronic flash unit, a power pack, filters and an abundance of film. Next came the recorders and tapes, batteries, books, pens, pencils and paper.

I packed medicine and medical supplies in the third case: quinine, tetracycline, penicillin, sulfa powders, medicine for diarrhea, dysentery, worms and conjunctivitis, and medicine for jungle fungus and other skin diseases. I put in more than Sjam and I would require; there would always be a need for medical dispensation.

I stuffed a few clothes into my sleeping bag and backpack. Two pairs of Levi's, two shirts, two pairs of socks, underclothing, a bandanna handkerchief and jungle boots.

I would wear my Borneo safari hat, the one that had been given to me by an old Dyak man years ago. He'd wanted to offer me food at the time but he didn't have any. I remember he apologized when he gave me his hat.

I said a difficult good-bye to my son, Jmy, and took a long, last look at him standing there at the Los Angeles International Airport.

And then I turned and boarded the airplane to begin the strangest adventure of my life.

(2)

It was two years since I had seen Sjam. She hadn't changed a bit. We didn't need to get used to each other again. We just picked up where we had left off.

Sjam was wearing an orange-and-yellow cotton dress with the sleeves rolled up to the elbows. A tall red fur hat teetered around on the top of her head.

"Hi! Get a job with a circus?"

"The cannibals will love it," she said. "I hear they've got a thing for *red*. When customs gets through banging the daylights out of your camera cases, we'll go to Immigration and get your visa extended. Then we've got to drop by the police station and get permission to enter West Irian."

Sjam was breathing through her mouth. She was excited. So was I.

Immigration apologized for their San Francisco office and validated my visa for three months, thus giving me permission to stay in Indonesia until January 4, 1973. They recalled my association with the Sargent-Dyak Fund, Inc., and said they were glad to have me in their country again.

On the way to the police department, Sjam told me Indonesia was getting ready for another presidential election. The preparations had already caused some anxiety within the country. She wanted to be sure everyone clearly understood that I wasn't in Indonesia for political reasons and that my purpose in West Irian was solely to photograph and study the native people for a proposed book.

When we arrived we found the police extremely selective in the people they allowed to roam through the West Irian territory. The Indonesians are automatically afraid of foreigners and the motives of anyone wanting to go to Irian are thoroughly examined. If the attending officials had not remembered me from two years before, I doubt that I would have been given permission to enter West Irian for a period longer than a week. Still, I was asked to fill out the six "request forms," in triplicate.

(3)

Sjam and I buckled ourselves into the seats of a DC-9 and listened to the engines roar before takeoff.

Eight hours later we touched down on the airstrip at Biak, capital of Biak Island, West Irian. We peeked through the airplane window to study the people that made up the Southeast Asian crowd. Their smiles flashed whitely when they saw the plane. Its arrival gave them their only touch with the outside world.

The people were mostly Indonesians. The baggage men and janitors were Papuans, the native people of New Guinea. Their hair was black and kinky. They had flat-spread noses, full lips and the dark-brown eyes that reflected their Negroid ancestry. All of them showed well-developed muscles.

We grabbed the suitcases and other gear and walked half a block to the Biak Hotel to spend the night with the heat and the mosquitoes. The next morning we flew to Jayapura, capital of West Irian.

The flight time from Biak to Jayapura in a small two-engined DC-3 is about two hours if everything goes well. There were bucket seats in a row on one side of the old aircraft. The noise of the engines was ear-splitting but it indicated that the motors were running. The passengers comprised of Indonesian police and military personnel, and there was one white-skinned missionary, looking very much out of place in the dark-colored group.

The air was choppy and we were relieved when the old plane touched down on the runway and skidded to a burning stop in Jayapura.

(4)

New Guinea island, of which West Irian is one-half, is the second largest in the·world next to Greenland. The island sits in the ocean north of Australia like a giant sea gull and stretches 1,500 miles from tip to tail, covering an area of 299,310 square miles.

There was some spice trading during the period of the Shrivijava Kingdom (A.D. 700–1300), but not much. After the kingdom terminated, the Sultans of Ternate and Tidore in the Moluccas, moved in.

The European explorers also began to arrive in the sixteenth century.

The island was officially discovered by two Portuguese sailors, d'Abrue and Serrano, in 1511, but no claim was ever staked for the Portuguese empire. The sailors were simply not interested; searching for spices, they had come from the west, across the Indian Ocean, and apparently missed seeing what few spices the island produced.

When the Spanish explorer Inigo Ortiz de Retes sailed east across the Pacific in 1545 and arrived on the sandy shores of the island, the land looked promising to him. He hoisted the Spanish flag at a point east of the mouth of the Mamberamo River, located on the northern tip of the island, and gave the island its name, *Nova Guinea* (New Guinea). But in time Spain showed no more interest in absorbing the territory into her empire than the Portuguese had.

In 1606 the first Dutchman, William Jansz, appeared on the New Guinea coastline. A parade of foreign invaders followed him, but by the middle of the seventeenth century the Dutch sailors controlled a strong trade center on the island.

When the Germans and French began to appear on the eastern horizon, the Dutchmen, in 1828, proclaimed the western half of the island a possession of The Netherlands. The British raised their flag at Port Moresby in 1883, and the Dutch spread their field of influence to the Moluccas in 1901.

A human stream of exploring expeditions began to penetrate the interior of the land. One of the first was headed by Dr.

H. A. Lorentz in 1909. Seventeen years later a Dutch-American expedition, led by Dr. M. Stirling, successfully contacted the natives in the interior and gave them the name Dani.

In 1938 Richard Archbold discovered the whole Grand Baliem Valley. The Archbold expedition was sponsored by the American Museum of Natural History in New York for the purpose of gathering flora and fauna from the island. Archbold flew over the central highlands of New Guinea and saw the Valley lying approximately 5,000 feet above sea level. It was forty miles long and ten miles wide. And it contained a whole population of naked black people completely unknown to the outside world.

A few missionaries had come to the island before the Japanese occupied it during World War II, in 1942. The Japanese gained a strangle hold on the northern and western parts of West New Guinea and held them for two years, but the south coast and interior remained unpenetrated. In 1944 General Douglas MacArthur rammed his way into the capital city, Hollandia, and established a base at nearby Lake Sentani.

On May 13, 1945, when just about all the shooting had quieted down, a C-47 loaded with military personnel crashed in the Baliem Valley. The bodies of twenty-one Americans lay scattered over the land but three people survived the disaster: WAC Margaret Hastings, John McCollum and Kenneth Decker. A feat of great imagination, but a risky one, rescued these people. Paratroopers who were dropped into the area built a runway, and with the help of a glider plus American know-how, the survivors were brought out.

After World War II, Indonesia had her own private little war with The Netherlands. She declared her independence on August 17, 1945, and after four years of intermittent warfare the official transfer of the Dutch sovereignty to Indonesia took place two days after Christmas in 1949. But the territory of West New Guinea was not included because there were Negroes living there, and the area remained under Dutch control. The Dutch, in their continuing efforts to colonize West New Guinea, established a government post in 1956, in Wamena, a spot located deep in the interior of the southern part of the Baliem Valley.

Four years later Pierre Gaissea filmed the west coast of the island and the Harvard-Peabody Expedition explored the Baliem Valley in 1961.

President Suharto of Indonesia, at that time a general, believed the Dutch territory should be incorporated into Indonesia. He formed the Mandala Command on January 11, 1962, to "liberate" West New Guinea from Dutch rule.

The Dutch saw no reason to give up a land they believed to be theirs. Shots were fired over the territory between the two contenders; some people were killed and many were hurt.

On October 1, 1962, the United Nations stepped in to help settle the dispute. They administrated until May 1, 1963, when the territory was turned over to Indonesia with the condition that, prior to 1969, the people of West New Guinea would be able to express their wishes either to annex themselves to the Indonesian Republic or to be independent.

The first thing Indonesia did was to give the land a new name, an effort to show possession. They called it Irian Barat, or West Irian, but that was all they could do. The Papuans who lived in the land resisted every Indonesian effort to penetrate the area because they felt the Indonesians were there without license.

On April 9, 1969, Indonesia set up a government in Wamena, and three months later West Irian became a part of Indonesia through something called the "Act of Free Choice."

Indonesia did not employ the one-vote per one-man system in the Act of Free Choice election. They used their traditional *musjawarah* method, meaning consultations which lead to some kind of consensus. They announced the "unanimous desire" of the West Irian Papuan people to become part of Indonesia.

Then the Indonesians changed the name of the capital city, Hollandia, to Kota Bahru. When Sukarno became President, the Indonesians renamed the capital, in deference to their leader, Sukarnapura. But when Sukarno fell, the Indonesians endowed the town with a third name, Djayapura. Their current effort is to change the spelling of Djayapura to Jayapura and to rename Irian Barat, Irian Jaya.

Jayapura is a town of about 30,000 inhabitants, with an additional 90,000 people living in the surrounding area. Although the town was built by the Dutch, it is an Indonesian city today. It faces the sea and is surrounded by beautiful mountains, but the town itself is ugly, hot, dusty and dirty. There are a few new houses for the UN officials in charge of aid, and of course, there's the Hotel Negara, the government-operated hotel.

There are no roads or trails from Jayapura to Wamena. The high mountains and swamps between the two points are insurmountable barriers. The only means to reach the Baliem Valley is by air. The small missionary planes are costly. We decided to wait for the Indonesian domestic airline, Merpati, to fly us there. Merpati is without a timetable of any kind. When it is in operation, the departures depend entirely upon the weather and the mood of the pilot. And one is no good without the other.

Sjam and I busied ourselves around Jayapura the best we could. We charged through the streets like nervous horses, searching for the native Papuan people, hoping they would provide us with a hint of what was to come. But we were disappointed. We couldn't find any. Jayapura is filled with Indonesians, mostly those from Java. They seemed unhappy at their fate of being "stuck" in such a remote, miserable place, working at whatever the duties of their jobs. Few, if any, had even bothered to learn the local dialect.

One day we went shopping. We bought knives, shovels, more medicine, beads and shells to give to the natives, if we ever reached them.

The following day we called on the West Irian military commander, General Acub Zanail. Zanail heads up a program called Operation Koteka which is supposed to put clothes on the Dani and teach them to speak the Indonesian language. *Koteka* is an Indonesian word which refers to the penis-sheath covering worn by the men.

During the meeting General Zanail expressed his enthusiasm

about my writing and photographing the Dani in the Baliem Valley. He gave me a letter of recommendation to support the endeavor. I promised him a portfolio of pictures of the people he was supposed to be "civilizing."

Zanail's attitude toward the Dani was paternalistic. He referred to them as "children." He had, at one time, promised the world to put clothes on all the natives by the end of 1972 through his Operation Koteka. But now, since the year's end was fast approaching, he confessed that "clothes really aren't so important," and that he only "want to make the Dani happy." Zanail said that the Dani cut off their fingers for some reason or other, and he was certain these self-inflicted amputations made them an unhappy people.

After four long days of waiting, Merpati scheduled a departure for Wamena. Sjam and I arrived at Sentani Airport long before dawn and far ahead of any other passengers. We watched a man in gray overalls and brown straw hat place a long hook beneath the cockpit of a small aircraft and pull it out of its hangar. He parked it on the taxiway and brushed at the cockpit window with a blue rag. Something on the glass stuck and the man spit on his rag and tried again.

The pilots arrived wearing snappy-looking blue jackets. Beneath the jackets were white, unstarched shirts, open at the collar. Both of the men appeared to be nervous.

Someone placed a wooden crate below the single iron step that swung out like an arm from beneath the plane's door. Sjam and I boarded and inched forward to sit, one behind the other, on the left side of the plane. The right side was stacked nearly to the ceiling with boxes and crates. On top of everything perched a few dozen eggs in gray cartons, and five or six oranges in a plastic bag.

There were only three other passengers on the plane. A young couple sat directly behind Sjam and a military man behind them. We had never seen these people before, but flying in a plane with only five seats tends to make one feel very close to one's companions.

Sjam and the young woman struck up a conversation during the first few minutes before takeoff. It was an attempt to ease the nerves of flying in such a rickety old plane. The woman's name was Mrs. Sumitro. Her husband was an Indonesian government price-control agent stationed in Wamena. Mrs. Sumitro invited Sjam and me to stay at her house, provided we arrived there at all. The Sumitros turned out to be lovely people.

Something similar to bronchitis sneezed out of the single engine beneath the cowl. It kept coming until the small propeller spun around a few times and caught. A tremendous vibration throbbed through the aircraft and when we began to bounce up and down in our seats, we didn't have to look out of the tiny windows to know we were moving. The old plane jerked down the runway, got up speed and lifted, fell back, lifted again and we were airborne, at least for the time being.

We flew over Lake Sentani and into the center of clouds that hung in the sky like huge white cauliflowers. To fly through them was like plowing in cotton. The plane jumped around, protesting, rattling and creaking from the stress the turbulence in the clouds had placed on its wings.

When the clouds broke we looked through the holes and saw craggy, mountainous country below us. Between the mountains was a trackless jungle, one filled with tall trees and an occasional swamp here or there. It promised to be a deathtrap if our plane was forced to crash-land.

As we flew over the rough, forest-clad mountain terrain, the enormous shoulders of mountains pushed up through the clouds on both sides of our plane. Below us the jungle rivers serpentined through thickly wooded valleys and flung out their muddy coils in all directions, adding to the hostility of the wilderness.

Then we saw the Baliem River; we had been watching for it. It was big and wide, and looked exactly like a good jungle river should look. It snaked over the land with a mind of its own, meandering and wandering wherever it wanted to go. It was fed by little mountain streams. It emptied itself into the Arafura Sea on the southwest coast of the island.

On the right, the mountains had thrust their humps into the sky and were crowned with heavy popcorn clouds. On the left of the plane was another set of jagged escarpments, but their peaks were covered in mist.

After an hour of flying, we were beginning to feel the size and nature of the country. It was no wonder this land defied transportation by ordinary means.

And then, suddenly, the mountains ahead of us separated a little and we entered a long, narrow pass through the escarpment that encircles the Baliem Valley. We must have been flying at about 10,000 feet, but the snow-capped mountains stood higher than our plane. Below us, the terrain flattened out onto the floor of the green, fertile Baliem Valley. The land looked nearly gentle.

The Grand Baliem Valley covers an area of 400 square miles. In the northeast part stands a limestone cliff about 1,000 feet tall. Below that cliff, sweeping downward over the Valley floor, we saw the first signs of life for some time. The land was dotted with little round rooftops, sprouting like mushroom caps, and smoke was rising in lazy coils from some of the shacks.

The villages were shrouded in banana trees. Beyond them were beautiful gardens, imprisoned in a mosaic network of stone and wood walls. Some of the gardens swept up the hillsides in a succession of impressive terraces.

At least 50,000 Dani were estimated to live in the Valley, with an additional 50,000 somewhere in the outskirts. Sjam and I craned our necks to see if we could pick out just one person, but the plane spiraled downward toward the Wamena airstrip at such a rate that any standing figure zipped by unnoticed.

After the old plane landed and taxied to an asphalt ramp area, Sjam and I were the first people to disembark. We had a hunger to see everything our eyes could bracket. Neither of us were prepared for the sight that faced us.

The Dani.

Lots of them—men, women and children.

They were astounding and they were unbelievable. And they were august-looking and very beautiful. The men stood behind the barbed-wire fence enclosing the airfield. They were round-faced, black people. At first all of them looked alike because they were near to nakedness.

The men wore tubular gourds, *holims*, to assure their modesty. The yellow sticks somehow seemed to accentuate their nakedness. The *holims* came in every thinkable shape and size: long and short, straight and curly. They were held in place with a string looped around the testicles and another around the upper torso of their bodies.

Holims are grown in the village gardens, we learned later. Sometimes heavy stones are tied to the ends of the gourds to encourage them to elongate during their growth. A stone placed beneath a growing gourd will produce a bend or curl. The length and design indicates the social and economic status of its wearer. No man would be without a wardrobe of them, not even a *kepu* (poor man). Often a man deserving a two-foot-long *holim* is seen wearing a shorter gourd to accommodate the work in his garden. But he invariably changes it before going home to the village at night. The *holim*, the single piece of dress worn by the Dani men, serves many purposes: modesty; proof of bravery, wealth, manhood; and as an additional reward, it keeps the flies off a tender area.

The Dani men had covered their faces, chests, arms and shoulders with black soot and pig fat. They believe the grease makes them handsome; they also believe it keeps them healthy and protects them against the cold and the mosquitoes. Without this black grease-paint make-up, the Dani feel unhappy and nearly ugly.

Some of the men had stuffed their hair into fiber nets packed with dry grass to give their heads a balloon effect. Others had saturated their hair with pig fat and then pulled the long, kinky strands into springlike coils that dripped over the head from the crown; the whole affair resembled a small beehive. They were beautiful arrangements, and indicated the elaborate and time-consuming effort of the Dani men to be gorgeous.

A few of the men had painted a black stripe beneath their eyes. Nearly all of them wore ringbeards on their faces, but there were no mustaches. The Dani pluck out this unwanted hair with a pair of tweezers fashioned from a broken twig. The men regard the hair found in places other than the head and beard as untidy. Great pains are put into its removal from the arms, legs, buttocks and even the genital area.

What the men lacked in clothing they made up in accessories. There were wide necklaces (*walimos*) made from small snail shells (*nassa*) that had been sewn together, and *mikaks*, or large platelike shells (*Cymbium*) tied around their necks. Those without shell necklaces wore *yopos* around their necks —shredded string fibers rubbed with pig oil to give them a magic power to keep evil spirits away. A few men wore *tipats* —cut and dried pig testicles that hung over their chests in long black strips.

There were colored beads (*werrakkboak*) around the necks of others, beads that were left over from the Dutch era. And there were a few *murikakas*, necklaces made from thousands of spiderwebs squeezed into single strings and then soaked in pig fat to activate their magic.

Nearly every man wore *tekans*—wrist and upper-arm bands woven from pandanus fibers, some with pigtails hanging from them (*wamare*). The bands were useful as well as decorative: they served as a carrying place for a spare cigarette. One man had a whole bunch of squashed pig scrotums tied to his *tekan*. They must have been new because the flies were still after them. The ornament was a reminder of a dandy party he had attended and it kept the evil spirits away at the same time.

Some of the Dani wore a band of greased bird feathers on their forehead; others wore a single row of cowrie shells. There was one man with half of a metal zipper tied around his head. That was probably the biggest prize of all. A few wore a *kud*, a halo of *cabanee* bird feathers, around their elaborate hairdos. The halos were red and white and beautiful.

There were two older fellows leaning against a fence post who had inserted white boar tusks (*nyawak*) through their nasal septums. The holes in the men's noses must have been enormous to accommodate the large tusks. One pair hung down like fangs and the other pair turned skyward, rather like a cat's whiskers.

There were also holes in the men's earlobes. Some of the

Dani carried a small bamboo harp (*pikkon*) there. They must have been sizable holes, too.

Jabees (buttock leaves), fashioned from fibers and leaves and sometimes plastic twine, hung down from rattan strings tied around their waists.

The motivations for the men to ornament themselves could have been many. Coming into town to "show off" would be excuse enough to decorate to the hilt. The headdresses, shells, beads and other adornments are also worn during battles, pig feasts or to make an impression on a girl. It depends entirely on what a man has in mind.

The most highly decorated Dani is not necessarily the most important man in the crowd. Sjam and I learned much later that the most dangerous, wealthy and powerful man in the Valley wore nothing but a bunch of twisted string fibers around his neck, and *tekans* so old they were nearly unraveled.

The boys wore miniature replicas of the *holim*, those who could keep them in place. They looked unusually clean and healthy.

The women were not as gorgeous as the men, and they wore more clothing. Their *yokals* (skirts) were made up of *buen* (orchid) fibers which had been woven into quarter-inch bands. The bands were wound around the women, well below the waistline, in fact below the hips, to form a skirt. Loops of fibers fell to the knees in the front and back and were tied up in a bunch on the sides of the skirt. Magic and imagination, probably, held the skirts in place, along with the help of thick thigh calluses. Later I learned about the calluses through the necessity of doctoring them while in the villages.

The women wore long carrying nets (*nokens*) woven from *yoh* tree bark. They hung from the top of the head and covered their back and buttocks. Some of the women wore three and four nets at a time. They carried children and sweet potatoes in them. One woman carried a small pig in hers.

A few women, a very few, wore a single strand of cowrie shells around the neck; others wore string-fiber necklaces.

The little girls wore *kem* grass skirts called *thalis*, which made them look like young hula dancers. The grass had been cut, washed, dried and then rubbed with pig oil and soot, again an assuring measure against the evil spirits.

The faces of the Dani reflected their Negroid ancestral origin, a race more closely related to Melanesians than any other Pacific people.

There was no self-consciousness in the Dani. They were unaware of the shock Sjam and I felt at their half-naked appearance. Some of the men stared at us without restraint; others pretended a lack of interest which probably covered their amazement, and possibly amusement, at our appearance. Although every Dani village in the Baliem Valley had seen or at least had heard of the white people who had come to their land, few had ever seen a six-foot-tall redheaded female in men's clothing and a milk-chocolate-colored Indonesian in a red fur hat walking down the road, armed with camera equipment that must have looked nearly lethal to them.

Mr. and Mrs. Sumitro led us down the dirt road toward the center of town amid a growing group of curious children who picked up our gear and carried it in a gesture of hospitality. They looked at us out of the corners of their eyes and then nearly strangled themselves with giggles. The boys giggled as loudly as the girls. Sometimes they made fresh starts to become straight-faced but it didn't last long; they burst out giggling again. They giggled all the way to the marketplace.

That marketplace, surely, is the only corner of its kind in the world. Half of the merchants are nearly naked and the other half are fully dressed. They sell their wares side by side. The sight seems incongruous and nearly unbelievable.

At the far end of the square, booths had been built for the Indonesian merchants who had goods to sell. The Indonesians, however, had invited the Dani to enter the marketplace in an effort to let them sell their produce and learn something about economy. There were rows of picnic tables set up on a concrete floor under a tin roof. Those tables were operated by the Dani.

The Dani women, heads down, straining against the weight of their heavy carrying nets, were streaming into the market to find a spot on a table or bench where they could display their netted produce. They were a people intent on their business, a people with things on their minds, things that had to be done. They arranged and then rearranged their goods on the tables. Although no one seemed to work very fast, things were put in order quickly and efficiently.

The Dani end of the market was a crowded place. The men moved around with the women and their bodies gave off an odor of smoked bacon. It could double the appetite if one was hungry, but it did nothing for Sjam, who is Moslem and therefore set against pork.

Whatever the Dani had to sell had been grown or produced in the native villages. There were dry goods: *nokens, yokal* bands and *thalis,* and *holims* standing up like breadsticks in a basket. These were sold to other Dani if they were not grabbed up by a passing visitor as a souvenir of his visit to the land. There were sweet potatoes and cabbages and other garden produce. All of it looked choice and fresh.

The Indonesian merchants sold wares that came in cans, plastic bags and in bottles with screw-top lids. The things were labeled with prices high enough to compensate for the transportation costs to fly them in.

The merchants had a special "low-high" price on items for the Wamena shoppers, and a "high-high" price for someone like me. They could look you straight in the eye and sell you black shoe polish when you really wanted red. And since the label was written in Indonesian—why, you simply took his word for it and were happy to buy it.

Some of the things the merchants sold must have looked curious to the Dani—a plastic fly swatter, for example, or a lady's garter belt or a can of mint-scented aerosol. By their very appearance in the booths they possibly created a false feeling in the Dani of need for them. A Dani would have been thrilled to possess just one of those curiosities, to have and to hold and to show his friends, whether he understood its purpose or not.

From the display of goods in the marketplace, I couldn't help noticing that while the Dani *produced* everything they needed for survival, the Indonesians depended on the airline to fly their food and clothing in to them.

I realize that I have repeatedly made the distinction of calling the Dani, the *Dani* and the Indonesians, the *Indonesians*. This would anger any Indonesian bent on Indonesianizing the Dani population. My purpose is solely to identify the indigenous people of the Baliem Valley as such, and to present a less confusing picture to the reader. It should be noted, however, that the Indonesians have had a difficult time remembering that the Dani are now "Indonesians," too. Usually the Dani are referred to as "those people." Even Sjam, an Indonesian born in Sumatra, could not quite get used to the idea that the Dani were supposed to be Indonesians. I guess it has something to do with the Dani *look*.

Mr. Sumitro's house was located directly behind the marketplace. The house was made up of a single cement floor covered over with a tin roof. The roof had been flown into the area, piece by piece, until there was enough to keep the rain out. The market and the house stood in the center of Wamena.

Wamena smells of urine. That is its characteristic smell.

There are spots in the town that are ruined by the reckless dumping of rubbish and debris from canned goods and other things that come in papers and plastics.

There are houses nestled in neat little flowering gardens, too, with white stone paths leading to their front door. One house had words painted on it that said the world was coming to an end.

Wamena wears the face of the military, a Franciscan mission, the many government officials and a police population. Most of them eat too much, drink too much and generally overindulge in every excess they can think of to entertain themselves during the long, dull evenings.

For some reason unknown to me, there is an obvious lack of force in the military. The concentration of power is found in the buttons and badges of the policemen and in the pageantry that goes on down at the police post. The police are armed with rifles, machine guns and small hand pistols. They never walk the streets of Wamena without them.

For the visitor there are certain routines that must take place at the police post. The official "signing in and out" of town is one of them. The post is about a block away from the Sumitros' house. We left our gear in one of the two bedrooms in the house and walked to the police post. As a visitor, I didn't think too much about the required registration. Sjam was impressed, however; she had never been required to sign her name anywhere in all of Indonesia.

On our way back to the Sumitros' we saw a young man standing on the flat chunk of cement that served as a footstep to the house. His name was Aem. He was the Sumitros' houseboy.

Aem was a Dani.

He had left his mountain village a year before, to seek work and some kind of fortune in Wamena. He was about twenty-two years old and heavy-set, with muscles that had come from hard work. He was barefoot, wore short brown pants and a white T-shirt.

Aem had "modernized" himself by growing a mustache. Above the mustache were flashing eyes that were filled with mischief. Below it was a winning smile that made you smile in return, whether you wanted to or not.

Around Aem's wrists and upper arms were yellow plastic *tekans*. They were the only plastic *tekans* I ever saw.

Aem got by because people thought he was harmless, but he was unsafe to be around. Sjam and I were to become sorry victims of both his deadly thoughts and actions.

Apparently the Sumitros had told Aem something about my purpose for being in the Baliem Valley.

"There's a funeral going on over there," he said in Indonesian. He pointed toward the northwestern section of town. His voice seemed shy, his eyes glittering with excitement.

It was nearly four o'clock in the afternoon and Sjam and I were tired. We hadn't eaten since we left Jayapura and we still had to unpack our things, but neither of us could resist the opportunity to attend a Dani funeral. I grabbed my camera case and Sjam's hand, and with Aem in the lead, we started off toward "over there."

The footpath veered around and behind the police station

and then buried itself in a sweet-potato garden. Our feet slushed around in the mud until the path reappeared again, dried out under the sun's fierce energies. In those places the path was the consistency of hard rock. The trail was never straight and seemed to have no direction.

It was on this footpath that Sjam and I received our first lesson in Dani walking. Aem gave it to us.

Dani walking has to do with Dani feet. To remember a Dani is to remember his feet. The Dani foot is big, flat, strangely mis-shapen, and with the toes spread wide apart. Sometimes a Dani is a little pigeon-toed, an arrangement which makes for sure-footedness when climbing hills.

Aem had a fine pair of Dani feet and an easy walk to go with them. His thighs, ankles and knees swung freely and without effort. His shoulders were set well back and his hips were thrust forward.

He walked so fast that nobody could keep up with him. His huge, splayed feet moved like lightning over the path. He never changed gait, not even when he came to a hill. He bent slightly forward at the waist, caught the elbow of one arm in the hand of the other and leaned into his walk, his body ahead of his racing feet, and plowed up the hill. When he arrived at the top there was no change in his breathing.

(Over the hundreds of miles Sjam and I walked in the Valley, neither of us ever caught on to Dani walking. We eventually trained our feet to move along most of the time, but we were never quick or sure-footed when climbing rocks or plodding through mud. I fell down more times than any single individual in town, and Sjam ran a close second.)

After the first ten minutes in maneuvering this footpath, our muscles cried with tension, and yet the path stretched inter-minably in front of us. We tried to reassure each other that the funeral was worthwhile, despite its distance.

Twenty-five minutes later I stopped to photograph a small black bug crawling across the path. In truth, I simply could not go on without rest. Sjam pretended to admire the country-side. She couldn't go on, either.

The three of us sat down. Several Dani women passed by,

looked at us with interest and murmured softly *"Laok"* ("Hello"). They should have said *"Nocksu"* ("Hello"), the proper address between women, but they mistook me for a man.

When we started off again, our muscles ached more than before we had rested. We heard footsteps behind us. Kulmut, a friend of Aem's trotted up to join us. He stayed with us until we reached the entrance of the funeral village and then he ran away. He was afraid he would be killed if he entered another tribe's village.

(Several weeks later I met Kulmut in his own village. He had just killed his first man and he said he'd never leave his mountain environment again. The news was startling to me. I wondered what had prompted such a thing and why he'd never leave his village. I hesitated to ask. I was still somewhat of a stranger in the land.)

The funeral village was settled in a little gully surrounded by banana trees. A six-foot-tall stockade made up of rough planks and tied with rattan vines encircled the village. The wall kept the buildings inside from view. The palisade, with pointed posts sticking up here and there with dried grass on top of the places in between, ran around the village in a rectangle. On the short side of the rectangle were two slotted entrances. The high one was used by people, the low one by pigs.

From behind the wall rose wails and sobs. The sound was pitiful. The voices cried in unison, a chanting choir, crying mournful coyote sounds as though hearts would break and never mend again.

"This is Potikelek village," Aem whispered. "Wait. I'll find Chief Kekele and tell him you're here."

In a few minutes, Aem returned with the chief.

Old Chief Kekele was just barely able to totter toward us on his thin, knobby legs. He visually frisked us as he came. He was an old, old man with dried-up prune skin and a gray beard that glistened in the yellow sunlight. His eyes were wet with tears. There were stain marks on his cheeks where a few had run down his face and dried there. He wrinkled his old brow in thought, spoke softly to Aem and then turned and walked in little shuffles back toward the village wall.

"You must wait here until they kill all of the pigs," Aem said. "Kekele says your clothes will frighten the animals."

By the time Chief Kekele came back to get us on his wobbly knees, Sjam and I were covered with millions of jungle flies. They never left us, not even when Chief Kekele motioned for us to follow him into the village. We passed through the entrance in the stockade and walked by the long row of seated women on our right. The women had covered their bodies with red and yellow clay as a sign of mourning.

The Dani men were dragging dead pigs, about seven of them, to a place in front of the main house in the village at the far end of the courtyard. We followed Chief Kekele to the house and were told to sit beneath its grass eave.

The house was round with a grass roof; it looked like a Dani beehive hairdo. Just as I sat down there was a sudden movement behind me. I twisted my neck around to see a black face poke through the entrance of the house. The man smiled and jumped his eyebrows up and down at me. I supposed this eyebrow-dancing was a sign of greeting and welcome.

The Dani men covered their dead pigs with long jungle grass and then retired to a corner of the yard to smoke. The women began to wail louder.

Chief Kekele whispered to Aem that the deceased had died from an infection in his hip. Whatever the cause of his death, the crowd and the sacrificed pigs indicated that the man's life had been important and that he had been needed.

I felt that the Dani had created a new thing in funerals but I couldn't put my finger on it. Whatever it was, it had the strong feel of truth in it. The funeral was a very real situation, a garden of misery, pathos and tragedy. There was no escape from the sounds and smells and tastes of it. But there was something else, too.

Suddenly there was a scream outside the village walls. Chief Kekele spread out his hands and shrugged his shoulders in a gesture of resignation.

"We go to my house and eat bananas," he announced. "My

house is in the next compound." He pulled himself up and shambled down the courtyard toward the entrance.

Reluctantly Sjam and I left the funeral scene and followed the chief to an adjoining compound where he motioned us to enter the main house.

"That's the *men's* house," Aem said. "Women aren't allowed to enter it!"

We pretended we didn't hear him. We wanted to see the inside of a warriors' house.

The round house (*pilai*) was about fifteen feet in diameter. There were no windows, but there was a slotlike entrance that provided both light and passage. The door was very narrow and very low. You had to get down on your hands and knees to crawl through it. I suppose some people might balk at having to crawl through a doorway on their hands and knees, but Sjam and I could hardly wait to get inside the house.

"Give me a boost through," Sjam yelled over her shoulder as she lowered herself to the entrance. She poked her head through the door and then withdrew it. She stood up, turned around, and aiming with a fine accuracy, she backed in.

I got down on my hands and knees and started to crawl toward the door. Halfway through, I got stuck. I was all inside except from the waist down. The leather strap on my camera case had caught on a piece of wood in the doorway, so I couldn't go forward or backward. Sjam got underneath me and worked the strap free. I crawled all the way in and sat down quickly in embarrassment.

It took a while for our eyes to get used to the dim interior. There was a soft, dry grass on the round floor. In the center of the room was a small open fireplace. It was an arrangement indicating that if you were accustomed to sleeping stretched out, you'd have to change your habit or move to another place.

The ceiling was so low that you had to crawl if you wanted to move around. It even scraped the top of your head in a sitting position.

Chief Kekele came through the door after us. He crawled on his hands and knees to a hole in the ceiling and pulled down a great bunch of bananas which he placed in front of us. Sjam and I ate four bananas and the chief ate the rest, right off the stalk. He opened each banana at its end, covered the fruit with his mouth, chewed and swallowed. There must have been twenty-five bananas on that stalk. Their rapid disappearance testified to Chief Kekele's appetite and to his remarkable devotion to bananas.

Getting out of the *pilai* was no easier than getting into it. Sjam improved on her style by going out headfirst. I managed to get hung up again in just about the same spot as before.

When we reached the village entrance we saw an albino. His skin had burned and peeled and burned again from his naked exposure to the jungle sun. Black Dani men surrounded him, gently guiding him along the footpath in the direction of the funeral.

Chief Kekele pointed out a shortcut to Wamena. We thanked him for his kindness and promised to return.

It was dark when we arrived in town. The people should have been asleep but there was too much excitement down at the police station.

Two men had just been brought in from Angrouk.

They were charged with having eaten two of their enemies.

(5)

There is a magic in the Baliem Valley that comes with early morning. The quality of that magic is changeless. It comes nearly every day.

It begins before the sun breaks out. The mountains are veiled in clouds and the fog drifts through the Valley and hangs over the houses in Wamena. It is a short space of time that seems forever and strangely nostalgic.

Then the sun fights a pathway through the clouds. The sky turns blue and the mist dries up. And the magic time is gone.

Wamena awakens. There are the soft whispering sounds

made by house slippers on cement floors and the sounds of people hacking their throats clear of mucus. The smell of burning kerosene rises into the air as little pots of rice boil for breakfast.

The Dani walk in from their villages with arms crossed and wrapped around their necks, hugging themselves against the cold. The merchants in the marketplace turn on blaring radios to drown out the calls to prayer coming from the mosque.

This morning Sjam and I helped the Dani to open their market spots. We sorted and arranged their produce. When the goods were displayed to everyone's satisfaction, we bought one of nearly everything they had to sell, produce and dry goods.

We had to learn a whole new system of arithmetic to do it.

When the Dani thinks of money, he thinks in terms of pairs. He has to see the pairs on his fingers and toes. If he must use more than twenty digits—why, there's always someone standing nearby with a set of fingers and toes he can borrow and look at.

The Dani must *show* you how much a thing is. I bought a cabbage from one old fellow. He put up his fingers to see its price. There was a cigarette burning on the table in front of him. He took a deep puff from it first, to tide him over while his hands would be tied up. Then he pressed his little finger and ring finger to his palm and held them down with the thumb of his other hand.

Two hundred rupiahs.

The Dani have names for their numbers, but not many. An astute Dani could perhaps count to ten by ones. But that's not usually the case. It's the style to think in pairs. When a Dani shows you two pairs, there are four fingers pressed to his palm. If he needs another pair, he joins the thumb up with the thumb on his other hand.

Mr. Marpaung, the chief of police of the Jayawijaya district, was rarely seen at the police post, so in the afternoon Sjam and I went to meet him at his home. It was a two-block walk from the Sumitros'.

Mr. Marpaung was a man with whom no one interfered very

much. He was a huge man with full lips and a wide mouth that often appeared to be laughing. But there was no humor in his eyes. Something threatening came out of them.

I wanted to ask Mr. Marpaung to suggest an outlying village where I could work and observe the culture of the people uninfluenced by change, without the threat of becoming someone's dinner.

Before he would talk to me, he asked to see my papers. It was fortunate that the man remembered my name and my activities in Borneo. He relaxed, almost, and invited us to enter his house.

During our talk Mr. Marpaung's face showed little emotion. He told us that the villages in the Valley were all pretty much the same, one as good as the other. He warned us, though, against forcing the natives to do something against their will.

He said that cannibalism was a thing of the past in the Valley area. And then he confessed he was still being pestered with it in Pyramid (about thirty miles northwest of Wamena). Two local men had been eaten there two months ago. Further, he admitted that last month the cannibals had eaten four women in Oxibil, a village about thirty-five miles to the east. His words seemed to contradict his statement that cannibalism was "a thing of the past."

The only serious problem that had occurred in the Baliem Valley, he went on to say, was a native uprising against the Indonesian government. But that was a *long* time ago. Four whole months ago.

When Sjam and I left Mr. Marpaung's house, I couldn't get over the feeling that I had looked into the face of a tiger.

Father DeHeinz lived at the Catholic mission in Wamena. Sjam and I visited with him for an hour or so. He told us he'd found the people in the Baliem Valley tough and resistant to change. He confessed that the missions had had little success in converting the Dani to Christianity.

Father DeHeinz advised me to work alone, independent of the missions. He believed my chances of acceptance by the Dani would be greater. He was a nice man, that Father DeHeinz. I wish I could have known him better.

It was getting late in the day, but Sjam and I wanted to visit one more person—the district chief, whom I shall call Mr. Sunaryo.

I find it difficult to write about Sunaryo without bitterness, which is unfortunate. He was the man who would initiate the move to force me to leave Indonesia.

Sunaryo was knock-kneed and possessed an untidy, pear-shaped body that was highly perfumed with expensive toilet waters. He tried to appear accommodating by smiling all the time. He was more dangerous because of it.

Sunaryo was never, by any chance, a man like other men. He was a greedy man and some of his goals were downright evil. The most undesirable trait in his personality was his racial hatred for the Dani.

I was not alone in my feelings. Sjam viewed Sunaryo in the same light, only her prejudice was stronger.

When Sunaryo invited us to accompany him to Pyramid the next day, neither of us could muster a glow of gratitude. But we told him we'd go. We didn't want to jeopardize our relationship.

(6)

The Dani had built the road between Wamena and Pyramid. They scraped off the jungle brush on a strip of their land and then they gave the road to the government. As a reward for their land and their efforts, Sunaryo meant to pay the Dani with clothes.

The "clothes" turned out to be sarongs. Sunaryo gave a few of them to each participating village. The sarongs were wrapped in transparent cellophane bags. The natives, without even opening them, sold them at the marketplace in Wamena the next day.

When the morning sun warmed the night chill a little, Sjam

and I boarded Sunaryo's jeep to begin the trip to Pyramid. The auto had been flown into Wamena, piece by piece. It had been assembled in town, and although some of the parts were still missing, there were enough delivered to make the car run. There was a small truckbed in the back of the jeep and Sjam and Sunaryo sat inside it. I crawled in up front with the driver.

A few miles down the road a little river cut across our path. The water was green and very clean. On both sides of the river grew lush grasses and ferns. We crossed the river on a rattan-tied log bridge and rattled on toward a steep hill. Terraced gardens stretched above and below the road. There was a fence on the right side of us. I watched a fat brown rat slither over the fence and run onto the road. The rat saw the car, bolted and skidded to safety behind a small woody shrub in the ditch.

The planted gardens soon fell away behind us. We drove through a plain of abandoned fields, swamps and patches of brush. The land shifted and moved in the golden sunlight.

We passed over another bridged gulch. It should have had water flowing in it but the bottom was choked with dry grass. The gulch was so deep that none of us wanted to stare down very long, not even the driver.

At noon the air turned hot and the earth smelled dry and good. Occasionally, in the far distance, we could see mushroom tops of the native houses spotting the landscape. The villages seemed hushed and somehow expectant.

With the early afternoon came the gnats and flies. They circled our heads in halos, even inside the jeep.

As we neared Pyramid, a few Dani men jumped out onto the road and tried to outrun the jeep. They found the auto amusing and were delighted with its speed. We were going about seven miles an hour, but just about every Dani kept up with us and a few even passed the car.

In Pyramid, Sjam crawled out of the truckbed. She was angry about something. Sunaryo climbed out of the back end and quickly disappeared.

The Dani watched Sunaryo go and they smiled after him. They didn't like him. They knew Sunaryo didn't like them.

Sunaryo disapproved of everything they did because it was not what he did. Sunaryo even found contempt for the way they dressed because he was handing out sarongs to a people who had never asked for them and didn't want them.

Sjam had reached her boiling point.

"That Sunaryo wants us to live at his house and not at the Sumitros'!" she said. "He's nasty and dirty-minded. Besides that, he's a crook. He's been using his government position to fatten his own pockets. You know what he wants me to do?"

Sjam's voice came out in a dry squawk.

"He wants me to organize native dances in Wamena so he can get the money in admission fees. No money for the Dani, just for him! He said they'd do it because he's with the government. He's also been taking stone axes off the natives. Been selling them to the tourists!"

"What'd you tell him?"

"I told him to go to hell!"

With Sunaryo out of sight, the Pyramid Dani had moved in around us. They were strong, healthy-looking people with an average height of about five feet, seven inches. They were wide-shouldered and narrow-hipped, with long and straight legs.

I saw two albino children in the village. Later I talked to Sister Margaret at the large Catholic mission built on the hill above Pyramid. She remarked how badly these children were in need of sunglasses. I looked at the Dutch beer, Danish butter, English cigarettes and Australian jam on the shelves of the mission's dining hall and I wondered about the price of a pair of sunglasses for children who were nearly blind from the sunlight. The following day I tried to get those glasses in Wamena.

The sun went westerly, took on an orange color and then dropped over the horizon. The clouds were illuminated with pink fringes for a while. Then night crept in and darkened the twilight.

It was midnight when we arrived back in Wamena. We thanked Sunaryo with false enthusiasm and then overtipped the driver to ease the guilt of our insincerity.

I spent a sleepless night. I worried about where I was going to work. I wondered which village would be safe to live in and how Sjam and I could enter it.

I could have saved myself the trouble. The following day I met Kelion.

(7)

It was a rosy morning. I was sitting on the Sumitros' front porch watching the Dani stream into the marketplace. Suddenly a black figure, splashed with areas of white, streaked across the watershed ditch and disappeared near one of the booths.

I jumped up. I ran down the road and around the corner into the marketplace. I stood on tiptoe, looking over the heads of the people in the crowded market. And then I saw him.

He was imposing in height and pitch-black in color. The relationship between his person and his decorations was anything but casual. His head was ornamented with every kind of feather thinkable. There were furry white dog tails tied to his upper arms. He wore a *holim* that reached to his shoulder. A huge white *walimo* covered his chest. The *walimo* gave him the appearance of a walking billboard.

I felt I wanted to talk to him, find out who he was.

When he saw me, he grinned. He was with some friends. When they saw me they grinned, too. They knew me: the jungle's "Associated Press" had been busy banging out bulletins of my arrival. Word had doubtless filtered to the village subscribers in the innermost parts of the Valley.

I rose to the bright bait of his flashing smile and walked over to him. There was a calm strength shining from his eyes as he murmured "*Narak*," man-to-man talk. His voice was controlled and soft.

I bought a box of assorted cookies, and shaking the package a little, I encouraged him to follow me to the Sumitro's grass garden. Sjam and Aem came out of the house to join us.

"Aem, please ask him what his name is."

The man cleared his throat, spat and said "Kerik."

I thought he said "Kelion." The misunderstanding gave rise to the way Kerik took title to a new name for himself. He never allowed anyone to call him Kerik again.

Aem brought out some glasses filled with water. I handed Kelion the package of cookies. He didn't know what they were but he regarded the package with joy. When he figured out how to open the box, his joy changed to rapturous thanksgiving.

He sipped his water whenever we sipped ours. When it was gone he began to eat the cookies. Somewhere he had learned to talk while he was eating and he never stopped talking. No word or bite was missed until he had finished eating every cookie in the box.

During the time it took for him to gobble his way through the box, he moved only once. That was because the sun had changed position and he wasn't sure what the sunlight might do to the cookies.

Kelion said he'd found it strange that I would buy him a box of cookies. He was charmed with the idea, but he couldn't quite understand it.

I asked Aem to explain my mission to Kelion. I think I even dignified it a little by calling it an expedition. I stressed that I was neither with the missionaries nor with the government. I'd come with my interpreter, Sjam, to write and photograph, and I wanted to live in a village with the Dani. I promised I would try not to change or upset their way of life.

I told him I was not poor, I had my own food and I would be willing to pay in knives, shells, money or sweet potatoes for lodging.

While Aem translated, Kelion's eyelids fell down sleepily, which, I learned later, meant that he was as alert as a hungry hawk.

Kelion sucked his teeth to dislodge a piece of cookie and

then grinned broadly. He promised to take us to his village. He also promised to protect us while we were there. I was going to ask him what he meant to protect us *from,* but his next statement was so startling that I forgot.

"You can sleep in the *pilai* with the men. Sjam can sleep in the women's house."

Kelion thought I was a man!

In the end we were able to halfway convince Kelion I should stay with Sjam and the women. Mostly, he viewed the whole thing with suspicion.

Kelion held down a pair of fingers in the palm of his hand. He told us that when the sun had gone across the sky two times, he would return to Wamena and take us to his village.

"Where is your village?"

Kelion stood and pointed his finger toward the east.

"Over there," he said.

(8)

When the sun crosses the sky "two times," it usually means that two days have passed, but two days had come and gone and Kelion had failed to arrive in Wamena.

Maybe he wouldn't come at all.

On the morning of the third day Sjam, a police interpreter and I set off for Pikke village. Pikke was located in the northeast, about a two-hour walk from Wamena. I understood there was a mummy "living" there. It was something I wanted to see.

It was ten o'clock in the morning. The sun fired its heat down on us as though it were our personal enemy. The air was hot, but it was clear and clean.

We walked for a while on a road nearly wide enough for an automobile. Then it narrowed into a Dani footpath and seemed to wander by itself through a thick forest. There were great swarms of enormous flies in there, more than I want to think about. The flies could bite right through one's clothing and they often did.

An hour later we came to the Baliem River. It was too muddy to be beautiful. The gulch was deep and it made the river look mean. We walked over the cable-suspended bridge; it was like trembling on the edge of a trampoline.

Pikke village perched on the top of a hill on the other side of the bridge. It was not a high hill, but it was steep. We plodded up and sat down on a rock to catch our breath.

A few kids came up to satisfy their curiosity at closer range. We were disappointed when they told us there was no mummy in Pikke. The mummy, they said, was located farther down the Valley, in Aikima village, another full hour's walk away.

Reluctantly we started off again on a footpath that took us through a great grassy plain. On the left were high jagged mountains spotted with white limestone. Some of the powder had blown down and covered parts of the path. The Valley stretched flat on the right side, filled here and there with tall grasses. Beyond were rambling, cultivated fields of sweet potatoes and taro.

The trail looped around the shoulder of the mountain on the left and abruptly disappeared into boulders. A little committee of Dani men, cutting their way through the boulders, was coming toward us. The leader of the group looked like a moving billboard.

"I wonder if that's Kelion?"

"It sure looks like him," Sjam said.

Kelion was shambling down the rocks with his companions and picked up speed when he saw us. He didn't appear surprised that we were not waiting for him in Wamena.

Kelion knew we were on our way to see the mummy in Aikima. Hulolik, the chief of Aikima, had alerted him. I am uncertain how the chief knew we were coming.

It was in this boulder pass that Sjam nearly lost her red fur hat. Hulolik was reduced to the point of madness with desire for it. He tried it on several times. Then he held it in his hands and petted it until the hat was nearly bare of fur. One of the Dani retrieved the hat and passed it back to Sjam, but Hulolik

Grand Baliem Valley (Southeast end)

········· Alliance boundaries   • Jiwika
·—·—· Author's trail with Kelion
—— Author's trail with Aem
········· Established trail
🏠 Author's
    house

N

KURULU MULIMA

Wenebuborah
Punycul   Lagora River   Taburobak
Wamholik   Kumina
WIYAGOBA
• Aborokdek
• Feratsilimo
Mulima
• Wamhalilmo

Tumagonem
SILO Mapilakma
ROCK
OPAGIMA

MULIMA
SIEPKOSI   • Abukulmo

Haratsilimo   Elima

Baliem River

Aikima

Aikhe River

Pabuma •

Lunagima
Molapua
Yumugima

Hiyasi
Telebaga

• Pikke

Yumugi River

Kusagima
Werenebagal
Kotiape

Hulekama

SIEPKOSI
ANALAGA

Obasia
Leihukma   ANALAGA
Huan River   ABULAKMA

Wamena

• Konisa

• Pugima   Miles
            0   1   2

had to be forcibly restrained from snatching it off her head again. In the end, Sjam promised to give Hulolik the hat before she left the Valley. The promise restored the chief's sanity for the remainder of the afternoon.

The footpath on the far side of the boulder pass turned into hard rocks, stony and sharp. The Dani leaped daintily over the path with sure feet and joy in speed. Sjam and I were set in noisy motion. We scrambled along with shoe leather scraping the path, legs brushing through the grass and arms flailing around in the air to maintain balance.

Kelion made us feel a little better—he was a clumsy Dani. Not slow, just clumsy. When Kelion walked, he either lumbered or galloped. He had never acquired the knack of walking like other Dani. He was forever stubbing his toe on every rock in the path, no matter how far to the right or left the rock lay.

Nothing can be more conspicuous in a land inhabited by naked black natives than the intrusion of fully clothed creatures moving across their horizon, especially if one is wearing a red fur hat. Our little parade alerted every Dani within miles of our presence. They ran to Aikima for a closer examination of us.

Aikima, like all other Dani villages, is really a collection of little compounds running in all directions and surrounded by a single fence. No one knew how old the village was because time is not measured in years or months. No one knew how many people lived in the village, either. The Dani have a habit of coming and going, and it is hard to keep track of everybody.

We climbed through the slotted entrance (*thop*) of a compound, struggled across the courtyard and collapsed in front of the *pilai*. Immediately we were surrounded by men and children. There were no women in the crowd; they were hard at work in their gardens.

I was amazed at the friendliness of the people. Everyone seemed excited about our being there. The children crowded in closer to examine my white skin. They touched my hands to see if the color would rub off and then they ran to a corner to hold a congress. Giggles came from the group when they peeked back at me to verify the marvel of the color. They pressed their knuckles against their teeth to smother some of the chuckling noises they made.

The men, in a mood of good manners, appraised Sjam and me with natural restraint. They released a little emotion when I pulled out my red bandanna to blow my nose. They lifted their eyebrows at each other, and a couple of them laughed out loud. I didn't feel they were laughing at me, but at the curiosity of seeing an event which probably appeared ridiculous to them.

One of the men began to grind his molars together. It was a strange sound—a sound which became somewhat enlivened when a chorus of five or six men ground away at the same time. The activity reflected a man's mood of preoccupation, nervousness, sometimes anger, often despair, and once in a while they gritted in the sheer satisfaction of it. Molar grinding covered just about everything.

Kelion had gone to sleep, a rattling snore coming from his mouth. He was lying flat on the ground, his huge feet sticking straight up in front of him. Kelion, we learned, loved to be warm and comfortable, but the combination made him go to sleep. Sitting in the sun in Aikima for any stretch of time was more than the man could bear. If he didn't move around, then he couldn't stay awake very long. Kelion thought everybody was that way.

Above the loud snoring noise, Hulolik tried to explain about the mummy in his village. His eyes were as bright as a sparrow's because of his interest in the subject. All the while Hulolik described the mummy he never mentioned its name, for fear of summoning it.

This male mummy is perhaps the most remarkable, if not the gaudiest, curiosity in the Dani culture. According to Hulolik it was found lying in the fields when the Dani came into the area to build the village of Aikima. They believed it to be an ancestor, and endowed with great powers. The people prayed to the mummy, sacrificed pigs to it, and even rubbed its stony legs and arms with pig oil. As a result a few local wars were won, the sweet potatoes grew larger, and the women suddenly became fat and attractively saucy.

The mummy was credited with performing all these miracles and the people elevated the petrified rarity to the position of divinity.

Some of the other miracles the mummy had performed were a little vague, but it was obvious that the people needed this good-luck omen to run their personal lives. I was almost reluctant to ask to photograph a thing so sacred.

Sjam and I crawled on our hands and knees into the *pilai* to see the mummy. Everybody else in the village followed us in. Chief Hulolik pointed to the hole in the ceiling and motioned for me to go up there.

There was no light in the second story of the Dani *pilai*. I could feel a thick bedding of soft grass beneath my hands and knees. I cracked my head against the low dome-shaped ceiling. When everybody had crawled up through the hole, the second floor was a very crowded place.

Sjam produced a matchbox and struck a light. Now I could see to aim my camera at the dimly lit mummy propped against a side wall. I was prepared for and expected 500 volts to go through my flash equipment, but I had forgotton to prepare anybody else. To this was added the surprise of something like 1,000 volts suddenly coming through the light unit for some unknown reason. It caused the hasty departure of half of our hosts.

Chief Hulolik ordered the Dani to lower the mummy to the first floor, where I could photograph it more easily. The mummy was in a seated position, the head bent slightly forward. It was a masterpiece of preservation: the skin was stretched tightly, black and rock-hard. The figure was undecorated except for a *holim* and a brown carrying net on its bald head.

Kelion had slept through the whole thing. His snoring, if anything, was louder. It was no easy job to awaken him. He finally opened his eyes, rose and mountainously shook himself. And then he began to hum in order to stay awake.

Chief Hulolik would not let us leave Aikima until Sjam promised again, on the mummy's ghost, that she would give him her red fur hat someday.

When we started back down the path to Wamena, one of Kelion's companions joined us. The Dani never goes anywhere alone, since danger is always lurking around and there's a certain safety in numbers in case of ambush.

Kelion was alert every minute during the long walk. He watched the movements of the birds, the tall grasses flanking the path, and his eyes never stopped scanning the high mountain ridge.

Sometimes Kelion sang to Sjam and me to encourage us in our walking. He slowed down when we walked slowly, and if we hurried going down a hill, he hurried, too.

It was night when we reached Wamena.

Aem was waiting for us at the back door of the Sumitro house. Although he did not appear happy to see Kelion, he shared his sleeping quarters with him for the night.

(9)

Morning found Kelion a worried man. He had spent the whole night thinking about an honest way to get a set of pots and pans. Considering that the Dani have no cooking utensils of any kind, Kelion's worries were unusual, and the fact that Kelion's thoughts were *honest* was astonishing. He believed that "thinking honest" could strain the mind. He usually devoted all of his energies to making wide circles around that kind of stress.

Kelion did not abide by the principle of private ownership of property, especially if it was small enough to be carried off quickly. Whenever Kelion was in town, any article smaller than a breadbox was in jeopardy of having its ownership changed. There was no size limit on anything he found lying around in the Baliem Valley.

In a sudden impulse of good will, Kelion rejected the idea of relieving some Indonesian in Wamena of his cooking utensils. In the Sumitros' backyard, Kelion approached me with his pots-and-pans thoughts.

As his story took shape, I understood that the Dani *roast* their sweet potatoes, but Kelion wanted these utensils to *boil* the potatoes for Sjam and me during our stay in his village. By the time he had finished with the telling of it, his voice had risen to a new, high sweetness and a tear had squeezed out of his right eye.

Not only did I buy Kelion the pots and pans he wanted, I bought him a knife, spade, axe and a colorful string of beads. And I merged from the whole deal with an inflated sense of having been given the honor to do it.

Kelion's friend appeared to help transport our things. There was a great contrast between our things and theirs. They carried a twist of home-grown tobacco; our equipment incorporated suitcases, backpacks, camera cases and a red fur hat. Our appearances did not lessen the contrast. The men wore *holims* and feathers; Sjam and I were clad in boots, pants, shirts and hats. We must have been a stunning group to look at.

Aem wanted to go with us to Kelion's village. He said he could be useful to us as an interpreter and pack bearer. We had no reason to suspect him of impure motives and were happy to have him along.

When Kelion finally stopped horsing around with his new pots and pans, the men took up their burdens. It was a matter of amazement how they carried all that stuff during the many hours we walked without any sign of fatigue or weariness.

We bettered our walking time to Pikke by seven minutes. At the pass through the boulders, we walked a right angle to Aikima. The side valleys came into view with their large cultivated fields, spiderwebbed with well-traveled footpaths.

After three hours of walking without rest, Sjam and I were tired and sweaty. The Kleenex in my shirt pocket was wet with perspiration. It fell apart in my hand when I tried to use it. Kelion had his troubles, too. He had tripped over a wild flower. He blamed it on a ghost, but it was a wild flower. His feet flew up in the air and he landed with a great thump right in the middle of his pots and pans.

We sat down by the pathway to rest. Kelion played his *pikkon* (harp). His intention was to take our minds off our thirst. The harp was made from a little piece of bamboo about four inches long, and its tone was soft and lovely.

While we were resting, we went through the ceremony of the bananas.

A woman came trotting down the footpath toward us carrying a highly desirable stalk of bananas. As a rule, one tribe will never eat the food of another, for fear of being poisoned, but Kelion wanted the bananas, although we were resting in territory unfriendly to him. I supposed he either knew the woman or had resigned himself to toxin.

Kelion barely survived the shock of our buying the stalk. He had something against giving money for things he could just as well steal.

Kelion ate more bananas than anybody else. He threw the skins in the hot sunshine on the path—the Dani believe their stomachs, if not their ankles, will swell up if the banana skins do not dry in the sun. I threw my peelings with Kelion's. I did not mean to support his belief, but it wouldn't do any good to take chances with it.

Aem and Kelion were talking together in soft whispers. Suddenly their voices raised in pitch and volume. Sjam and I sensed something was wrong between the two men. Aem turned a deaf ear to Sjam's questions and refused to answer her.

An hour later we came to the Aikhe River. It's a joy just to look at it. There are little green five-fingered ferns growing on the sides where frogs hide during the daylight hours. At night the frogs croak across the watery surface and their bellows can be heard for miles around. Fish are swimming in the river, and graceful dragonflies zip over the surface. And it's a well-behaved river: during the dry season there's still enough water for swimming and wading; it hardly ever floods its banks in the wet season. The Dani come down to drink from it all year round. They fill their water gourds (*sigi-sigi*) from it to take back to their houses. The Aikhe is a grand little jungle river.

The Dani jealously guard their rivers against contamination. No village is ever built near a river's banks to pollute and poison the waters with the careless dumping of sewage and other toxic wastes.

When we left the Aikhe River, Aem was angered about something. Sjam and I wondered why he was upset.

"There," he said, pointing to a little cluster of round huts in a banana grove," that's Kelion's village. The name of the village is Tumagonem, and Kelion is chief. We don't have to go any farther. We can stay there."

Aem lead us to the village entrance and then fell back a little. Kelion didn't know what to do for a moment. Then he motioned us through the *thop*. We hobbled in, half wilted from our long walk, and collapsed inside the entrance.

The village was laid out exactly like every other village in the Valley, except that it was smaller. There were only two compounds; one had been abandoned. The fence was still there, but the house lumber had been carted away for use somewhere else.

There are four different structures in every compound. At the far end of the courtyard, facing the entrance, is the *pilai*, where all the men and young boys sleep. The position of the *pilai* is unchanging. The slotted door faces the village's entrance and enables the men within the *pilai* to see who is passing by, friend or foe.

The courtyard is rectangular, sometimes oval. A kitchen longhouse (*hunila*) dominates one side. Inside the *hunila* are individual fireplaces for the families that live in the compound. The kitchen is primarily the domain of the Dani women. But sometimes men, children and piglets enter the structure, where they occasionally eat together. More often, the men stay long enough to gather their roasted sweet potatoes together and then return to their own *pilai* to eat them.

Opposite the kitchen longhouse are small replicas of the warriors' house, the *abiais*. These round little houses belong to the women of the compound. They provide sleeping facilities for wives, babies, single girls and women relatives.

The fourth existing structure in the compound is the rectangular sty (*wamai*) for the pigs. It is a covered house, divided into stalls because pigs have thin tempers. They do not get along with one another for very long without fighting.

Despite my long hair, lipstick and nail polish, it was a matter of constant wonder to me that the Dani men considered me to be a man. Sjam and I were invariably invited into the *pilai* to sit with the warriors.

The *pilai* was no sudden development. It was designed by men far ahead of their time, men who were aware of their own needs and who could anticipate the needs of their children. The *pilai* used by the Dani ancestors was fundamentally the same as that used today.

The *pilai* is the permanent seat of the compound, a place for all men to relax and be happy. It boasts a living room (part-time dining room) and a bedroom. The sleeping loft is directly beneath the hemispheric roof. It is divided from the ground-level living room by a cane floor.

In the living room the men hang tobacco leaves to toast and pork to smoke. There are family water gourds propped up against the walls. Each *pilai* carries some of its past with it, for bows and arrows are kept close at hand. There are family fetishes and sacred stones hidden in secret places in the walls.

The *pilai* is a model of neatness. Within its walls is found just about everything a man would need or want to be content. The grass is clean and dry, there's food and tobacco, and a little fire in the hearth for warmth during the chilly evenings.

The Dani never build a fire large enough to burn down the house. The smoke runs up the walls and seeps into the hayloft to subdue the mosquitoes.

The *pilai* in Tumagonem sprang to life when the men returned from their daily work. Sjam and I faced the prospect of living with a people with whom we had little in common, particularly clothes, color or language.

By arriving in Tumagonem, Sjam and I had penetrated deep into the Baliem Valley. The faces of these native people reflected their fear at the mere sight of strangers. The Dani probably thought we were going to try to stop their wars, convert them to Christianity, steal their pigs, stone axes, and bows and arrows, and maybe their women. By the same token, Sjam and I regarded the Dani as natives who might kill us for one reason or another, and at worst, eat us alive.

To do something helpful is a good vehicle for getting someone to understand one's intent. I gave medical attention to the many sick and injured in the village, and when we recorded their voices on our tape recorders, the Dani were fascinated with the playbacks. Many of them had never seen a match struck, and its lighting prompted every man present to quickly roll his own and come up for a light from the match.

Sjam and I found that we did not have to understand what a Dani was saying to understand what he was feeling. If he laughed, we knew he was happy, and during a sullen, quiet moment, we knew we had probably committed an error in either procedure or protocol.

We learned that the hour of waiting for the miracle of the roasted sweet potatoes to appear was the hour of entertainment in the *pilai*. The men invented their own pleasures without the advantage of money. They were found in conversations —great, long, never-ending ribbons of conversation. People saved up all day on the good things to tell and they recounted them during this evening hour of pleasure.

Even Kelion managed to stay awake during this time. He loved to listen to conversation. He was always disappointed when things ran dry. This night, when Kelion was sure nobody had anything more to say, he left to collect the daily ration of roasted sweet potatoes from the kitchen. He brought them back to the *pilai* in one of his new pots. Huddled near the fire, the men peeled and ate their potatoes and saved the skins for the pigs.

They all ate well, but Kelion stuffed himself to the point of discomfort. He had an incredible appetite and was hungry almost all the time. It was reported that during one hunger seizure Kelion had eaten fifteen large sweet potatoes, a variety of garden vegetables, a stalk of bananas and a roasted piglet all by himself.

The men in the room belched appreciatively and grunted

happily. Kelion searched through the grass on the floor to find a good straw to pick his teeth.

The Dani bed down for the night promptly after suppertime because their land is one without lanterns or lamps. It was only seven o'clock in the evening, but the Dani didn't know that. They have no clocks. They depend upon the sun to regulate their days. They had found it trustworthy, since there was no way for anyone to tamper with it.

Sjam and I were happy to retire. We were exhausted. The men invited us to sleep in the *pilai* but Kelion half suspected we might be women, after all. He didn't want to take any chances with it. He led us to an *abiai*, which must have caused great astonishment, if not grave concern, among the Dani women in the village. They believed we were men, too.

Sjam got down on her hands and knees, poked her head through the door and crawled through its opening. I followed her in and sat down on a grassy floor saturated with the penetrating odors of pigs and pig fat. A little kennel arrangement had been built in the back of the *abiai* and a white piglet had been installed there. He grunted at our intrusion and inspected us through the slatted partition with his pink eyes. Then he flopped over and went to sleep.

Our suitcases and other things had been piled up on one side of the room. I was amazed to see that the Dani had stolen none of our equipment. Somehow even Kelion had managed to keep his hands off our property.

Kelion was busy boarding up the entrance of the *abiai* and with such permanency that Sjam and I were prisoners until the following morning.

There is no changing into pajamas in the jungle. It's incongruous to the Dani way of life. You come as you are and that's as ready as you will ever be. Sjam and I took off our boots, however. We swung ourselves upward through the hole in the ceiling into the sleeping loft. We crawled around in the deep, soft bed of grass amid the mass of sinister mosquitoes flying about. They were all wide awake because no fire had been built downstairs to smoke them to sleep.

We lay down in the grass nest and were immediately visited by little black fleas and grayish-white lice. They had come to bite us. Even our clothing did not keep them away. They crawled down inside and munched away on whatever tender spots they could find. It may seem strange to think that one can become accustomed and actually bored with their presence, but it happens. The fleas and lice have staked a claim in the Dani world. Sooner or later one learns to live with them.

Many people, I suppose, would refuse to sleep in such a place. Once inside, you can count on never standing up again; there is a lack of lighting, ventilation, running water, plumbing and electricity, and you must sleep wrapped around the center poles that come up through the floor into the sleeping loft, where the fleas and lice crawl over you all night.

But the house is cozy and rainproof and you wouldn't want a warmer place to sleep.

(10)

It's a tossup between who wakes up first in a Dani village—the pigs have a slight edge over the children. The children wake up the women, who open the sty. The pigs run outside into the courtyard to root and churn up the dirt with their tough, flat noses.

The women pad across the yard to the *hunila* to roast sweet potatoes for breakfast. The little children walk about shivering with the cold; they rub their hands together to keep their fingers warm and hug themselves while waiting for the potatoes to get done enough to eat.

Great morning noises come from the *pilai*. There's hacking and spitting and coughing as the men stir about inside in an effort to wake up. When the door planks are removed, you can see a little glow from the freshly stoked fire and the red tips from cigarettes smoked while the men wait for their breakfast.

Kelion and Aem came through the doorway of our *abiai*. Kelion's feathers were cockeyed, and he had grass in his hair. Apparently he had slept on his face because the white strip down the center of his nose was smeared. He borrowed my hand mirror to fix his make-up and adjust his ornaments. I stepped outside in the courtyard to meet the women of the compound before they left for work.

After I met them I was nearly sorry I had done it. It is difficult for me to criticize a people I love, but the Dani women were more than I could take. When I think of them, the memory response it sets up still leaves me trembling. I was afraid to be with them and I spent most of my days in the Valley thinking up ways to avoid them. I simply did not have the physical strength or mental stamina it took to hold my own with the Dani women.

The Dani women are full-hipped, big-bellied creatures. When they get together they are a robust, boisterous, rowdy bunch. Their energy is volcanic and sometimes downright harmful. They are without restraint of any kind in both thought and action. Sjam and I spent many hours trying to teach them gentleness, but we could have saved ourselves the trouble. They are not only dangerous, they are incurable. To criticize their behavior was useless because they were insensitive to it.

Aem told the women in the courtyard that I was a woman, too. They viewed the idea with curiosity. Some of them shoved in a little closer to get a better look. One old woman with a runny nose knocked my hat off my head and ran her fingers through my hair. My blouse was opened and the women took turns peeking inside at my underclothing. Another woman squeezed my bosom. Then she turned to convince the others that I really was a woman. The announcement created a pandemonium so grand that even some of the men stepped outside of the *pilai* to watch it.

"Mama Wyn! Mama Wyn!" they screamed. And then they smacked the daylights out of me. I was jostled and hustled around in the dirt. They slapped me with big loving punches. The punches were repeated and improved upon with such elaboration that the breath was finally knocked out of me. As far as I know, I have never been discourteous to strangers. But now I began to fight tooth and nail because these women appeared bent on destroying me.

I would still be lying in that courtyard if Kelion hadn't opened my gate to freedom by yelling a few well-chosen threats at the ladies. There are no words to describe the sense of relief I felt when I crawled back into the safety of the *abiai*.

The Dani women do not love men as much as they love one another, but there was no indication of homosexuality between them. The women are compulsively devoted to one another because they work, eat and sleep together. They spend what other time they have in drawing attention to themselves to acquire the love and admiration from one another which they need to be happy.

In all fairness, the Dani women are loving people. You could have great fun horsing around with them, I suppose, if you had the strength of Samson. But it was no wonder that their unique behavior kept them from being invited into the *pilai*.

(11)

The Dani who live in Tumagonem found themselves together for a variety of reasons. The most important one was that they get along with one another, and in one way or another, they are related.

Everyone has his job to do. In the early-morning hours the women leave their village to tend to their sweet-potato gardens with their digging sticks (*mileh* or *wieleh* or *poel*). They take a few hot coals from their morning fire, wrap them in grass and carry them to the fields so they can light and smoke cigarettes while they work.

The children gather the pigs together. They herd the animals along behind the women on their way to the gardens. The young boys usually tend the pigs, and the girls help with the cultivating and planting.

The babies are carried in their mothers' carrying nets or are left in the villages with older women who can no longer work in the fields.

The men do the heavy work. They build houses and cut wood to clear the land for new gardens. They turn over the topsoil and dig huge ditches and canals for irrigation.

Both men and women know how to weave skirts, nets and wristbands. The children learn by watching and can pick up weaving at a very early age.

Except for the information regarding the Dani's belief in their origin and religion, nothing is kept from the children. The Dani transmit their culture to the children every moment of the day. Each child is told and shown what he must know to survive. By the time the child is five or six years old, he has had exposure to nearly every facet of Dani life.

A woman plays an important role in the Dani economy because she is a living medium for exchange. A group of women, married to the same man, makes that man a wealthy individual.

Every boy dreams of becoming a *kain*, although he knows that his dream, for the most part, is futile. A *kain*, great overlord, is believed to be appointed by the gods found in the sun and the moon. A *kain*'s power is measured by the number of wives and pigs he has, the number of gardens he owns and the number of men he has killed. In the old days a *kain* was required to have twenty or thirty wives and hundreds of pigs to be considered wealthy enough to accept the god-given appointment of leadership. By today's standards a *kain* with five wives and a handful of pigs is a very powerful man, and one with great social prestige and economic status.

If a boy's father is a chief, it does not mean the child will inherit chiefdom. Village chiefs are chosen through demonstrations of their bravery. There is a demand for the constant performance of brave deeds to maintain such a reputation. When a chief loses favor with his people, he voluntarily thinks of retiring. The people are quick to follow a brighter, more promising warrior.

It is interesting that the *kains* and chiefs do not rule their people with coercive power. Their authority is found in their great influence over the people.

Below the village chiefs are a few aristocrats who have one or two wives and a small herd of pigs. The remainder of the male population are bachelors or *kepus*. A *kepu* is an individual who has never killed a man and therefore has failed to win the admiration and respect required to marry. He has no wife, no children, no pigs, no garden and very few friends. The Dani do not feel sorry for him. They simply wait for him to do something to elevate himself to their standards of acceptance.

(12)

Aem had told us that Kelion was the chief of Tumagonem. Aem had lied. A man named Asuan was chief.

Chief Asuan was the laziest man in the Valley. His father, Nilik, had been a great *kain* in his day. For a while, Asuan had tried to keep up with his father's reputation. He had managed to kill eight men and then he quit.

Not only was Asuan lazy, he was slow. He was slow even when he was running. The Dani used to ask Asuan questions but he took so long to answer that they simply stopped asking him anything.

Asuan believed that three fourths of every day should be spent sleeping, and the other quarter devoted to resting. Outside of killing men, he couldn't do anything. There was nothing he wanted to do, so he never learned much.

Despite the fact that Asuan's quality of genius was found in his laziness, he was greatly respected in Tumagonem. Asuan became chief when his father-in-law, Old Pum, aged into a senility that lessened his youthful menace to both men and women. Sjam and I had to watch ourselves when we were around Old Pum. He was senile, but he had moments of recovery. During those lapses he loved to pinch a girl on the hip.

Old Pum, Asuan, Kelion and Aem were sitting in our *abiai* when the discussion about the pig came up. Kelion was casting about in his mind how to get it started. He wriggled his toes to keep the flies off while he did it. He made a few false starts and then blurted it all out at once: "I want to kill a pig for you!"

The reader should be alerted to the fact that the Dani do not kill their pigs for food alone, but they are sacrificed only for very specific purposes. The understanding must be clearly agreed upon by all concerned prior to the animal's death, or the situation could result in an embarrassment. A dead pig could initiate a kinship, an appeasement to the gods, a welcome, a life for a dying man, a placation of a ghost, rain, drought, or a person could find himself suddenly married. And it is not impossible that all of these things could be incorporated into a single pig's death.

"Kelion wants to kill a pig for you," Old Pum repeated.

"Why, that's very nice of him," I said. "What for?"

"He wants to honor you as a returning warrior to Tumagonem," Asuan drawled.

"A returning *warrior?*"

Kelion put his chin in his hands and grinned broadly. There was sort of a gaiety about him that was difficult to trust.

"Mama Wyn," he said, "you give me pots and pans. You give me shovel and knife and beads. I want to kill a pig for you."

The value of this gift was the measure of the Dani. If I accepted, Kelion's dignity would never be taller.

I agreed to the killing. An immeasurable satisfaction settled down on Kelion. He crawled over to the doorway and out into the courtyard to catch the animal for the sacrifice. He was humming to himself as he went.

When Kelion returned, he had a gray piglet beneath his right arm. His left hand was tightly strapped over the animal's snout. He was smiling broadly. There was a look of triumph in his eyes.

It had taken Kelion just about ten minutes to practice his

profession: he had stolen the pig from a neighboring village. He described its theft with zest and color. His honesty about the whole thing was nearly exotic.

It is an honorable and acceptable occupation for the Dani to steal pigs. The crime lies in getting caught in the act. The thefts usually take place when the pigs are playing in the gardens during the daylight hours. The chances for abducting a pig from a compound sty at night are slim. I understood, though, that Kelion had successfully swiped at least half a dozen animals at midnight. These accomplishments had given him a certain professional reputation he was to enjoy the rest of his life.

Kelion was proud of this pig and wanted me to inspect the animal for my approval. But I have never been fond of pigs; they have always seemed rather unattractive to me, and I find some of their habits disgusting. I couldn't see myself getting close to Kelion's pig.

Old Pum helped me. He creaked up from his sitting position in the *abiai*, leaned forward and pinched me. I was the first one out in the courtyard to look at Kelion's pig.

As pigs go, it was a dandy little animal. I managed to give it a pat on the head. Then Kelion called for his bow (*sike*) and arrow (*wim*) in preparation for the kill. Asuan held the pig's hind legs and Aem squeezed his hands around the animal's ears. They stretched the pig out between them. Kelion stood about two feet away from the pig, aimed his arrow and fired.

Listening to a dying pig is worse than looking at it, although both are frightening. When the men have the pig in the air, its eyes are staring wide open in terror and it is protesting loudly. Then the arrow punches its way through the pig's heart and a sudden belch of blood spews out. The animal's screams split one's eardrums.

Aem and Asuan put the dying pig on the ground to wobble around by itself until it gave a last, groaning cry, a little quiver and went limp. It was dead.

Kelion heaped up some firewood and pulled a thong of rattan (*mol*) up and down through a piece of hardwood (*chimo*) shaped like a fork (*apemakelok*). He dropped to his knees and blew at the hot little friction spot until a blaze leaped up. Then he held his pig over the flames to singe off the bristles.

Kelion cut up the pig with a bamboo knife (*wampalin*) in a matter of minutes. When the knife got dull, he pulled off the splinters with his teeth, making it sharp again. He cut beneath the jaws and made slits down both sides of the pig. After disemboweling the animal, he broke the ribs from the spine with his stone adze. "Men are cut up and cooked the same way pigs are," he remarked.

I didn't have time to investigate that statement because the women were entering the courtyard. I looked for an escape. Inside the *abiai* I hung cameras and tape recorders around my neck. Armed with sharp corners, curves and angles, I was a cutting menace to anyone who came near me. The stratagem met with such success that I used it many times during my stay in the Valley.

Kelion only had one wife and I liked her very much when she kept her distance. Her name was Wenybake. She was always laughing. She never stopped. Sometimes she said something but nobody ever remembered it. One was left with her laughter, not her words.

Wenybake and the other women converted a hole in the ground into a Dani Dutch oven. They lined the hole with *lukwaka* grass. The men picked up hot stones with long wood tweezers and placed them on the grass. *Sowa, towa* and *bapaweka* vegetables were placed on the rocks, and leaves were spread over them. The men positioned another layer of hot rocks on the leaves. The pig was placed spread-eagle on top.

Water was sprinkled on the hot stones to encourage steam. The *lukwaka* was brought up from the sides, gathered at the top and tied with a length of rattan. The oven looked like a steaming haystack.

It took about an hour and a half for the whole thing to cook. When the bundle was untied, the vegetables looked a little overdone, but the pig was toasted to perfection.

Kelion carried the roasted piglet into the *pilai* and spread it out on clean banana leaves. Each hoof pointed toward some cardinal point. The men of the compound and a few curious

Dani visitors stared with grave solemnity at the little pig. The offering of a sacrifice is a very meaningful moment in the Dani culture.

I was given the liver to eat, as well as the kidneys, heart and a piece of roasted brain. These are the choicest parts because there are not many of them. I found them a bit of a shock to the palate, but if I didn't think about them too much, they were acceptable.

The people were momentarily thrown off balance when I tried to share my meal with them. Kelion explained that a gift cannot be taken back, not in any form. Tomorrow, he said, I would have permission to share the pork with friends outside the village. Meanwhile it would hang in my sleeping loft, where the rats could not get at it. I was unaware that there were rats in the hayloft of the *abiai*.

It was late afternoon, and Kelion wanted to sing. We walked to Silo Rock, which is a natural watchtower. In the days before the government came, the Dani erected watchtowers (*kayo*) all over the Valley where men stood guard watching for the enemy to come. Now they're outlawed, however, so the Dani use the towers found in nature for their lookout stations. Silo Rock is one of them.

The men sang for two hours without stopping, never singing the same song twice. They made up most of the pieces as they went along, belting them out in pure ecstasy. They sang war songs, funeral songs, love songs and some songs that were just plain nonsense. One man would start out, feeling around in the air for a tune. The others would come in with a harmony that seemed more accidental than anything else. Sometimes the songs had no lyrics. There were no musical instruments to accompany the songs. Aem translated a typical song for us:

"During the Mulima war, her husband was killed. She cannot forget him. She still roasts sweet potatoes for him. She keeps hoping he will return so her work will be easier. But he does not return."

The men sucked in their breath and whooshed during this song to indicate the sadness of its theme.

It was almost dark when we returned to Tumagonem. The village was deathly quiet.

Inside the entrance, the men froze. There was someone crouched in the darkness near the *pilai*. I heard Kelion's breath catch in his throat.

The figure stood up from his squatting position and came toward us. His body was black with pig grease and soot. His color made him fade into the blackness of the night. He was holding something in his hands.

"Do you want to buy my stone axe?" he asked softly.

"No, I don't think so, thank you," I said.

Kelion coughed abruptly.

The dark man nodded. He walked a wide circle around the frozen men and disappeared into the night.

Sjam and I crawled into our *abiai* and lighted the small candle we'd brought with us. The men came in and sat down. They were shaken. They kept their eyes glued to the grass floor. Some of them rolled leaves into cigarettes and took lights from the little candle, then sucked noisily on the cigarettes.

No one said anything.

Sjam and I sat staring at the candle. We watched the little spear of light point upward until the candle grew shorter and shorter, and then, finally, burned out. We were left sitting in darkness.

"That man," Kelion whispered, "that man is a *kain!*"

"He's a *kain?*"

"Maybe it is better, Mama Wyn, if you had bought the stone axe from the *kain*."

"Why?"

Kelion wasn't prepared for a question like that. He couldn't figure the answer.

"The *kain* is Obaharok," Asuan said apologetically.

(13)

We were invited to a funeral in Punycul village. Kelion didn't want to go, saying he had to toast tobacco and do some other things. He wouldn't have time. Sjam and I sensed something was wrong, but we couldn't put our finger on it.

Aem seemed happy for the first time in several days. We suspected it had to do with Kelion's staying at home, for the two men had not been getting along for some time.

The day was hot and the sun was blindingly white. It left dark shadows between the leaves in the sweet-potato-carpeted Valley. There was no breeze to relieve the heat. Even the swallows were too warm to warble. They sat hidden in little groups under the acacia leaves waiting for the cool of the evening.

Aem walked with us to the entrance of Punycul and then deserted us. I supposed he was afraid he would be killed by strangers in the village.

Sjam and I climbed through the *thop* and wove our way between the many mourners in the courtyard toward the *pilai*. I'd brought an axe to give to the family of the deceased—it is Dani tradition to exchange gifts at funerals.

Aem's departure had left us with the inconvenience of being without an interpreter, and I didn't know what to do with the axe. However, the clarity of the Dani mind recognized my predicament; abruptly three men stood up in front of the *pilai* and chanted, "Wa, wa, wa, wa, wa . . ." It was an expression of gratitude for the gift and to inform the ghost of the deceased that he had been remembered.

Not only does one leave something at a Dani funeral, one takes something away. I was presented with a small, squealing piglet. I was grateful for the past experience of patting Kelion's pig on the head, but it did not fully prepare me to hold such an animal in my arms.

A young Dani was watching from the sidelines. With quick understanding, he relieved my distress by handing the wiggling pig to a woman nearby. She would take charge of it for the time being.

The boy motioned us to sit down in a shady spot beneath the eave of an *abiai*. He sat down, too. We found that he spoke a "pigeon," Bahasa Indonesia. He told us his name was Winoco and that he'd come from a nearby village called Wenebuborah.

Winoco was a young boy, fifteen or sixteen years old maybe, with big brown friendly eyes. He had beautiful black greased hair with little white lights in it. His body was terribly scarred, marked and dotted with wounds that come from pointed arrows. He wore a necklace of tiny blue beads. When I admired the beads, the compliment caused him to take them off and tie the strings around my neck.

Winoco explained the details of the ritual we were attending. It was an *ilko* (death ceremony), he said, not a funeral (*warema*). The deceased was Lokop, the former chief of Punycul. His body had been cremated more than two months before. He had been a chief of some importance. Because of the Dani's desire to honor him with as many pigs as possible, it had taken them nearly two months to collect them.

Meanwhile Lokop's ghost, which was released at the time of his cremation, had been roaming around the village causing all kinds of mischief. The ghost wanted Sike to perform the *ilko* as soon as possible.

Sike was the new chief of Punycul. He was a very young handsome Dani with wide, high cheekbones and dazzling black eyes that pinched shut whenever he smiled. There was a black stripe painted beneath his eyes. The stripe meant that Sike had won his chiefdom title through bravery. No man is allowed to blacken his cheekbones unless he has killed another man.

Chief Sike oversaw the killing of the many pigs the Dani had brought to honor Lokop. Then he went into the *pilai* to sing the usual funeral songs with the men. The women, their bodies covered with clay, wailed alone in the *hunila*.

Wherever the Dani congregated, I was invariably impressed with the oversupply of women present. There were many young girls, pestering everybody with their liveliness, many middle-aged women busy with whatever they were doing, and many ancient-looking women sitting around like ornaments in the village. Winoco said that the abundance of women was a result of the wars that had killed the men. There had been no major wars since the government came in, but not enough time had passed to even things out.

Winoco offered a little information on the Dani attempt to maintain the natural balance of the population. He was prompted by the fellow sitting next to him, a man of age and experience. The Dani women, we were told, refuse to bear more than two children. If they thought they could get away with it, they would have none at all. The Dani women want to work in the garden, herd around their pigs and cook in the *hunila*. They consider children a nuisance to their industry.

Most of the women resign themselves to bearing one or two children. If they find a third is on its way, they induce self-abortion with the help of a sharp bamboo stick.

After a child is born, the Dani father practices sexual abstinence until the newborn is five or six years old. Upon the birth of a second child, the wife usually denies a man his marital rights entirely. Strangely enough, the husband shows little concern or anxiety. One has the impression that the Dani men possess very weak sexual interests.

The Dani man is strongly devoted to his children. He loves them dearly and spends much of his time beating his wife if she abuses them.

The sun was hanging low in the sky. It looked like a big drop of red blood. Suddenly the village became hushed, and a black-sooted man crawled out of the *pilai*. He stood facing the courtyard. Every head swung toward him and quickly swung back again. Then people sat still, their eyes fixed on the ground.

The black man was middle-aged, small and wiry. He wore no decorations except for a few frayed string fibers around his neck and a black hairnet on his head. His *holim* reached to the top of his shoulder.

He wore a ringbeard on his soot-covered face. The soot had been wiped away beneath his eyes and down the bridge of his nose. He looked over the villagers with eyes that saw and ears that heard. He tested everything to find out if what he saw and heard was true or not. His mind made little notes of some of the things he wanted to remember.

And then he looked in our direction.

He nodded slightly and made a sharp entry into his mental notebook. He walked the length of the courtyard and disappeared through the village entrance. He was followed by several warriors.

The man was Obaharok.

(14)

Life in Tumagonem had suddenly turned ugly.

There was a feeling of deadness about the people. The once kind and hospitable natives had become aloof and detached to us.

Sjam and I couldn't figure it out. Asuan, and even Old Pum, evinced a complete loss of interest in us. Kelion's nerves seemed a little thin. This morning he went out of his way to kick a rock in the courtyard. He sat down in the ditch outside the village entrance and spent the whole day there.

We knew there was an animosity between Aem and Kelion. They hadn't spoken to each other for several days. They went their own ways, moving about silently, and they kept their heads down when they passed each other. There was no greeting between them.

We wanted to know what was going on but were afraid to ask Aem to interpret. We'd felt a small distrust of him ever since he'd lied about Kelion being chief of Tumagonem. We didn't know it at the time, but Aem had sent a set of unattractive rumors around the compound. Whatever they were, they worked against Sjam and me. Aem's motives for authorizing the rumors were not clear to us until later.

Sjam gritted her teeth and set her heels to solve the problem.

After she had nearly threatened to murder Aem in our *abiai*, he blurted out, "Kelion says you must leave the village. There's no room for you here! The women want their house back."

Aem crawled to the other side of the *abiai* to change his thinking. He sank back against the wall, exhausted with emotion.

"There's no wood here to build you a house. Kelion doesn't like you any more, either!" he said triumphantly.

It seemed an unbelievable thing.

"Tell Kelion we'll leave for Wamena in the morning," I said.

(15)

The day had the quality of dying to it.

The trek back to Wamena was terrible. No one spoke. There were no sounds except for the rustling noise made by our legs whipping awkwardly through the grasses.

Nearly all the villagers went with us, even Chief Asuan. The women and children carried our belongings on their heads and backs. Wenybake carried my piglet in her carrying net. In Pikke the pig became restless. She sang a soft lullaby to comfort the little fellow. But when the animal was asleep again, there were no more sounds from anybody.

The natives were sad. Only Aem seemed happy. I supposed he was glad to be returning to Wamena.

Sjam and I walked along trying to search for a truth, for an understanding of what had happened, for the relation of one thing to another. But nothing related, nothing fit together, nothing made sense to us.

We guessed that the natives of Tumagonem had somehow failed to weather our good intentions toward them. We had given them food when they had not asked to be fed. We had given them knives and shovels, but they had never come to us for tools.

The natives had given us things we could never forget—
things like trust. It's a terrible responsibility when you know
someone trusts you. A trust is a very fragile gift.

They had given us shelter and friendship without plan of
profit and with no idea of payment. One can't buy that kind of
kindness, not with money.

I looked at Kelion, his black ringbeard glistening in the sunshine, and I wondered, What can I do now? How can I get
along without him? Good-natured Kelion, a man with no
ambition beyond food and sleep and the entertainment of
stealing once in a while.

I watched Asuan walking alone. Lazy Chief Asuan, who
wanted nothing more than to lie down all day and let the life
of the Valley flow around him without lifting a finger to make
it go.

I remembered Old Pum, whose gay warrior-life days had
been reduced by age to pinching girls whenever he got the
chance.

I was so saddened by the thoughts of leaving the people of
Tumagonem that even the rowdy, uncontrollable Dani women
were suddenly beloved to me. I was almost sorry I had hung
cameras around my neck to keep them away from me.

Sjam and I felt we were waiting for something that would
keep us together before we reached Wamena. It was like
waiting for a miracle that never happens and you know it will
not happen. The waiting for it makes the hurt worse.

When we arrived in Wamena, Aem entered the Sumitros'
house, and Sjam and I turned to say farewell to a people whom,
for some unknown reason, we were leaving.

We shook hands with Kelion.

"*Nit warok hat ninom motok dogosak*," Kelion said huskily.
There were tears in his eyes. Then he turned and led his people
down the road to return to Tumagonem.

I watched the little group move along, all the time hoping
they would come back and ask me to go with them. I watched
them until they became tiny specks of pepper on the horizon.

And then they were gone.

(16)

"Aem, what does '*Nit warok hat ninom motok dogosak*' mean?"

"Where'd you hear that?"

"Oh, I just heard it. What does it mean?"

"It means, 'We want you to stay with us, forever.'"

Handwriting BY KOLO

CHAPTER TWO

Kolo

(1)

I woke up in the morning with raw and burning skin from not having taken off my clothes for days and days. I itched all over from mosquito and flea bites. I'd sprained my right ankle in leaping over a ditch the day before. The joint was stiff and swollen.

It had not rained in Wamena for a whole week. The rain barrels were almost dried up. Sjam and I took a bath in a pail of water and washed our underthings in the suds.

In the late morning we paid a visit to Police Chief Marpaung and told him we'd returned from Tumagonem.

"Why? Didn't anyone ask to marry you?"

"There wasn't any wood in the village to build us a house. We were inconveniencing the natives by living in one of theirs. What do you mean, didn't anyone ask to marry me?"

"Oh," Marpaung laughed, "don't be surprised if they ask you to marry them! It's a common thing, you know. Marriages make them rich!"

"No, no one asked me to get married, as far as I know."

"Well, what are your plans now?"

"Aem has invited us to his village. We'll probably go tomorrow. If we like it, we'll pack in and stay for a while. I'll let you know."

When Sjam and I returned to the Sumitros' there was a group of natives waiting for us on the front porch. All of them needed medicine. The jungle's "Associated Press" had been knocking out news bulletins, again.

I was puzzled by the injuries on one of the young Dani men. The locations and types of wounds were unusual. Deep holes had been burned into his right arm. He had been burned between the buttocks. There were lacerations crisscrossing over his back as though he had been whipped. One of the ugly gashes needed sutures.

"What happened to you?"

"I was beaten."

"Who beat you?"

"The police at Jiwika."

I looked up at Sjam. Her brows were knit together in a frown but she made no comment.

"Sjam, take my camera and get a shot of this."

I emptied sulfa powder into the open wounds and covered the burns with ointment.

"Why were you beaten by the police?"

"They stole my pigs and they didn't want me to tell anybody."

I dressed his wounds and advised him to drop by the government hospital to have stitches taken in the deep cut on his scapula, but he shook his head and headed back toward the mountains.

(2)

Aem was electric with joy.

This gay rapture was the result of an agreement Sjam and I had made with him. We promised to visit his village for the day. If we liked it, we would return to stay for a while.

Aem appointed himself as guide-interpreter. It was not a job he was well suited for. Sjam and I suspected he'd largely contributed to whatever the misunderstanding in Tumagonem, but we were uncertain of the extent of his mischief and neither of us wanted to accuse the boy of things he possibly did not do.

The morning sun shone with such eagerness that it seemed to take the color right out of the landscape. Ten minutes outside of Wamena we entered a dense bamboo forest. Aem leaped with sure feet through the trees and came out on the other side without a scratch. Sjam and I lost our way somewhere in the middle of the forest and thought we were going to be entombed in there forever. We scrambled over the slimy earth beneath a giant umbrella of bamboo, slipping and falling over rocks embedded in the mud, fighting to find our way out. When we finally emerged from the grove, we were winded to the point of having to sit down and rest.

There were tall jungle grasses growing where the bamboo forest left off. Beyond them stood rows of acacias, causarinas and eucalyptus trees. The great trees dipped their roots into the banks of the Baliem River. Here the river was lazy and slow.

It was a beautiful place to be. The air was liquid-filled and warm. The sun, throwing a hot shine on the river, fired sparks on the surface so bright that they were blinding to the eye. The grasses around the trees grew thicker and greener than elsewhere because they drew more water from the river and the dripping trees. The foliage above and around us was so heavy that the sun couldn't get through. The spot beneath the trees was shady and almost cool.

At this crossing the Baliem River was forded by means of a Dani homemade raft. Once there were two rafts in service, but one had already fallen apart. The good raft, an affair made of three logs tied together with rattan lengths, was stationed on the other side of the river. We sat down on the riverbank to wait until we saw someone who would ferry it across to us. When it finally arrived, we were faced with problems.

It required one's undivided attention to cross the Baliem River on a three-log raft. The wood was wet and slippery. The raft was half emerged in water and any additional weight put on it, would sink it out of sight. The Dani stood on the raft and poled it from one side to the other, but standing is a risky venture for a Westerner wearing heavy jungle boots. It was safer to sit down on the raft, although your backside would be quite wet upon arrival at the other side of the river.

A group of natives came rustling through the grasses to meet us. After exchanging a few words with Aem, they skipped down the bank and poled themselves across the river.

"They said there's a funeral going on in Abulakma," Aem said. "That's my village. One of my brothers died there yesterday."

"Is this a good time to go to the village?" I asked.

"Sure," Aem said offhandedly.

I was surprised at Aem's insensitivity to the death of his brother.

When we came out of the woods it was easier to see the landscape around us. There is so much variety in this southeastern part of the country that it is hard to know where to start to describe such a land. One thing sets off another.

We were walking on a stony path surrounded by short brown grasses that had an abundance of multicolored wild flowers growing in them. Beyond the grasses, the Valley floor swept upward, climbing the high mountain walls on the south and west. The lowlands stretched for miles to the north and east. The plain was banded, here and there, with trees where little rivers encouraged their tall growth.

The entire Valley was covered with gardens. They were walled in with white stone fences high enough to allow people to enter but to keep the pigs out. The pigs moved slowly along the spiderwebbing paths, eating as they went.

The landscape was breath-takingly beautiful, but it was

difficult to walk on the stony paths, which went around rather
than through the gardens. The distance was doubled by their
many cutbacks in direction, and sometimes the paths went
straight up a hillside. Sjam and I climbed the hills, scrambling
around in the rocks on our hands and knees, and we slid down
the steep descents on our hip pockets. It's no lady's job to
walk anywhere in the Baliem Valley.

We heard the wailing of the natives in Abulakma long before
the village came into view. Dani funerals, like funerals everywhere else in the world, are grim affairs. The quality of the
Dani feelings is no different than ours.

When I entered the courtyard, my white skin and foreign
"look" caused an awkward silence to hang over the people for
a few moments. When the Dani recovered from the sight of
me, they returned to their business of providing the cere-
monialism required for the pacification of the deceased.

More Dani men and women arrived, their bodies covered
with clay as a sign of mourning. The women dropped off at
the kitchen to join the other mourners inside. The men walked
the length of the courtyard and stood before the *pilai*. The
chief of the compound began a mournful chant, calling out the
name of the dead man. The warriors bowed their heads as
though in prayer and chanted their bereavement in unison.
They rubbed their thighs with their hands, piled up little rocks
with their feet, and from time to time wiped at the tears that
were streaming from their eyes.

It is an awesome sight to see the Dani men cry. They possess
feelings as fragile as glass, and when they are hurt, they weep
bitterly. Weeping seems to leave them with their souls nakedly
exposed and makes them appear enfeebled and pathetically
defenseless.

The Dani women cry like coyotes. They shake with such exaggerated grief that their mourning strikes a chord of insincerity. But their loss is very real. It is usually the women
who suffer the longest.

The importance of the role the deceased played during his
lifetime as well as the manner in which he died determine the
grandeur of the funeral. An accident, illness or old age does

not command as much attention as the death of a hero. Certainly a *kain's* death would bring about an enormous funeral from his own people. It would probably move his enemy to a celebration of a different sort.

All funerals are occasions for pig feasts because something valuable must be given to the deceased's ghost and family. Friends and relatives who don't have pigs to offer bring cowrie shells, *walimos, mikaks,* feathered headdresses (*cabanees*), furs, carrying nets and other things.

The gifts are presented to the chief or to the most important man in the compound. He chants a series of gentle cries, "Wa, wa, wa, wa, wa," to inform the ghost that they have arrived and that the dead man has been remembered.

The deceased at this funeral was a man who had died of a heart attack. His body was propped up in a chair (*pia*) in the kitchen. The chair was made of bamboo and is the only piece of furniture ever made by the Dani.

The women were crouched facing the corpse, crying. They brushed and swatted the body with sweet-potato vines to keep the flies away. Sometimes a woman would reach out and stroke the dead man's arm or leg.

The corpse had been dressed with a long *holim.* Later he would be greased with pig fat (*wamano*) and decorated in death with the ornaments he would have wanted to wear in life.

The shell strands (*yerak* or *honnaboen*) that had been brought to the funeral were draped around the corpse's head. They streamed down from his shoulders in six-foot lengths and would adorn his body until the pigs were eaten. Then they would be redistributed among the important people at the funeral and those who were owed a debt.

At funerals, as well as on any other occasion that requires pig killings, the men have more work to do than the women. They had made the *pia* and now were preparing to kill and cook the pigs. Later they would construct the pyre to cremate the deceased.

Although the number of pigs to be killed varies with the importance of the deceased, the steps in the killing (*wamwaria-*

gai) never change. Two Dani hold the pig by the ears and hind legs and stretch the animal between them while a third shoots a blood-letting arrow (*wim*) into its heart at a distance of about two feet.

The animal is lowered to the ground to run around until it bleeds to death. Sometimes a Dani accelerates the process by stepping on a fallen animal and gently pressing his foot against the heart to expel the blood and stop the muscular action.

The slaughtered pigs are arranged in a row in front of the *pilai*. The feet of one pig are placed to touch the body of its neighbor. This unifies the animals as a single gift to the deceased's ghost.

The chief marches down the row of dead pigs and shouts out the names of the donors to inform the living as well as the dead man that the gifts are all present and accounted for. Then the animals are separated. The men cut off the pigs' ears and scrotums, and large circles of skin are sliced off with the tails. While ears are roasted and eaten, the tails and scrotums will be dried and worn as ornaments by important men.

Now the Dani dragged the animals over to a fire in the courtyard and burned off the bristles. Clean banana leaves were spread on the ground, on which the pigs were eviscerated with sharp bamboo knives and cut into large chunks. Some of the better parts of meat were hung on an improvised line. They were saved for eating later. The remaining pieces, including the thick fat, were taken away to be cooked in the steam pit.

The pig cooking (*isatare*) is a sharp example of the sophistication of the Dani mind. The method is neat, hygenic and safe. Few Dani have ever died from food poisoning.

The cooking pit is cleaned and lined with *lukwaka* grass. Layers of hot stones are placed between the green vegetables, sweet potatoes and pork. The whole bundle is tide up at the top. Water is sprinkled on the oven to produce steam for thorough cooking.

Rodents find themselves of sudden significance in a Dani funeral. Dogs hunt the *cuscus* (mouse opossum) and other furry marsupials. They are brought in to be roasted and eaten at the funeral gatherings. As far as I could learn, the animals' importance lay in their rarity and difficulty to catch.

Sometimes, during the first day of a funeral ritual, a muffled human scream can be heard in the distance. More often, the screams are heard the following day, when not so many people are around. The screams come from little girls who have offered their fingers to be cut off to placate the deceased's ghost. It is a physical demonstration of grief. The Dani believe that without it, the ghost will feel unloved and ill-remembered.

And this is a true thing. All Dani girls are expected, sooner or later, to give up their finger joints. When they are called upon, few ever balk at having them cut off.

The amputator, usually an experienced Dani man, raps a sharp blow to the "crazy bone" in the child's elbow to anesthetize the hand. Then he chops off a single finger joint with a stone adze. The finger is thrown on the funeral pyre at the time of cremation. If the finger is cut off on the second day, the joint is burned in the kitchen fireplace.

Sometimes the men cut their ears and fingers to show grief if their loss is of a very deep and personal nature. Often young women will beg to have slices cut from their ears to indicate that their grief will remain permanent. (During my stay in the Valley, I doctored sliced ears and finger stumps because the Indonesian government hospital refused to touch such patients)

The Dani treat the wounded fingers with *oeka* leaves and dress the hand with pressure bandages made from *hum* leaves. The girl holds her arm up in the air until the blood stops flowing and all dangers of infection pass.

The men sit talking quietly while they are waiting for the pork to roast. Often they tweeze each other's beards or roll bark fibers on their thighs to make threads strong enough to weave nets at some later date.

When the pig is cooked, the oven bundle is dismantled. The pork is cut into smaller pieces with bamboo knives. The meat and vegetables are divided among the men and women. The people wait until every guest is served and then they eat in silence. When they are finished they rub their greasy hands on their hair or bodies to clean them.

The Dani men build the pyre for the cremation ritual (*hele-kirikare*) from rough logs measuring about seven feet in length to a height of four feet. The corpse is taken from the *pia* and placed on the smoking pyre in a reclining position with the head toward the sunset. The *pia* and additional logs are carefully arranged on top of the pyre to provide a good draft for complete consummation.

At this moment the chief of the village shoots an arrow through a little bundle of grass held by another Dani. This act releases the deceased's ghost. Several men and a few boys run with the grass bundle toward the entrance of the village, yelling and screaming to chase the ghost on its way out of town.

When the pyre has burned down, the guests depart for their own compounds. Those who remain think of tomorrow and the sadness it will bring. The people must gather the bones of the dead man and place them in an *oak*, a small wooden box located behind the men's *pilai*.

(The villagers in Abulakma mourned for a period of one week with ritualistic chanting, wailing and eating of pig meat. Then they settled down into their normal routine of living again. I did not have time to investigate any further aspects or stages of the Dani funeral, but I had the impression that the Dani dead are not easily forgotten. They are remembered, in fact, with ceremony at other pig feasts closely tied to religious functions, and in particular to the wedding ritual, of which I was soon to become a part.)

The sun had gone behind a hill, leaving pink clouds hanging on the horizon. It would soon be dark. If we wanted to cross the Baliem River on a three-log raft in daylight, we would have to hurry or we would be stuck in the jungle for the night.

The sky was gray when we reached the river. Night had fallen when we walked into Wamena. The darkness gave off a chilly aloofness that reminded man of his littleness and loneliness in the world.

(3)

Aem desperately wanted Sjam and me to live in his Village of Abulakma. Since we had found the natives very friendly to us on the day of the funeral, we decided to return to Abulakma and establish our headquarters there.

It was six o'clock in the morning. Sjam and I were busy packing our things in Wamena, preparing to leave with Aem for his village, when I looked out the window and saw a young boy leaning against the Sumitros' back fence.

"Winoco!"

"*Laok*," he said. His voice was shy and apologetic.

"You're a long way from home. What are you doing in Wamena?"

Winoco dropped his head and looked at the ground while he put his mind through the preparation of answer. He itched with self-consciousness because everyone was looking at him, waiting for him to say something.

"I decided I'd follow you," he said as a simple matter of fact.

Sadness came into his eyes and suddenly he looked lonely. "You can go around in circles just so long. I've been sitting in my village thinking and thinking. My mother and father are both dead. I've been wondering where I should go and what I should do. I decided I'd go with you."

Winoco had arrived in Wamena with a stunning new greased hairdo and everything he owned, which was nothing.

He smiled and looked around for something he could do for us. He picked up a box of canned goods and an aluminum suitcase. "I will carry these for you," he said. "I will live in Abulakma and help you there. I can speak Indonesian and Dani for you."

Winoco's abilities were becoming apparent. Aem's fulltime job with the Sumitros meant he would have to return to Wamena in a few days anyway. Winoco could be put on salary for odd jobs and translating.

Villagers from Abulakma arrived to transport our goods. We had more help than we could use and nearly enough strong arms to move all of Wamena. The natives picked up rice sacks and cases of canned cooking oil, corned beef, pears, cookies and catsup, noodles, camera cases and suitcases, backpacks and sleeping bags. One of the women in the crowd nestled my piglet in her carrying net and hung it from her head.

As the little party of bearers trotted down the road toward the bamboo forest and Abulakma, Aem hung back, squatting down by the Sumitros' house. He looked as though he weren't going to move. His face was pinched up in a black frown and his eyes stared straight ahead; his broad-mindedness did not include Winoco's intrusion. He felt the whole situation was getting out of his hands.

"Aem, we really need someone to translate for us up there while you're working in Wamena," I explained. "And Winoco can get water for us and maybe cook, too." I got no response.

Sjam yelled at Aem. Whatever it was she said moved him up off the ground and into a step fast enough to join the others.

When we arrived in Abulakma everyone in our little parade had a new name, with the exception of Aem, who didn't want one. Sjam and I were surprised to see how easily the old names were tossed off and the new ones stuck. I felt hard put for names toward the end of the list. I named one boy after my son, Jmy. This brought a sharp cry from Winoco. I renamed Winoco "Mi Hijo," which means "my son" in Spanish. I named the last two men after "dove" (La Paloma) in Spanish and "butterfly" (Le Papillon) in French.

It was about three-thirty in the afternoon. We'd arrived in the courtyard of Aem's compound. The people from the funeral next door interrupted their mourning long enough to visit us. They seemed pleased about our being there.

Mi Hijo was afraid of these new people. He hung back behind the entrance of the compound, wrestling between duty and fear. When he finally gathered his courage, he crept in close enough to hear the Dani talking. Then he became perplexed. He couldn't understand what they were saying. He felt he should understand the Abulakma Dani because he looked like them. They were the same in stance and shape. They even wore the same decorations.

The Abulakma Dani are a good example of how tight little

groups are held together on islands of isolation through regional hostilities. Mi Hijo's village was no more than sixteen kilometers away as the crow flies, but the prevailing animosity between the people guaranteed the maintenance of many, many dialects between the northern and southern parts of the Valley.

Mi Hijo quickly learned the Abulakma dialect. Before I left the Valley he had learned three others, improved on his Bahasa Indonesia, and had mastered the English word "Hello."

Eluguno and Eadeke were Aem's father and mother. We called Eluguno "Papa Aem." He was short and heavy and very strong. His beard surprised us a little because it was so gray. He was the head of the compound and one of the nicest people I ever met in the Valley. He was not a chief because he simply did not want to be. "Chief" meant putting on certain airs and keeping a reputation lively. Papa Aem was too old to want more than a quiet, peaceful compound to live in.

Being near Mama Aem was like sitting in a flower garden next to a volcano. She constantly held a Dani cigarette in a long reed holder but she never smoked it because she never stopped talking. Mama Aem was animated to the point of danger. When .she spoke, one stood at a distance to avoid getting hurt.

I told the villagers of my mission and thanked them for allowing us to enter the compound. I said I would be living with them for a while and promised to try not to disturb them too much.

Mama Aem asked me if I was going to make her husband rich. "Rich" meant more pigs or wives for Papa Aem.

I told her I believed he already had his hands full.

(4)

There were only three structures, besides the pigsty, in Aem's compound: the *pilai*, kitchen and one tiny *abiai*. Didek was Aem's grandmother. She slept in the *abiai* along with Mama Aem and a whole squadron of children related in one way or another to Aem's family.

In the interest of space, Sjam and I were told we could spend the night in the *pilai* until Aem built a house for us. It was probably the first time in history that two women spent the whole night on the ground floor of a warriors' house in West Irian, with real live men sleeping upstairs. We sat in a circle watching the lazy coils of smoke rise from the dying embers of the fire and flatten themselves against the low ceiling. A few cockroaches crept through the grass carpet to bite us. When they found we didn't taste any better than the Dani, they left us alone.

Without a word the men left, one by one, to climb up into the loft to bed down for the night. Le Papillon was the first to go. He was followed by Mi Hijo, Aem and a boy I had named Amigo. Papa Aem stayed on and on. When he was satisfied they were all asleep up there, he swung himself through the hole to join them. Bits of grass fell down as he scooted some boards across the entrance to the loft and closed it up.

I believe he slept on top of the entrance all night just to be sure that Sjam and I weren't disturbed by sleepwalkers.

(5)

Our new house was built in one day. It was an amazing thing when it was finished.

The excitement of building a new house was intense. Even the mourners from next door came over to help. They brought their own tools with them.

The most important tool in the carpenter's kit is the stone adze. The adze is a piece of hard stone that has been sharpened on limestone outcroppings and bound into a wood handle with rattan lengths. The Dani chops downward with the adze. When he applies the right pressure in the right direction, he can fell a fairly large tree in a matter of minutes.

The stone axe looks like a wooden club with a rock embedded in the end. It is used to split wood.

The Dani have hammers but never use them to drive nails because they don't have any. The hammers are large, flat rocks. They can sink a center post into the ground in no time at all.

Sometimes small pieces of flint and boar's tusks are used to cut vines. More often a Dani will cut the vines with his own teeth.

The men and women worked together leveling the ground for the new house with their digging sticks. When it was flat and clean of grass, Aem laid out a large circle of vine in the shape of an *abiai*. Then he changed his mind and placed some rough planks in a rectangle on the site.

It was difficult for Sjam and me to stay out of the designing of the house. We had ideas about its height—we wanted to stand up inside it—and we thought a small window would be nice to let in the fresh air. But we kept quiet. Aem was the architect and builder; he deserved full authority over its construction.

The front and back walls went up first. Pairs of posts were thrown into the ground and set with a hard rock hammer. Rough boards were slipped in between the vertical pairs, and bamboo vines were used to lash the boards in place.

After the end walls were finished, seven-foot forked poles were placed in the middle of the house for the pitched roof. A wood beam was laid in the fork. Reeds were tied to the beam and extended down to the walls, then long thatch grass was tied to the reeds. An additional layer of grass was carefully laid on top. The grass roof was trimmed at its lower edge with a stone adze hit against a board.

At this point it became apparent that Aem had made an enemy of himself to some of the carpenters. He had shouted at them, believing it made for clarity. A few of them resented his bossy behavior and left the compound in a huff. He let them go with a wave of his hand. He stood back, hands on his hips, surveying the rectangular house with an appraising eye.

The entrance was small. It had been boarded across the bottom so the pigs couldn't get in. The structure was tall enough for standing up in the middle. There was plenty of head room when sitting against the side walls.

Aem could find no fault with it. A smile spread over his face.

The remaining carpenters raised a bamboo-reed platform a foot off the ground in the part of the house meant for the sleeping area. The only drawback, we learned, was that the space below provided a dandy place for rats to move in with their families. They had all kinds of freedom in there and knew they could never get caught.

A fire pit was dug in the floor on the other side of the house, and grass carpeting was installed for sitting. According to Western standards the little thatched house was a pretty grim abode, but Sjam and I were overjoyed with the idea of being proprietors of this split-level marvel. Everyone in the compound crowded inside the house to evaluate the architectural wonder that had been built in a single day.

Aem lit a fire to drive out the mosquitoes, which were unmerciful. We had disturbed their nests when we uprooted the grass they lived in. This action gave them enough reason to double their biting efforts on us.

The children were splitting bamboo lengths with their teeth and peeling off the outer bark to weave a mat that would separate the bedroom from the living room, when we heard soft footsteps in the courtyard.

The children dropped their bamboo pieces and looked at one another. Mi Hijo and Aem exchanged a glance and turned their heads toward the door. Papa and Mama Aem shared a common dark cloud over their faces.

Abruptly, a man's figure filled the little doorway. He was half stooped over, one hand resting on the doorframe. He poked his head into the house. Then he raised his face to look at us.

Obaharok.

He was accompanied by two of his warriors.

"*Laok*," he said softly.

When Aem recognized Obaharok, his eyes glazed over and you could see a rage building up in him. It pulsed through the little veins in his temples in hot jumps. His breathing became fast and hollow, and it came in intervals.

Mi Hijo wished he weren't there at all. He pushed himself into a corner and tried to squeeze himself out of sight in it. He wasn't angry. He was afraid.

Papa and Mama Aem were afraid, too. Mama Aem didn't know why she was afraid, but one look at Papa Aem's terror-stricken face was good enough reason to feel a fear without questioning it.

Obaharok stepped over the wood barrier in the doorway and into the living room. The two warriors followed him and sat down on either side of Sjam. She looked hemmed in.

Obaharok felt no shyness about himself and therefore he had no shyness with strangers. He climbed up on the sleeping platform, crossed his legs and sat down next to me. I hoped he didn't know we were sitting in the bedroom of the house.

Obaharok sat as though his back had been permanently starched with whalebone. He kept his back as straight as a board even when he leaned forward. When he turned from side to side, which he rarely did, his back was still straight. Obaharok never tired from sitting up straight.

I had never seen Obaharok at such close range before. His head was covered with the same black hairnet. He had stuck a single white feather in the front of it. His eyes were small and deep-set in a face that was very black. His teeth were slightly crooked because they were crowded into a mouth that could not accommodate them. There were places in his beard that were gray. I guessed his age to be about forty-five.

Obaharok's appraisal of the people in the house was instantaneous. There was an air of acute attentiveness about him, but his eyes did not move around. It would be very unusual for him not to know everything that was going on, wherever he happened to be.

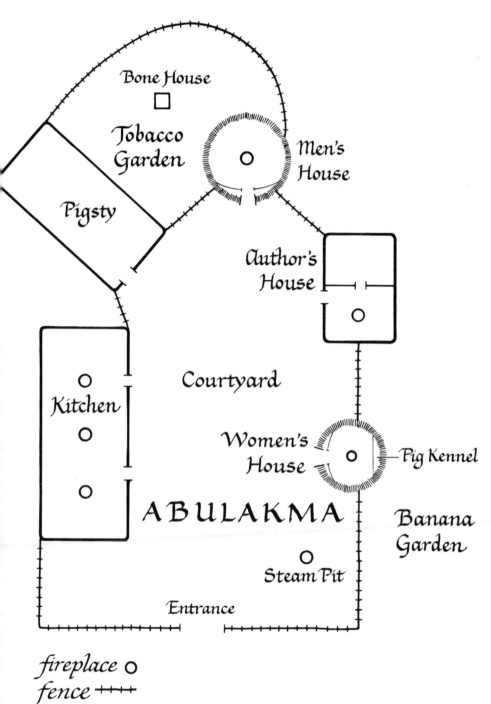

Bone House

Tobacco Garden

Men's House

Pigsty

Author's House

Courtyard

Kitchen

Women's House

Pig Kennel

ABULAKMA

Banana Garden

Steam Pit

Entrance

fireplace o
fence ++++

Obaharok was at ease with himself, and he used that quietude to ease others. He conversed lightly with his two men to get things going. None of us knew what he said because the dialect was foreign to Aem. Mi Hijo wouldn't have understood even if he had been listening.

There were Indonesian cigarettes on the floor. Obaharok leaned forward and picked up the pack. He turned it over in his hands, took out a cigarette and looked at it. "This," he said in Aem's dialect, "this is honest work. The paper is thin and the tobacco is packed tightly inside. This is a true thing."

Obaharok's voice was soft. "Do you plan on living here in this house?" he asked me.

"Yes, for a little while."

"Did you have my permission to build such a house?"

I swallowed hard. "Uh, no. I'm sorry. I didn't know I needed your permission. It's not really my house, you see. I will be using it only as long as I am here in the Valley."

My mind flashed back to the maps I had seen in Police Chief Marpaung's office: this whole territory of the Valley was considered by the Indonesian government to be under Obaharok's jurisdiction. According to the people in the southern area, however, a man named Kolo was chief of Analaga district, of which Abulakma was a village. A village without a chief was placed beneath the ruling chief's jurisdiction; in this case, Kolo oversaw Abulakma but lived in Obasia. Old Dialec was Kolo's father, still chief of his *own* village, but beneath his son's rule.

Obaharok and Kolo had been enemies for some time. Suddenly the building of the little house in Abulakma placed me in the middle of something nasty. I had not received permission for its construction from either Obaharok or Kolo; in fact, I hadn't even met Chief Kolo.

"I should fine you one large pig for building such a house," Obaharok said. He measured the size of the animal by raising his hand three feet off the floor.

"But no matter," he added quietly.

There was something very gentle, nearly dear, in Obaharok's face, yet something alarmingly ferocious, too. It had to do with the look of success he had about him, an enormous success born of method. You felt that anyone close to him would be influenced forever by what he said or did. The influence and force of the man revealed itself in his neat thinking.

"I understand you are here to write a book about my people," he said. "You must come visit me when you can. I will show you my gardens, my pigs, my villages and my wives, if you are interested."

"That's very kind of you. I hope you will come visit Sjam and me in Abulakma as often as you like."

"I will return," he said simply.

Obaharok nodded to his warriors. And then he left.

(6)

Sjam and I didn't meet Chief Kolo until after Aem had returned to work in Wamena.

We had asked Aem to take us to Kolo's village on several occasions. Each time he offered one reason or another for not going. His excuses invariably lacked conviction, and a few of them were even astonishing. One evasion had to do with the accusation that Kolo's wife had sexually attacked him in his own compound. I wanted to ask Aem a few questions about such an event, but his gaze was so ferocious that I abandoned the notion of asking him anything.

In the beginning it was difficult to know what to call our house because of its shape and function. Naming it even puzzled the natives. It was a combined kitchen (*hunila*) and sleeping quarters for two women (*abiai*). The architectural framework did not resemble anything else in the Baliem Valley. The Dani had no word for it. In the end, they finally settled on calling it simply "house" (*uma*).

It had become a matter of habit for the Dani in the area to head toward our *uma* every night after work. They came for a variety of reasons. The sick needed medicine, the farmers asked for new vegetable seeds, the children wanted to play. And all were curiously fascinated with the tape recorder.

The Dani never understood the principle of the machine and expressed no interest in learning the mechanics of it. They felt amazement but no fear at the contraption. Their fondness to hear their own voices on it kept a standing order going for batteries down at Wamena. I believe the recorder scattered nearly a carload of exhausted size C's over the Valley before we removed it from the area.

The tape recorder, during these evening fiestas, began to bring people together in the *uma*. They were people who had previously prided themselves on hating and despising one another. Enemies suddenly became friends, neighbors became relatives, and kinships were reaffirmed and bragged about for the first time in years. I suppose it was the beginning of some kind of social revolution in the Dani world. A little gladness began to penetrate from the *uma* into the compound. It gradually built and spread out into other compounds and finally into the surrounding villages.

The activities, laughter and singing forced a premature gaiety into the funeral compound next door. When those people showed up, the girls still had their fingers and ears in bandages.

Sjam and I had discussed to what extent we, as guests in the area, should become involved with the people. We decided to permit ourselves to give the Dani things like medicine, foods, tools, clothing, tobacco and books, and pens and pencils for the children, in return for their kind hospitality. We were reluctant to change their existing traditions and laws, however. And we refrained from expressing our ideas or opinions on any culture, whether Indonesian, Dani or American.

There were times when we had difficulty skirting some of the problems concerning the demands made upon the people by the Indonesian government. Sometimes the Dani men asked us why we thought they had to wear clothes. They said they knew the government was unhappy with them because they wore *holims*. But they didn't have any money to buy clothes and they had no way of getting it. And once you had clothes, you had to buy soap to wash them. If they tore, why, you would have to buy needle and thread to mend them. Apart from the problem of economics, there was the problem of sweating inside the clothes. This was a disgusting thought to the Dani.

During these nightly sessions, Mi Hijo translated. Sjam and I began to understand a little more about these southern Dani. We found them to be a remarkably kind and open people. They maintained the same sense of wonder at the structure of life. They wanted from life exactly the same things we wanted: security and love.

There were sharp contrasts, too. Just to listen to the men talk of the good old days when they played "war" made us realize the vastness in our cultural differences.

Sometimes the people told rumors. A Dani would begin a rumor by whispering it. As the story went around the room everyone improved on it. Everyone in the *uma* believed the rumor for at least the rest of the evening and sometimes even until the next day. Then another rumor would take its place.

The content of the rumors had to do with ghosts who stole pigs, or the sun being angry with the people because it hadn't rained for several days, or about a single individual who had run off into the jungle swearing he'd never return.

When the Dani ran out of rumors, the tape recorder was brought out. Sjam and I listened to endless hours of yodeling songs which became nearly silly to us before the people tired singing them.

Then a sleepy dullness would settle over the people. Their eyes and voices grew weary. The children would fall asleep in their mothers' arms. Sometimes the men collapsed on the floor and dozed off.

Wood was precious in the area. When the fire died down, Sjam would bring out a candle. As the candle grew shorter and shorter, the people would gradually thin out and disappear into the night. By the time the candle had burned down and sagged sideways, almost everyone had gone. The village settled into a fine sleep.

One night I looked up to see three dark figures who had

remained behind. Now, these people should go, I thought, but they didn't. They would probably stay for weeks and weeks.

"Ma," Mi Hijo whispered, "Ma, my uncle and Kolo are here."

Mi Hijo had discovered an uncle living in the area he didn't know he had. This was in itself not an unusual thing. It was the style for unhappy women to run to the enemy during wartime to better themselves. If they were young and useful, they usually married into the tribe. If they were old and ugly, then the enemy might kill the ladies and often ate them. Apparently, a few wars back, some daring creature from Wenebuborah had bolted across the enemy line and tied up with the Analaga forces. The action resulted in a marriage, which thereby produced an uncle for Mi Hijo, though probably more through Mi Hijo's desire than through Wenebuborah blood. And Uncle Abinyai was Kolo's best friend.

"Light another candle," I said to Sjam. "We're finally going to meet the boss!"

In the glow of the candlelight, Kolo's head was bent slightly forward. He wore no decoration except for a coil of red plastic around his neck and a band of greased bird feathers on his forehead. His head was covered with a black hair net.

When he raised his face he showed neither fear nor amiability. It was a black face, blackened with soot and pig grease, upon which he had cultivated a fine black beard.

Kolo did not seem glad to see us. But Kolo we discovered later, was never glad to see anybody. He had a sour eye for the whole world and he took pride in showing it. He was a set-apart, lonesome-looking man with a mouth engraved by bitterness. His greatness had receded the day Obaharok defeated him. It left him with a look of hatred. He sneered most of the time, whined with self-pity and he was a professional at practicing sickness.

With this kind of crumbling character, Kolo's disposition was unpredictable. Sometimes he put on quite a handsome face, but only when he felt like it. Most of the time he was just plain hateful-looking.

Kolo's real name was Umataok. When he learned it meant "under, beneath," he took a new appellation for himself. As a boy, had he worn clothes he would have been the kind of a kid who acted too big for his britches.

On impulse rather than ability, Old Dialec, Kolo's father, had handed him his reins of chiefdom. Through Kolo's mean, irritable and greedy character he managed to hang on to the title, even in the face of his defeat.

Kolo had one wife. Only one. I don't know how she stood him.

When I first met Kolo, I made an error about his intelligence. He never said very much. I believed he was a silent man with deep, wise thoughts. Instead, Kolo turned out to be a man with hardly any thoughts at all. Having rejected the idea of having thoughts of his own, he rejected the thoughts of others. He possessed a rubber brain. Any ideas passing his way bounced off without leaving so much as a small dent.

Chief Kolo was the most difficult man I had to work with in the Valley. I knew he was capable of great hatred and cruelty, a man who knew and practiced revenge whenever he could. Fortunately, Kolo took a shine to me. At one time he even thought he wanted to marry me. The idea improved his character and gave rise to an unbelieveable sweetness of disposition. He even surprised himself with it.

The first night we met Kolo he asked me two questions in the same breath.

"Obaharok was here, wasn't he? What did he want?"

Somehow I felt I shouldn't tell Kolo that Obaharok wanted to fine me for building a house in Abulakma.

"I met Obaharok before. Sometime ago, in Tumagonem. He is a friend."

Chief Kolo brooded for a while over the statement. He left the *uma* without saying a word.

(7)

One night after the others had left, Mi Hijo hung back in the *uma*. He looked as though he had something on his mind. He stood on one leg and then the other. He sat down and took a sudden interest in his fingernails.

"Mi Hijo?"

"Ma," he whispered, "Ma, do you think you could be my mother? I mean, I want to be your son. My mother is dead, you know. I guess I want to be your son more than anything else in the world."

"Why, I'd be honored if you were my son, Mi Hijo."

"I'd have to kill a pig to make it stick. That's the way it's done. We tell everybody that I'm going to be your son and then I kill a pig. I don't have enough money right now but I'm saving every bit. Pretty soon I think I can buy a little pig for the ceremony."

I wondered if Mi Hijo was going to suggest a raise in his salary.

"I'll tell you when I have enough money. I don't know how much I need yet, but my uncle knows. He knows about how much pigs cost and all. My uncle's a very smart man."

"Well, fine, Mi Hijo. You let me know."

"Ma, can we keep it a secret right now? Just between you and me?"

(8)

I suppose the quickest way to earn the respect of the Dani is to walk around their countryside and pretend you're not afraid.

Sjam and I spent hours every day, with our hearts in our throats, walking between the villages in the Analaga district trying to display some kind of courage and valor. We got away with it.

The Dani allowed us to roam around unharmed. I think it

was because the children helped us. We found them playing games in the footpaths near the compounds. Those who recovered from the shock of seeing us followed us and in a way protected us with their presence.

Mi Hijo carried the medical kit in addition to the camera cases. I never found a child without some kind of scratch on his leg, if not something worse. Giving first aid got things going. The children let me practice medicine on them because they liked the "stuff" that stung. It was red and when it dried on their skin it wouldn't rub off, not even with spit.

The children followed us until we reached a new compound. Then fear would overcome them and they disappeared into thin air.

At home the children reported our brave conduct to their village chiefs. The chiefs mistook boldness for leadership. They arrived at the stunning conclusion that I was some kind of a tall white chief, followed around by a chocolate-colored *kepu* name Sjam. Sjam liked the *kepu* idea. She promptly plugged it by announcing to everyone she had no house, no gardens and no pigs.

When we found the children they were usually engaged in some kind of game. Mi Hijo tried to explain one contest to us, but we were still baffled by it. Two boys had armed themselves with hard, pea-shaped berries (*yalie*). They were firing them at each other with bent twigs. No one kept track of the hits or misses. No score between the two was ever arrived at. There was no winner.

The game the children loved the most was banned by Indonesian law. It was called "kill the hoop" (*siqoqo wasin*) and was more in the nature of war preparation than just plain fun. A child would throw a bamboo hoop into the air. Any boy with a spear (*teboe teboe*) in his hand would aim and throw it through the hoop's center. There was no more to the game than the cooperation between the throwers and the skill required to get the spear through the hoop in the air.

The kids made small balls from dried grass bound with rattan string, but I never saw a ball game. They tossed the ball to themselves and sometimes threw to someone else.

The boys love to hunt. They make their own bows and a variety of arrows. Hunting is limited to the bird population because there are few other animals around. A favorite arrow is a five-pronged one (*suap*) made of *yoli* wood and is used to kill large birds. The boys knock the stuffings out of small birds by hitting them with a *topo,* an arrow with a hard wooden ball on its end.

The Dani have no quivers to carry their weapons. The extra arrows are held vertically in the hand holding the bow while the arrow in use is being shot.

These bows and arrows are some of the rare artifacts found in the Dani environment. Generally, the Dani are without art. They've found no place for such a thing in their culture. There is relatively no painting, drawing or sculpturing. One finds craftsmanship in the Dani weapons, adzes, *yokals* and *nokens,* and shell and feather decorations.

During our long walks through the Dani countryside, Sjam and I learned about agriculture.

To ask the Dani about agriculture is like asking about themselves. The people relate to their gardens in a very special way. Long ago, food raising became a necessary and vital thing about which there should be no nonsense. The Dani went to work on the problem with industry.

There are three kinds of farming in the Baliem Valley. One is found in the compound garden (*hakiloma*), where bananas (*haki*) and tobacco (*hanom*) are raised. (The Dani had the smoking habit long before anybody from an outside civilization showed up. But they have yet to manufacture any kind of intoxicant). They know the value of potash and they place their fire ashes around the young tobacco plants.

The other two kinds of farming are found in the hills and on the flat plains of the Valley. The great gardens deal directly with the business of raising the food the Dani like the most, the sweet potato (*hipere*). The potatoes constitute 85 percent of the Dani diet. There are over seventy different kinds of them.

The Dani also raise taro (*hom*), cucumbers (*iloe*), yams

(*pain*), sugar cane (*el*), and *hiperica*, which is a vegetable that looks like a fern. *Soa* resembles a young onion but tastes like an artichoke. The Dani also love spinach and raise different varieties they call *molin, kebee, nibie, hela, kipie-kipie* and *wietat*. Although all of them looked and tasted the same to me, you may depend that the Dani know the difference.

There are also some wild nuts growing around (*moli-moli*) and wild raspberries (*malikeb*), but they fail to raise the Dani's enthusiasm.

The climate in the Baliem Valley allows production all year round in a nearly pest-free area. The Dani work the land in cooperative groups of men and women (*yen-yoko*). First, the men ring the trees with their stone adzes, causing them to die. Later the dead trees are cut down. The shrubs are dug up with fire-hardened digging sticks (*tege*). The women burn off the light vegetation, and the men turn up the ground with sticks into soft chunks.

The gardens are separated by a geometric maze of irrigation ditches which are dug with *tege*. Sometimes a wooden paddle is used to plaster the sides and to throw the rich mud and silt, along with humus and manure, from the bottom of the ditch onto the raised gardens.

At this point the chief of the village tells the people which part of the land they will receive. The workers do not know beforehand; this prevents extra special individual effort on a particular piece of land. The land is allocated according to the number of women and children in a family.

The women and girls enter the gardens. The men may count on never returning to the site again. The women scatter sharp thorns around to keep them out. Sweet-potato cuttings are taken from mature vines and placed, two to a mound, in a hole made with the help of the digging stick. They are covered with a little dirt and stomped on by the woman's foot.

Then nothing is done for a while; the field is momentarily forgotten. Weeds invade the gardens and grow happily for three months, until the ladies come to pull them up by the root and burn them.

Little bridges called *mokat aku* are built in the gardens. They are made of little sticks. The bridges are used by the village ghosts to walk upon.

The vines begin to blossom and the roots beneath them swell to provide food for the Dani.

I have often heard people refer to the Dani as a "Stone Age people" and I've thought that surely, those folks failed to see the enormously sophisticated agricultural achievements of the Valley dwellers, who know no hunger.

(9)

I suppose it's inevitable that you'll get sick on a trip, sooner or later.

I woke up one morning in Abulakma with a high temperature and a fierce headache. I doctored myself with aspirin and self-pity and asked Mi Hijo what the Dani medical world could do for me. (I'd like to note that I have no medical degree. What little I may know about medicine I've learned from desire, demand and sheer desperation.)

Mi Hijo tried to convince me that a ghost had caused me to be sick. He said a ghost could make a person sick, an inert object could cause sickness, and sometimes injuries were caused by humans to themselves and to others. There were no other ways a person could get sick.

Mi Hijo was not overly concerned about my condition. He thought that no ghost in his right mind would dare to do a permanent damage to me. He told me to ask Chief Kolo to blow on my chest in short, rapid breaths. He had the "power" to get the sickness out. If that didn't work, then I should wear a *yopo* (string fibers endowed with magic powers) around my neck. It'd cure me and keep the ghosts at a distance at the same time.

Besides the *yopo* and the chief's breath, the Dani have concocted quite a remarkable medical kit for themselves. Their approach to medicine is a mixture of common sense and magic, logic and faith.

The Dani know the importance of blood in their bodies. If the blood becomes contaminated, little bamboo slivers are sent into the skin for bloodletting. A fresh wound must be cleaned before it is treated.

The Dani treat boils, jungle ulcers and pig bites with wood bark (*wip*) and roots (*heik* and *omaken*) and *pawih, beka jawi, apelagap* leaves.

Bandages are made from different kinds of leaves (*kaa, aniekoekoen, egenbpuga, hum*) depending on the size of the wound.

Skin diseases are treated with flower petals (*anekuku*). *Kelok* leaves are given to a person with dysentery. Sap (*hetali*) from the *sin* tree is burned near the sick person to clear up the air and chase away bad ghosts.

The Dani have their own acupuncture. They use a nettle leaf to transfer pain from a wounded area to a perfectly healthy spot on the body. It also gets the patient's mind off his former grief.

Mi Hijo told me about the lady witch doctors called *waganins* who exist in the Valley. He had never seen one, but he knew they had powerful saliva and muttered magic over the sick people. Spit and spells usually cured whatever the Dani medicine failed to correct.

"Ma, do you know what a *pupalep* is? It's a little nest that an insect makes, and when it dries out you can carry medicine in it."

"Like a pill box."

"I have one. Can you give me some medicine for it?"

"What kind of medicine?"

"Woman-medicine!"

"What's woman-medicine, Mi Hijo?"

"You have some, Ma. I've seen it in the little bottles in the medical kit."

I took a mental inventory of the bottles in the kit: aspirin, painkillers, antibiotics, vitamins, minerals, laxative and quinine.

"What does woman-medicine do?" I repeated.

"You just carry it around with you. The women talk to you and they want to get married to you. Can I have some?"

"I'll think about it, Mi Hijo."

(10)

The Day of the Cave came.

I had asked Kolo for permission to photograph the cave nearly two weeks before. I thought he'd forgotten about it. I should have known better; the Dani never forget anything.

The cave is a hole in the ground located near Abulakma. The Dani believe their ancestors walked out of it. (This cave should not be confused with the one at the mouth of the Huan River.)

If some guardian angel had warned me about the troublesome results of the Day of the Cave, I would have stayed home. We had several forewarnings about how unlucky the day would be, but none of us paid any attention to them.

First of all, Mi Hijo said he didn't want to go. He thought the whole thing was crazy. Ordinarily, Mi Hijo joined anything he couldn't get out of, but this was more than he could handle. He was afraid he would die if he visited his ancestors' cave.

Sjam pointed out that we would be without a translator. Mi Hijo frantically began to build up a backfire of courage to urge himself into going. And in the end he went, but only after we had solemnly promised that if he died at the cave, we would not leave his body at the site.

The sun signaled it would be a bad day, but we missed the clue. The great white ball shone with intensity right up to the moment when we were ready to leave the compound. And then it disappeared. Something covered it up, rather like an eclipse. I was so fascinated to see this accident of nature occur in the middle of the jungle that I overlooked whatever the omen meant. I don't think I believe in omens but I was living with people who did. Mi Hijo missed seeing the eclipse because he had his eyes shut. He followed the footpath by feeling it with his feet. He kept his eyes shut until we came to a bridge spanning a broad, shallow stream.

The bridge presented a real hazard to cross even with one's eyes wide open. It consisted of a single log, stretched from bank to bank, and there were of course no railings to hold on to when crossing. The Dani ran across the log, the mud on their feet leaving the surface slippery. The Dani must go first so they could come back and hang themselves halfway across from the other side to help you maneuver the log in hard-soled leather boots.

There were tall *sin* trees on the other side of the stream. Beyond them stretched a plain of dry brown jungle grass. Kolo had sent a guide along. He and Mi Hijo walked waist-high in the tall grass, flailing sticks at the long brown blades on both sides of the path.

The grassy plain left off suddenly and a hill began. We climbed its cliff on a narrow trail that had been carved into the limestone composition with adzes. The trail had not been used very much. Little rocks skittered beneath our feet. Some of them rolled over the side of the path and down the bank of the hill.

The guide told us the cave was embedded in the side of the hill below us where a forest of tall dark trees crowded at its back. He said we had to walk to the top of the hill, cut a wide circle and drop down to see the cave. No one ever approached such a sacred place head-on.

As we began our descent to the cave we saw our first danger sign (*silo*). It was a forked stick standing straight up in the middle of the path. It had dried grass stuffed in its V.

Mi Hijo looked as though he were ready to bolt. Even the guide was set back a little. It took him a while but he managed to burn a path around the *silo* at a distance he considered safe. We went on.

There were two more *silos* directly in front of the cave. Mi Hijo missed seeing them; he had closed his eyes again. The guide was pushing him along past the foreboding signals.

Somehow I had expected to see a life-size cave, one that measured at least the height of a Dani. I walked right by the cave without seeing it at all. The guide whispered me back to look at a hole no larger than a breadbox. The entrance was nearly covered over with green five-fingered ferns. The roof slanted sharply down into the ground behind the vegetation.

Now, in this holy place, revered by many and visited by few, I confess some rather unusual events began to transpire. The wind stopped whistling in the trees. There was a conspicuous absence of insects, including the common housefly known to inhabit every inch of the Valley. The sun had disappeared again. The air was filled with suspenseful expectancy.

Mi Hijo sat down as far away from the cave as he could. He began to feel the air for danger. Mi Hijo believed there were still some people inside the cave. He believed they were stone people, moving around, people who could talk and eat and sleep. Possibly one of them would walk out any minute. A sudden madness overtook the boy. He got up off his rock and approached the cave. He peeked inside. In the light of what he did, I tried to imagine how he must have felt.

When the photography was finished, Mi Hijo was the first one down the hill. His eyes were wide open all the way.

The sun came out and burned the air with its heat. A gentle breeze whispered around in the trees. Great blowflies swarmed around our heads in halos.

In the evening Old Dialec came over to the *uma* to tell us about the cave. Sjam and I loved Old Dialec even though we were a bit frightened of him. He was a man who balanced precariously between good and evil deeds.

Old Dialec was the chief ornament of Analaga because of his age and his glorious past. He remembered his old days with pleasure. He spoke of them so often that we were all afraid he might return to them. He had killed many men himself and caused the killing of hundreds of others. Often, when recounting old battles, he hooked his right index finger around the thumb of his left hand to make the gesture of shooting a bow and arrow. It made you feel as though you had been shot.

He had lived through many wars. The violent experiences

had marked his soul with roughness. And one rendezvous had put out his right eye with a well-aimed arrow. When Old Dialec talked he had to tilt his head back in order to see out of the good eye, which was set in a face that was toothless, dried-up and ancient.

I never caught on to the reason why this old, one-eyed warrior went around telling everyone he was afraid. I supposed he thought it was the style. But he didn't fool anyone very much. Old Dialec was afraid of nothing.

Old Dialec could give you many deep secrets of the Dani if he wanted to. Secrecy was a world in itself; it was a well-known field to him.

Old Dialec shuffled into the *uma*, his knees bent, with tendons creaking. He sat down near the fireplace. His one milky eye darted quickly around the room to make sure no children were present. Caves and such are never discussed in front of children. Information like that could be mishandled in a moment of childish foolishness.

Kolo and Abinyai came into the room. They closed the wooden door behind them. Mi Hijo moved in closer to hear better. Sjam and I waited for the old man to speak.

A fine peacefulness settled down on Old Dialec. He was quiet for a long time. When he saw that Kolo and Abinyai were waiting for him to speak, Old Dialec unfolded the story about the cave with a voice full of enthusiasm:

"God [*uwe namet mina pike*] made man and woman.

"God carved their bodies from a great piece of stone. He called the man 'Tabhe' [white skin] because the stone was clean and white. He called the woman 'Hesage' because she was beautiful.

"God went away and watched Tabhe and Hesage from a distance. He wanted to know if they could take care of themselves in the jungle.

"Tabhe and Hesage ate wild raspberries and nuts. They ate sweet potatoes they found in the ground. In the afternoon their white skin had burned and was painful. The man and woman covered their bodies with mud.

"In the evening Tabhe and Hesage found the cave God had

made for them. It was a warm place to sleep. They spent the night there.

"God was happy with Tabhe and Hesage. And God left them.

"In the cave a family was born to Tabhe and Hesage. Their children were black-skinned. The children left the cave to go out into the world to live. Their black skin protected them against the sun's harsh rays. The children built round houses like the top of their parents' cave.

"When the children were old enough to marry, Hesage transformed her white stone body into burning grass. Tabhe watched the flaming grass and then transformed himself into brown leaves.

"God came to throw the leaves on the fire. The burning souls of Tabhe and Hesage rose and entered into the stones inside the cave.

"The children returned to the cave and found the stones [wesas] containing the spirits of their mother and father. The children took the stones to their little round houses.

"Some of the children stayed in the cave to live. They are still there, but they are afraid to come out.

"We do not know much about the god who created our ancestors. But we know about our ancestors. Tabhe and Hesage were people of great glory. They were able to take care of themselves in a land that was not necessarily friendly to them.

"We know that in order to survive, we must live like our mother Hesage and father Tabhe. We know we must please them, for we are their children."

Old Dialec creaked up from his sitting position and slowly shuffled toward the door of the uma. He lifted up one leg with both hands and swung it over the board base. He pulled the other leg after it. And then he disappeared into the black night.

Old Dialec's story of their creation gave them the shape of yesterday and it provided the shape for tomorrow. It flourished because it bequeathed self-sufficiency to the Dani. It was both wise and beautiful to them.

Tabhe and Hesage are written deeply in the hearts and minds of the Dani people. The lesions are difficult to remove by missionaries preaching of clay beginnings. The Dani had carved their religious immortality entirely through the use of stone.

(11)

Le Papillon and a few other men had dug a deep hole behind the *uma* to provide Sjam and me with outdoor toilet facilities. When they finally stopped digging there was a huge cavity in the ground with an eight-foot diameter. The men put up a circular bamboo wall to enclose the hole. I photographed the half-finished structure.

And then the Day of the Hail came.

Hail was a rare thing. In fact, no one could remember ever having seen it before, except Old Dialec. He remembered he had lost a war the day it hailed.

The stones were the size of large marbles. They pelted down with a force that flattened gardens, ripped grass rooftops and knocked a small piglet nearly senseless.

To the amazement and consternation of the natives, Sjam and I made snow cones from the white marbles. We added sugar, longed for vanilla and ate them.

When the last trace of hail had melted away, the elders of the village came to visit us. The natives thought I was responsible for the hail drama. They were certain their Dani ancestors had seen me peeking at them when I photographed the hole of the outdoor john. The ancestors were angry; the Dani reasoned I caused the hail!

Kolo asked me to tell him the secret of creating such a phenomenon. I tried to recount what happens when rain passes through cold air, but I could have saved my breath.

Kolo remained convinced I had caused the hail. He made me promise never to do such a thing again.

The heavens supported my promise. There were no more performances of the Day of the Hail before we left the Valley.

The outdoor john remained roofless. The men flatly refused ever to work on it again.

(12)

"Ma," whispered Mi Hijo, "Ma, I think I have enough money now. Enough to buy a pig so I can be your son. Could we go to my village, Wenebuborah, for the ceremony?"

"Yes. Maybe we can see Kelion and Asuan on the way. Shall we leave tomorrow?"

"That'll be fine, Ma, just fine. I'm sure looking forward to being your son. I sure am."

(13)

No one knew how long it would take to walk from Abulakma to Wenebuborah. Only that it was far to the north.

We decided to go to Wamena and spend the night with the Sumitros. We'd strike out for Wenebuborah the following day.

Kolo resented the idea of our going at all. He whined and pouted. He pretended sickness to keep us in the *uma* where he thought we belonged. In the end, he promised to keep an eye on our house. We promised to return within a few days.

Mi Hijo, Sjam and I arrived in Wamena about noon.

Obaharok arrived about three hours later. "I am having a pig feast for *kanake* [religious feast] on this day," he said, holding down two fingers in the palm of his hand. "I need this much money to buy another pig." He held down four fingers, indicating four hundred rupiahs (approximately one dollar).

"And you want me to give you the four hundred rupiahs?"
"Yes."
Nobody had ever asked for money before. I was used to giving shovels, knives and seeds, but not money.
"I don't usually give money," I said.
Obaharok squinted darkly, nodded and left.
I felt uneasy.
I should have given him the dollar.

(14)

Aem wanted to go north with us to Wenebuborah, but the Sumitros were planning to give a party during the week and they needed him to work in the house. Aem made our night miserable with his whining disappointment. He filled the early-morning hours with threats against his employers. We were glad to be off and away.

It had rained during the night. The air was left polished clean. The raindrops still clung to the leaves on the trees, glittering like diamonds. Although they were worthless, they were beautiful.

Below the trees, rain water collected in small puddles. The puddles were crowded with visiting insects, worms and snails who had probably been thirsty for several dry days.

The smoke from the kitchen fires in the surrounding villages drifted up through the air. It gave off the sweet smell of burning resin.

The footpath was muddy. We slipped and slid until we reached Pikke. Then the sun burst out with heated energy and dried up the path, which made the walking easier.

A strong desire to see his friends again had come to Mi Hijo. He was filled with ecstasy and his blood boiled over with it. Mi Hijo was thinking about the ceremony, too. He looked like a pleased child. He smiled at everything and anything, and sometimes he smiled vaguely at nothing at all. From time to time he did a curious little tap step on the footpath, dancing on tiptoe in a circle. Then he'd slap his thigh with his hand and throw back his head and laugh out loud.

Outside Aikima, Chief Hulolik was waiting for us. Sjam's red fur hat bouncing up and down on the horizon had alerted him we were coming. He felt a momentary disappointment when he learned that we were not leaving the Valley. He shrugged his shoulders and resigned himself to waiting a little longer for the hat.

In Tumagonem, Chief Asuan and Old Pum seemed glad to see us. But Kelion was not there. They told us he was in Mulima, a place about an hour's walk away. Asuan agreed to take us to Mulima.

It was a slow walk. Asuan was the only Dani who walked slower than Sjam and me.

There were only two houses in Mulima. Neither of them had been lived in for years.

"Kelion is in Wiyagoba," Asuan remembered.

Wiyagoba could be reached by fording a deep river and walking an additional two hours uphill. We decided to go on to Wenebuborah.

Asuan, his big white teeth flashing in the sunlight, pulled Sjam over to the side of the path. He whispered something to her. Then he turned to walk back to Tumagonem.

"Guess what! I *think* Asuan just asked me to marry him!"

"Well, we've been warned."

When we arrived in Wenebuborah, Mi Hijo was so happy that his feet barely touched the ground. His black eyes shone with the pleasure of showing us off to his compound's people. He reported everything he knew about us. What he didn't know, he invented.

The people of Wenebuborah were good-looking and well-mannered. Mi Hijo told them of the great paradise he'd found in Analaga. The picture was so attractive that nearly everyone in the village wanted to return to live with us there.

Mi Hijo was about to install us in his small house when a woman with a runny nose came limping through the *thop* into the courtyard of the village. There was a cabbage leaf on the top of her head. She held her hand on the leaf to keep it in place.

She said she had walked a long time to reach the village, because she needed medical treatment. I lifted the leaf. Her scalp was split open; there were two nasty gashes, ugly wounds there. Her hair was matted together in hard knots with dried blood.

I asked her to tell me how it had happened. She said her husband had discovered that she had induced self-abortion. He had hit her on the head with his stone axe. This woman was the first of many abortion patients I was to treat during my stay in the Baliem Valley.

Night crept in like a stealthy octopus and covered us with its clammy cold. Sjam and I crawled into the soft grass bed of the *abiai* to become targets for the Wenebuborah mosquitoes. They swooped and power-dived into us. They zoomed up and circled to dive again and again. They were without mercy, those Wenebuborah mosquitoes.

"I wonder who the chief of Wenebuborah is," I said more to myself than to Sjam. "Maybe we can ask in the morning."

And then I promptly forgot all about it.

(15)

Mi Hijo was smiling again. There was a glow about him, a glow as though he had descended from kings which intrigued me.

"Sjam, someday that boy will be very rich and the Valley will be very proud of him."

Despite the surge of excitement that filled Mi Hijo, he was a little shy about it.

"Ma," he whispered, "I'll go get the pig now," and he said it as a matter of wonder at himself.

It took Mi Hijo quite a length of time to find the pig he wanted. When he returned to the village he was carrying a tiny, black, squealing bundle beneath his arm. The bundle was outraged at being carried away from its home so early in the morning.

Mi Hijo set about making a nest of clean grass in the middle of the courtyard. All the villagers came out to see. Sike arrived with Asuan. They stood in silent audience as Mi Hijo tenderly arranged the grass and placed the squealing piglet in the center. He hunkered down beside the pig and stretched his elbows out over his knees. With his right hand he scratched the piglet behind the ear. Then he gently stroked its sides until the animal was lulled to a calmness.

He was smiling and smiling. His heart seemed to burst with the unbelievable happiness that had invaded it. Sjam and I were leaning against the *abiai* when Mi Hijo looked up at us. He grinned. Then he looked down at the little piglet and studied it for a moment. A frown settled over his face. He glanced up at us again. And then his head dropped and he lost his smile.

A cloud moved over his face.

He stopped scratching the pig.

A sadness had entered his heart. Tears squeezed out of his eyes and splashed down on the piglet. They made big dark circles on the animal's dry skin. A little whimper issued from Mi Hijo's throat. His shoulders began to shake and his extended left hand jerked in shaking sorrow.

I walked to the little nest where the piglet lay asleep and knelt to touch Mi Hijo's hand.

"Ma," he said, sobbing to break your heart, "it's not good enough. The pig is too small and not good enough. Ma, I'm so ashamed."

Mi Hijo sniffed and wiped his eyes with the back of his hand. He did not raise his head.

"I gave all my money for it, Ma, but the pig isn't big enough. You should have a big pig with long teeth! I am not worthy. This pig is no good. I just love you so much, Ma."

It takes a lot of love, perhaps the greatest love, to spend

every cent you have in the world to demonstrate your affection. It must have been a frightening thing for Mi Hijo to lay out everything he had and then feel unworthy.

"Mi Hijo," I said, fighting back tears, "the pig is a promise of happiness, a dream that is golden and very beautiful. Look at your brothers, Mi Hijo! See how proud you've made them. Why, your dignity has never been taller."

Mi Hijo raised his head a little. He peeked out of the corner of his eye at his friends in the compound. He turned up his chin a little. He whispered, "Never taller, never taller," over and over again. He saw a little respect in the eyes of his friends and some admiration and nearly envy.

Mi Hijo was very quiet for a moment. A strong cough burst from his throat. Then he grinned a little, and his eyes brightened. He drew his head down between his shoulders and his smile was vivacious again.

"Do you really think it's good enough, Ma?"

"It's good enough, Mi Hijo. It's really good enough."

"I just love you, Ma. I just do."

(16)

Sike talked Sjam into buying a *cuscus* (opossum) fur for her red fur hat. He didn't have to do much talking. She thought the straggly *cuscus* was beautiful.

What it lacked in beauty it made up for in size. It was the bushiest *cuscus* in the whole Baliem Valley. It went twice around the headband of her red fur hat. The combination guaranteed to send Hulolik into further mad desire for it.

Sike, Asuan and Mi Hijo corralled a group of men to put on a concert at the river. In the middle of the third or fourth song, Mi Hijo stopped singing. He cocked his head to one side, the better to hear. He touched his lips with his index finger. The group became silent.

There were sounds of footsteps in the distance, sounds of bare feet pounding hard against the mud. A dark man came into view. He came at a heated run. When he saw us, he stopped. His body went limp with terror.

Suddenly he sighed with relief. He took a deep breath and shouted, "Mama Wyn! Sjam!"

"Papillon!" Mi Hijo yelled.

Asuan slowly waved Le Papillon with his hand into the group. Breathing heavily and noisily, he collapsed against a tree stump, exhausted. He closed his eyes and shook his head from side to side. His face was filled with deep anxiety.

"Mama Wyn," he said, trying to keep his voice even, "Obaharok has forbidden you to return to Analaga! He'll kill you if you try to go back. He's not playing. He has forty warriors sentried around with bows and arrows to keep you out. He says you entered the cave of our ancestors. He's fined you four large pigs. Obaharok's men have already taken one of Abinyai's boars."

The Day of the Cave!

Mi Hijo's look of hard concentration changed to a look of outrage. "She did not! She didn't enter the cave! She took pictures. She didn't go inside!"

For a boy who had had his eyes shut most of the day, Mi Hijo was not an ideal witness.

Mi Hijo's voice was bottled up in fury. His eyes were feverish. He thrust out his lower jaw and said, "We will fight Obaharok!"

"Kolo will fight, too!" Le Papillon said excitedly.

Someone let out a war cry. Everyone joined in. The cry floated upward and echoed through the sky.

"Sike," I said, "can you get a message to Obaharok?"

"I can go to Wamena and find one of Obaharok's men in the marketplace."

I wrote a note. Sjam and Mi Hijo translated it into Dani.

"Obaharok: Return Abinyai's pig. There will be no pig settlement until I talk with you in Wamena tomorrow."

(17)

I had hoped a good night's sleep might resolve yesterday's problem. It didn't. The night gave the warriors more time to gather their forces together. The courtyard at Wenebuborah was filled with men. They were still coming. They had dressed up in high gear. Mi Hijo looked like a feathered maypole. Le Papillon resembled his name.

The men were in the mood for war.

"Mi Hijo, tell all those people out there, including Asuan and Sike, that this problem is between Obaharok and me. There's going to be no fighting. And don't let anyone talk back to you!"

"Ma, they won't do anything until you tell them."

When we left Wenebuborah, the air was morning-gray but the visibility was good. We made excellent targets walking over the footpath toward Wamena.

I had no sense of being heroic in such an atmosphere. The war-painted warriors walked in front and back of Sjam and me. We picked up more warriors from other villages as we went along.

As the little army moved down the path, I thought about the Day of the Cave and remembered the Day of the Hail. I wondered how many other things I'd be blamed for before we reached Wamena. Well, I had refused to buy Obaharok's stone axe. I had built a house without his permission. I had paid him no social call to respect his position as the great *kain* in the area. And a few days ago, I had refused to give him a dollar.

My sins were numerous.

Obaharok's men watched us walking along the footpath from the hilltops. We entered the forest near Pikke and some of his men were watching there, too. They had bows and arrows, all right, but they weren't drawn.

We crawled over a large fallen trunk across the path. Sjam and I both fell down in the mud on the other side of it. I thought I had sprained my ankle. Worse, Sjam believed her leg was broken. We leaned on the shoulders of Mi Hijo and Sike.

We didn't care much whether our shirts soaked up their black pig fat or not.

Our party arrived in Wamena before noon. The marketplace was filled with waiting Dani. They followed us to the Sumitros' backyard and packed themselves into the fenced-in garden lawn.

Obaharok had not yet arrived, but Kolo was there. And Old Dialec, Abinyai, Mama and Papa Aem and a host of others from the Analaga district. The men had freshly blackened shoulders and faces. They had ornamented themselves with exaggerated elaboration. Those who had inserted boar tusks in their noses looked more ferocious than the others. All of them looked like they meant business.

Asuan was his usual slow. He came down the street with Mi Hijo and Sike, who had waited for him to catch up. They marched into the Sumitros' backyard to face Kolo.

Asuan and Sike had never met Kolo. They were enemies.

There was a fierce smile of pleasure on Kolo's face. There was anticipation, too. He needed the north to fight Obaharok. He wondered if he could get Sike and Asuan to pledge their warriors to him.

Kolo and Mi Hijo exchanged a careful volley of words. The men nodded in some kind of agreement.

Kolo had about twenty-five hundred men under his jurisdiction. Sike, Asuan and Mi Hijo could throw in an equal number of men. Since Obaharok reigned over five thousand warriors, it would be an even fight.

"Kolo," I said, "there will be no fighting."

Kolo's face turned dark and ugly. I supposed I had let his whole future down with that statement.

"Kolo, if you fight, I will never return to Analaga. No more medicine, no more food or shovels or knives. Nothing!"

Ordinarily Kolo never bothered to listen to anyone else's thoughts, but he inspected this threat from every angle.

"We must revenge!" Kolo whined, his voice reaching a higher pitch.

"It's between Obaharok and me, Kolo. You're not involved."

Kolo half slumped down on the grass. Old Dialec pinched him. He sat up straight again.

I glanced over the congregation of warriors. There were about one hundred men there, most of them chiefs. And I thought it strange, with so many people, that loneliness fell upon me.

Sjam and I walked into the Sumitros' house to wait for Obaharok to show up. I had lost interest in my sprained ankle. Sjam found her leg not worth mentioning any more.

We sat down on the twin beds, facing each other, and tried to think. The whole thing scared me. The Dani warriors out there on the lawn were high-strung, passionate creatures. They wanted drama and war and a powwow and—

"Sjam, I've got it. We're going to have a powwow, American Indian style, with broken arrow and war paint!"

I drew stripes on my face with lipstick and black eyebrow pencil. Sjam improved on the artwork with her enormous imagination. When we were finished I looked more baneful than any Dani who ever lived. And I was a good target for ridicule if the local Wamena officials saw me.

There was a sudden rapping at the window. A black face pushed itself up against the glass. The nose was punched down flat on the pane. It was Kelion.

"Kelion, why did you come to Wamena?"

"To fight Obaharok!" Kelion would join any kind of fiesta, regardless of its nature.

"Kelion, if you're not too clumsy, come on in here."

It took him about a minute before he stuck his big head into the doorway. He came shambling on into the room. He acted shy but he was still clumsy. He stumbled over a small stool before he reached a spot on the floor where he wanted to sit down.

His big eyes began to wander over the room, appraising and assessing the things he saw. Sometimes they dwelt longingly on an object he thought he'd like to have. It was not a good idea to lead him into such temptation. He had no resistance to it at all.

"Kelion, don't you take anything from this house!"

"Can I have that woman-medicine?" he asked, pointing to one of the three aspirin tablets on the table beside him.

"No, Kelion, nothing from this house. Or any other house in Wamena, hear me?"

"Yes, all right."

It didn't really matter what I said to him. You could talk and talk and Kelion would agree with you. Then he went right on with whatever he had planned to do in the first place.

"Kelion, did you hear?"

"Hear what?"

"Hear what I said. You are not to take anything from this house. Pay attention and listen."

Kelion's mind was whirling. "I have decided to keep my hands off the woman-medicine," he said, "if I can remember."

It was three-thirty in the afternoon. Obaharok had still not arrived. The stripes on my face had begun to melt. The Dani make-up was more enduring than mine.

"Obaharok didn't come," said Mi Hijo from the doorway. "He sent Chief Pesimeken instead."

My courage suddenly flowed away. A little chill of terror ran up my spine. Sjam dared me not to go through with it. The dare sent me with some hope but not much confidence out the door to face the great lump of gathered men outside.

With as much reassurance as we could muster, Sjam and I walked through the grouped warriors. I sat down next to a man whom I guessed to be Pesimeken. I had the feeling I was intruding into a men's club.

The exotic nature of my red and black war paint did not go without notice. Sike and Asuan gasped. I am certain Pesimeken felt horrified at my appearance.

The growing circle of warriors divided themselves into two teams and sat down. A few young boys trooped in. They stood on the sidelines and enclosed Sjam and me like a zipper.

The warriors stared at one another with animosity. Their excitement was high-pitched and uneasy.

Chief Pesimeken and I gazed at each other. Pesimeken was an old man. He had a flat nose and a wide mouth. Some of his teeth were missing. His face was lean and corded. His eyes were set deep in their sockets; something eerie came out of them. Pesimeken was old but his eyes were young. They had an extremely fast reaction time. He didn't miss a thing.

He was an intelligent man. His legacy was victory.

I opened the powwow with as much ceremonial seriousness as my melting warpaint would allow. It was not a stroke of strategy, it was ignorance of protocol.

"You . . ." I said in a heavy whisper. I cleared my throat and began again. "You are a great chief, Pesimeken, and I respect your coming here today."

When the sentence was translated into Dani, Pesimeken shook his head negatively. He said something to the warrior on his right. I thought he had already declared war on me. I hurried on.

"In my country, a broken arrow means peace," I said.

With trembling hands I broke the arrow in two pieces and placed the parts on the ground in front of Pesimeken. I was sorry to see one piece of arrow was much longer than the other.

"I understand that Chief Obaharok has accused me of entering the cave of your ancestors. This is not true. The entrance to the cave is so small that you cannot put your hand inside it."

Pesimeken's warriors leaned into the story. They watched Pesimeken swing his arm around and point to a man who sat nearly hidden from view.

"La Paloma said you went into the cave," Pesimeken said huskily.

"You did," La Paloma shouted. "You walked into it and I saw you!"

"She did not!" screamed Mi Hijo in a flame of scorching rage.

"Chief Pesimeken, I took a picture of your ancestors' cave. This is a good thing. If anything happens to the cave, if it were covered up, why, you'll always have a picture to remember it by. I didn't enter the cave."

The case rested.

Pesimeken cleared his throat and spat. When he spoke, his voice was bushy. "You are a wise chief for such white skin. I end this meeting. I will report to Obaharok in the morning."

Pesimeken's warriors looked up and questioned one another with their eyes.

In a moment of gratefulness I made a hasty promise. "Please tell Obaharok I will visit him in his village in a day or two."

The great lumps of men broke up into small knots. The knots moved off, walking to the villages they called home.

A tremendous snore rose from the corner where Kelion had gone to sleep.

Inside the Sumitros' house there were two aspirins left on the table.

(18)

White popcorn clouds puffed themselves up on the Wamena horizon. It was morning. The sun blazed a hot orange.

Obaharok stood on the Sumitros' front porch. He'd come with two of his warriors.

"You missed the meeting yesterday," I said.

"I call meetings," Obaharok said. "I am not called by others."

My heart flicked a little on a fast beat.

Obaharok untied the banana bark wrapped package he held in his hands. "This is my *wesa* [religious stone]," he said. "I will sell it to you."

I had agreed to buy the stone even before I asked its price.

One of the warriors stepped up and handed Obaharok a small round object. Obaharok turned it over in his hand. It looked like an acorn.

"This is woman-medicine," he said. "I will sell it to you."

I bought the curiosity without argument.

Obaharok started to leave. I wondered if Pesimeken had reported the outcome of yesterday's meeting.

"Obaharok, are we friends now?" I asked.

Obaharok did not answer.

"I'd like to come visit you in a day or two. Where is your village?"

"Ask anyone. All people know where I live."

And then he turned and left.

Kolo arrived in Wamena to escort us back to Abulakma. I think we set a new time record getting there. Kolo's constant complaining spirited us into running. He had spent the last few days remembering his past greatness. He felt a victory in warfare would restore his withered glory. He longed for that old time again.

"Ma, look!" Mi Hijo said, pointing to a spot of mashed grass. "Obaharok's men are just up ahead."

A few birds abruptly took flight from an acacia tree on the hilltop. Kolo said, "They're under the tree."

The men looked at us. They didn't move. Their bows and arrows lay in the grass beside them. We walked on without changing our gait too much. I wondered what it would be like to be shot with an arrow.

When we arrived in Abulakma, Sjam and I felt our bodies frayed and our nerves weary. Kolo was as fresh as a young weed.

"Kolo, I'll go to Obaharok's village tomorrow. Where does he live?"

"He lives everywhere. Lunagima, Yumugima, Hiyasi, Pabuma. How do I know where he lives?"

"Well, does he have one favorite village where he spends most of his time?"

"No, he lives in all of them. One night here, one night there. He's always hiding around so nobody will kill him.

Kolo practiced a little sickness. "I don't feel well," he said. "I'm going home. I may die by morning."

During our absence a guest had moved into the *uma*. The visitor was a little gray kitten. It was curled up by the cold fireplace and had made itself at home by going to sleep. When we stepped inside, the kitten stretched and looked at us out of slanted green eyes. And then it went back to sleep again. The rats under our sleeping platform weren't as safe as they thought they were.

We couldn't think of a finer name, so we called her "Kitty." Kitty became a permanent resident.

The afternoon waned. The sun went over the hill and left a heap of golden clouds sitting around in the sky for a while. Then a sliver of moon appeared. It drifted through the thin mist that had dropped into the Valley. It was a cold night. The sky was chock-full of sharp stars. The objects on the ground appeared still and lifeless.

Abulakma was hushed as though waiting for something everybody knew would happen. Sjam and I stood in the courtyard trying to get the feel of the place. Some great black bugs came winging in to visit us. They beat their bristly wings against our faces. We fled for the safety of the *uma*.

Kitty moved a little closer to the burning embers for warmth. The compound was very quiet. Even the rats beneath the bedroom floor had enough sense to keep still.

"Sjam, did Mi Hijo bring up those extra hatchets today?"

"Yes. There're some of the extra long knives, too."

The long knives were hard to come by. To possess one was every man's dream. They looked like machetes and measured a full two feet in length. They were very expensive and made fine gifts, especially if you were trying to make peace with somebody.

"I think we'll take a knife and shovel, maybe an axe, and start early in the morning to find Obaharok's village. Sjam, he must know that the entrance to that cave is tiny. If that's true, I can't figure his motives for giving me such a bad time."

"He wants war with Kolo," Sjam said, and added, "What do you think it'll be like to walk through Obaharok's territory tomorrow? He wouldn't dare kill a white woman, would he?"

(19)

Aem came into Abulakma sometime during the early-morning hours. Kolo sent word to the compound that a little child had fallen into a fire in Konisa village.

Aem led us over the spiderwebbing trails to Konisa and then abandoned us. Mi Hijo was shaking and trembling with the fear of being in a new place. But at least he stuck with us.

After treating and dressing the child's burns, we left Konisa. None of us knew where to go to find Obaharok. Sjam and I couldn't separate Obaharok's people from Kolo's people, and Mi Hijo was as much a stranger to the situation as we were.

Mi Hijo asked some women who were working in a sweet-potato garden where they thought Obaharok might be. The question sent them into the silent fury of industry again.

We asked everyone we saw for Obaharok's whereabouts. Some of the people replied and some did not. A few believed he was in Pabuma, others said he was in Yumugima. Some said he was in Molapua. If one of our informants pointed his finger during the conversation, we walked in that direction. Often it lead to nowhere. One time we walked for two hours to discover we'd completed a circle. Our efforts to reach Obaharok's village this day were futile.

"Let's go back, Sjam. The sun's about ready to set. I don't want to be caught out here at night. We'll start first thing in the morning."

We arrived at the *uma* as darkness fell. Kolo came to visit us. He'd experienced a marvelous recovery from his sickness and decided not to die, after all. He wanted to know where we had gone, with whom we had spoken and the number of men we had seen along the way.

He paid no attention to me when I told him about the burned child. His happiness at our unsuccessful efforts to see Obaharok had kept him from listening.

(20)

Aem flatly refused to help us find Obaharok's village if Mi Hijo came along. The dispute was settled by Mama Aem. She sent Aem back to work in Wamena.

When the sun had cleared the eastern mountain ridge and the ground began to warm under its heat, we retraced our steps to what we believed to be the village of Lunagima. Inside one of the compounds we approached an old woman who was scratching the soil around some new tobacco plants. She looked startled when she saw us.

"Mama, *nocksu*," I said. "Where is Obaharok?"

Sjam and I had forced ourselves to learn a little Dani in a desire to understand the people and speak for ourselves once in a while.

"He is here, he is there, he is everywhere. He is always with us," she replied melancholically and returned to her gardening.

Outside the village an old man shouted at us, "What do you want here, you strangers?"

"Obaharok," I stammered. "We look for Obaharok."

"He is not here. He is there." The man swung his arm toward the red-sided mountain behind us.

"What village?" I asked.

"Hiyasi," the old man said.

We started up the mountain. It was a rocky trail and so steep that we had to pull ourselves up by grabbing roots in the ground. Sometimes the trail dropped sharply before it ascended again. We climbed over and in between tortuous rocks and boulders that made every step painful. We scraped our boots over the sharp stones and felt the jagged points through the leather.

The path required constant vigilance to maneuver. By keeping our eyes glued to the ground we could not keep an eye on each other. I could hear the clanking of the shovel and knife Mi Hijo carried on his shoulder. They crashed against the boulders when he passed too close. It was only when the clanking stopped that I realized Mi Hijo had left us. The poor boy was scared to death in this territory. The contract of going on had been too large.

"I didn't even hear him leave," Sjam said.

"Well, we have a decision to make. Shall we go on alone, or shall we turn back?"

We were standing in a narrow valley pinched in between two tall mountains. There was a little river in the bottom of the valley. I picked up the cameras, medical kit and the shovel and waded across the river. Neither of us had any notion of turning back.

We entered the woods on the other side of the river and started up the mountainside again. The woods thinned. The rocks became boulders and the going was tougher. Halfway up we sat down to rest. We looked around for footprints and trampled grass and saw none. There were no birds in the area; I wondered what their absence meant. Sjam and I were quiet because we wanted to listen for sounds. And for a Westerner, that is a strange thing to do.

The spot denoted sort of a low note of lethargy. We moved off and started climbing again. Our feet slipped on the gravel in the path. Sometimes we lost the step we had taken. We plunged on and on, slipping and sliding. When we reached the top of the ridge we were panting with exhaustion.

Below us spread another valley, green and wooded. Nestled in the northern mouth was a tiny village. There was no smoke rising or any other sign of human life.

"I'll bet that's Hiyasi."

At the bottom of the steep slope the path leveled out and wandered into the trees. On the other side of the forest we reached a rocky plain. The village lay in front of us.

There was a strong feeling of secrecy about the place. We felt as though we were being watched. Suddenly a man sprang out from behind a boulder on the side of the trail and he placed himself in the middle of the path.

La Paloma!

He crouched, his arms arched away from his body, ready to spring at us.

We stared at each other. Neither of us spoke. La Paloma's greedy eyes fixed themselves on the shovel. I wondered if he would kill me for such a thing.

Abruptly he turned. He ran toward the village and disappeared behind the entrance wall. Sjam let out a tremendous sigh of relief. Her eyes were rolled upward, showing the whites.

We inched ourselves toward the village with the sideways movements of a crab. When we reached the entrance we peered inside. There was no one in sight, not even a pig in the courtyard.

"Sjam," my voice rasped in a hoarse whisper, "I'll go in first. Wait a minute and then come in behind me."

I dragged the shovel, medical kit, cameras and my trembling legs through the narrow *thop* and arrived on the other side still standing up.

The door of the *pilai* was open. I had the feeling there were people in there, but I couldn't see them.

The look and feel of the place were bad.

Suddenly a black face appeared over the top of the southern stockade. It was joined by another face and still another. And then black faces popped up over the northern stockade. Sjam and I were standing in a circle of cold eyes.

"My God!" Sjam gasped. "We're surrounded!"

The Dani showed us their bows and arrows. There is nothing playful about a Dani with a drawn bow and arrow. My heart jumped into my throat and turned my voice into a raw croak.

"Sjam, hand me the knife and the axe slowly, very slowly."

I put the shovel on the ground in front of me. Without turning around I reached for the axe and knife. When the tools were placed into my hands I put them beside the shovel.

We waited.

Minutes dripped by.

The village was motionless and the silence deafening.

Abruptly a bellow issued from the *pilai*.

"*Ukeemay!*" ("Enter!") It was Obaharok's voice.

The black faces lining the stockade swung momentarily toward the *pilai*. There was a rustling behind the fence. The warriors jumped down and ran around to the entrance of the compound.

I picked up the shovel, axe and knife and began to shuffle toward the *pilai*. I couldn't feel my feet touch the ground. My head was spinning dizzily. I stopped walking when I was near the entrance of the *pilai*. Whoever was inside could see me only from the waist down. I glanced back at Sjam. Her chocolate-colored skin had blanched to almond-white. Her eyes had practically popped out of their sockets.

We could hear the warriors plummeting through the *thop*. The sound of their running feet pounded hard on the courtyard ground. One of the men shouted and drew his bow. The cry brought a command from Obaharok inside the *pilai* and the man put down his bow. The others stopped running; they sat down in a row in front of the long kitchen like trained seals.

"*Ukeemay!*" Obaharok's voice belched explosively.

I wanted to take the gifts inside the *pilai*. I wondered if I should throw the knife and shovel in first and then follow them. I abandoned the idea, someone might be sitting in the entrance.

I left my cameras and medical kit in the first section of the entrance. I turned around and backed in, dragging the hardware behind me. The shovel got stuck on a side board and Sjam kicked at it from the outside with her foot. The shovel came loose all at once. It propelled me into the *pilai* in a hurry.

It was dark inside. I felt around for the shovel and found it next to the knife. Pushing both tools to the right side of the entrance, I sat down in the soft grass. Sjam scooted in, shoved the axe in my direction and then disappeared in the darkness on the left side of the entrance.

The air was heavy with the odor of pig fat. It was hot with the bodies of many people inside. You could hear the men breathing but you couldn't see them. When my eyes finally accustomed themselves to the darkness, I was alarmed at what I saw. There were twenty or twenty-five chiefs sitting in the *pilai*. They were dressed in long *holims* and decorated with feathered headdresses and shell necklaces.

Obaharok crawled out from behind the fireplace. When he reached the entrance he sat down, looking strangely neat without decorations. Compared to him, the others seemed over-dressed.

The chiefs straightened their shoulders and waited. I tried to think of something to say in Dani. I felt so enormously outnumbered and afraid that I couldn't even think of anything to say in English.

Obaharok began talking softly to his men. His voice resurrected a few Dani words in my mind. "You me friends, Obaharok," I said. "Here! Peace gifts!" I think I invented the word for "gifts."

I felt around in the grass for the knife and placed it in front of Obaharok. The handle on the shovel hit me across the chin as I pulled it out to place it next to the knife. The axe arrived with a sonorous ring when it clanked against the metal shovel. I hoped the quality of the gifts made up for their ungraceful presentation.

The chiefs leaned forward, the better to see. A few of them tapped their *holims* with their index fingers to indicate their surprise.

Obaharok bowed his head over the little symbolic center of friendship. He looked up at me, shook his head from side to side and then dropped his face to the floor.

"No one," he said softly, "no one has ever given me anything like this."

He folded his hands in his lap as though he were afraid to touch the gifts. He was quiet and unmoving. He looked rather desolate and defenseless.

"Thank you," he said simply.

By accepting these gifts, Obaharok displayed a fine balance between self-knowledge and understanding. The acceptance required tact and it required humility.

Abruptly Obaharok folded the palms of his hands together and raised them toward the sky.

"I think he's praying!" Sjam whispered.

The tense feeling had gone out of the dark *pilai*. The men relaxed. Obaharok ran his fingertips along the blade of the knife, then picked up the axe and fitted it to the palm of his hand. He smiled.

"I know you did not enter the cave," he said. "I was falsely informed. It's my mistake. Abinyai's pig will be returned in the morning." His voice was so soft that I could barely hear him.

My Dani had just about run dry, but I managed to ask if there were any sick people in the compound. My reputation as healer of the cut finger had spread around the Valley. The women, alerted that we were in the area, had already filed through the *thop* with their wounds and sick children. They were waiting outside. Sjam and I set up a first-aid station in the courtyard. Sjam couldn't stomach the nature of some of the injuries, but she sat near enough to me so we could talk.

"Well, I should have known better, Sjam. We already knew that the highest crime to the Dani was to go against human feelings. When I didn't bother to pay a visit to Obaharok, he must have felt deeply affronted. I suppose he thought my attention to Kolo and Sike and the others devaluated his position as *kain*. He's a symbol, Sjam. He needs recognition before all others."

"One of the chiefs in the *pilai*," Sjam said, "told me Obaharok is the son of the sun and the moon. He's also supposed to have special influence over the rain."

"I'm finished here. I think we'd better start back."

"I will go with you," Obaharok was saying. "You have come a long way. I'll accompany you back to Abulakma."

We left Hiyasi with Obaharok and three of his warriors. The men carried the medical kit and cameras. Relieved of those burdens, Sjam and I found it easier and faster to walk back.

As we turned onto the path into Abulakma, I thought I saw Kolo jump out of sight behind a tree.

Inside the compound Obaharok shook hands with Mama and Papa Aem. Mama Aem had her mouth open the whole time but no words came out of it. Obaharok said good-bye and quietly left the village with his warriors.

Mi Hijo was crying in the *uma*. He sat in a corner, his legs drawn up against his chest. His head was buried in his arms.

"Ma, Kitty is dying," he whimpered. "Someone . . . someone *crushed* Kitty's body."

Kitty lay on her favorite rock by the fireplace. She was not quite dead. Her eyes were closed, and her tiny body raised up and down in rapid little breaths.

"How did it happen, Mi Hijo?"

"I don't know. I just don't know, Ma."

Kitty raised her head and looked at us. Her body was broken and twisted. She arched her back, crying out with the pain of it, then fell back on the rock. Her tiny lungs filled with a last gasp of air before she died.

Sjam was frowning darkly. "Who was here last?" she asked Mi Hijo.

"Aem was still here when I returned," he sniffed. "Then he went."

"Where was Kitty, Mi Hijo?"

"After Aem left, Kitty crawled into the *uma*. She could hardly walk. She was dragging her hind legs. I helped put her on the rock there. Kitty came in right after Aem left."

Sjam and I looked at each other.

Neither of us dared to say anything.

(21)

If Kolo had seen Obaharok on the path, he made no sign of it. He came to the *uma* before the sun rose. He demanded to know every word that had been spoken and every action that had taken place at the meeting with Obaharok.

He was bitterly disappointed over the outcome of the meeting. Kolo felt the whole war situation had slipped from his hands.

"*Hano*" ["All right"], he said, more to himself than to anybody else. He stalked out of the house.

Word arrived through Wamena that a Dani in Wamholik

who had been injured by a falling tree, was dying. Wamholik village was adjacent to Punycul. We decided to try to walk straight across the Valley. It meant going through Obaharok's territory of Siepkosi and into Punycul. We left word with Mama Aem to tell Kolo we'd be gone for a day or two. And then we started off on the long march.

If we had been crows we'd have arrived in less than an hour, but walking corners around the angular sweet-potato gardens provided no shortcuts. The corners tripled the distance between the two villages. We spent nearly the entire day walking.

The Dani were waiting for us outside the village of Wamholik. They took us into the compound and pointed at the *pilai*. Then they stood in the courtyard and waited.

I crawled into the *pilai*. The dying man was lying on the floor next to the fireplace. There were huge blowflies feasting on the open gangrenous-looking slash that ran the length of his leg. The stench of decaying flesh was unbearable. I fought back the nausea rising in my stomach and stepped outside.

"Sjam, this man should go to the mission. It looks like gangrene is setting in. He's unconscious and burning with fever. I can't take this responsibility, Sjam."

Mi Hijo conferred with the Dani in the courtyard. A couple of older men shook their heads.

"Ma," Mi Hijo said, "they don't want to take him to a mission. It wouldn't do any good. They don't have a pig to pay to get him in. They say if he's going to die, they want him to die here, not in the mission."

I tied a handerchief over my nose and went back into the *pilai*.

(22)

We left Wamholik and walked on to Punycul. Chief Sike took us to the *pilai*. A few minutes later Aem showed up. He told us he had quit his job with the Sumitros in Wamena. And now, he said, he was free to wander around the Valley with us.

Sjam wondered if the Sumitros had fired him.

When the fire burned down to a soft glow, the men became drowsy. Their heads nodded sleepily. Chief Sike told Sjam and me to sleep on the ground floor of the *pilai*.

This was the second time Sjam and I were to spend the night on the lower level of a warriors' *pilai*. I can't say I could become accustomed to such a practice, even though the *pilai* is the safest place in the compound to be. It is a fortress with warriors in the hayloft who are ready to protect you from any kind of danger.

In the light of the great built-in defense upstairs, it was surprising to me that during the early-morning hours Aem crept downstairs. Sjam, in total darkness, actually connected a resounding slap on Aem's body and she screamed in English at a boy who understood only Dani and Indonesian.

The warriors thundered down from the hayloft and grabbed Aem. They dragged him out into the courtyard and through the village entrance. I don't know what they did to him, but when the warriors returned, Chief Sike assured us that Aem would never dare enter the village again.

(23)

The sick Dani in Wamholik had improved remarkably. He was sitting up in the *pilai* when we arrived. I left him a supply of medicine and promised to return within the week.

Sjam, Mi Hijo and I began the long trudge back to Analaga. Kolo would be angry because we'd stayed away for so long, and I wasn't looking forward to the confrontation.

It was noon when we reached the Aikhe River. The sun was

scorching. The perspiration poured off our bodies. There was not a dry spot on my shirt.

We ate lunch by the river. Lunch meant a handful of cold rice. By Western standards the meal might be shabby, but after a week's menu of potatoes, rice was a welcome treat.

"Ma, look!" Mi Hijo said, pointing to a group of warriors approaching the river.

"Why, that's Obaharok! And Sike and Asuan!"

I had never seen the three men together. Perhaps Obaharok wanted to smooth out his war alliance with Asuan and Sike. All of the men were walking fast. Even Asuan managed to keep up with them. When Sike saw us sitting on the river-bank, he broke into a run.

"The police want Mi Hijo!" he yelled from across the river. Sike raced over the bridge. He sat down next to us, panting. When Obaharok joined us, Sike handed Sjam a letter written in Indonesian. It was from the police post in Jiwika, a village north of Wenebuborah. The letter charged Mi Hijo with beating a woman the night before and demanded his arrest.

"Mi Hijo, why would a woman charge you with something like that?"

"If the police believe her, then I have to pay a pig!" Mi Hijo was going into a slow burn.

Mi Hijo refused to go to Jiwika to be arrested for something he didn't do. No one blamed him. The whole thing was ridiculous; Mi Hijo had never been out of Sjam's and my sight. But Mi Hijo's refusal to be arrested sent Sike into depths of despair.

"If I tell the police Mi Hijo won't come for arrest," he said, "they'll put *me* in jail!"

I didn't especially want to interfere in police business, but as an eyewitness, my involvement seemed justified. I wrote a letter to the police chief in Jiwika.

Sike dispatched himself to the police post with the letter and with new confidence.

Obaharok's mind made little notes on everything he saw. He was impressed with the letter-writing procedure.

"We will follow you and Sjam to Abulakma," he said. There was a glint of approval in his eyes.

With Mi Hijo in the lead, Obaharok and Asuan brought up the rear. Asuan set a new speedy pace for himself back there. He had never been so far from home. He was scared to death every minute we were on the trail, even in the company of a *kain*.

When we arrived in Abulakma, the men returned to their own villages. Kolo burst into the *uma*. He wanted to know who that "tall, skinny, slow man" was. He complained that too many strangers were coming into his territory. He asked me why I didn't stay home where I belonged, which meant inside the *uma* twenty-four hours a day. He looked angry enough to collapse and die.

Kolo's attitude was heartbreaking. It was unfortunate, and it was untimely. The north had taken a friendly interest in the southern people. I had no personal plot to disturb Kolo's delicate balance of things, but I could envision, with a little encouragement, a future of togetherness for these Dani. They could live in peace and friendship for the first time in history.

Kolo was firm and unmoving. I supposed he considered his foul pride an asset. There was nothing I could do right now.

Kolo's temperament was to become uglier before it sweetened, and Kelion's surprise appearance in Abulakma stimulated Kolo's disposition to a new nastiness.

(24)

It was about noon when Kelion arrived in Abulakma. He came with three other warriors.

It must have taken tremendous courage for Kelion to have gone through enemy territory. It was an action which required not only a strong heart but fast feet.

Kelion looked as though he'd come from one journey and was ready to start another one at a moment's notice. Perhaps he and the others had run across the Valley, I don't know. He seemed greatly relieved that he had reached the *uma* and hadn't been killed on the way.

Sjam had found a lemon somewhere. She made six glasses of lemonade out of that one lemon. It was thin, but good. Kelion drank his juice in a single swallow. He picked up my glass.

"Kelion, I will share my lemonade with you, half and half. But not all of it. Here, put the glass between us where we can both see it."

Kelion explained the reasons for risking his life to visit us. He'd learned about the incident with Aem in Punycul. He'd done a little checking around. He'd found that Aem was not a truthful person. He thought that Aem might have succeeded in his crime of lying if he had varied his routine by telling the truth once in a while.

Kelion had come to the stunning conclusion that Aem might *not* have served as a reliable interpreter.

"Did you really *say* you didn't like my people?" Mi Hijo translated.

"Kelion, did you really *say* you didn't like us?" I asked.

Kelion pursed his lips, frowned and shook his head. He qualified Aem with a single adjective.

"The boy is *kepu*," he said insultingly, warding the flies off the lemonade glass. "We want you to live with us. Please, Sjam, Mama Wyn, come back to live in Tumagonem."

"I think it'd cause ill feelings with Kolo, Kelion."

"Then have two houses! Keep this one and we'll build you another in Tumagonem!"

Sjam and I promised to visit the people in Tumagonem within the week. Meanwhile, we would think about the house.

When Kelion and the others left, I reached for my lemonade glass. It was empty.

(25)

"A new man in my village!" Kolo screamed. "Who was that?" The look in his eyes was one of fury.

"That was Kelion," I said. "I must leave for Tumagonem today. There's been a misunderstanding among the people there. We've got to straighten it out. I also promised to see the sick Dani in Wamholik. Kolo, if I'm causing you to be unhappy, I won't return to Abulakma."

"I allow myself to make a mistake once in a while," he said. "*Lu!*" ("Go!").

(26)

Kolo's messenger caught up with us at the Aikhe River.

"Kolo begs you to return whenever you are ready," he said. "Kolo said you can stay as long as you like. You can even bring people back with you if you want to."

Kolo's statement gave me a half-open gate to freedom and a sense of genuine relief.

The terrible duty of friendship began when we met Kelion, Old Pum and Asuan in Tumagonem. They begged us to stay with them. They promised to build a house for us at any cost. Kelion wanted to throw in a pig to close the deal.

If Sjam and I maintained two houses, one in the north and the other in the south, it would require a five-hour walk between them several times a week. It would be exhausting, but it would be worth it if friendship between the natives in the Valley would come about.

We agreed to the house. Asuan appointed himself architect, and Kelion left the village to hunt for lumber.

The next morning Sjam and I visited the police in Jiwika. We wanted to register my visa with the police and let them know we would be staying in the area.

The police chief struck me as a man incapable of great violence. "A native in Wamena," I began, "told me the police here in Jiwika had beaten him. And I was wondering if he was telling the truth?"

"*Biasa!*" ["Commonplace!"], the chief laughed. "Beating is the only way to handle these people. They don't understand anything else!"

(27)

When we returned to Analaga village, a change had come over Kolo. He was kind. He gave us sweet potatoes from his own garden and he didn't even want anything in return.

The Dani in Analaga, as in all other places in the Valley, sleep in *pilais* and *abiais* above a fireplace that keeps them warm during the cold nights; all Sjam and I slept above was a family of rats. For warmth we enveloped ourselves in bright-blue nylon sleeping bags, stuffed with an abundance of duck down. A zipper ran the length of the bag and across the end. We slept in our clothes inside the bags because it became colder as the night progressed. To compensate for its warm beginning, however, the zippers on the sleeping bags were invariably left open.

I was aroused from a deep sleep by a movement on the foot of my sleeping bag. Sjam was snoring explosively. It occurred to me that perhaps she was tossing around in a nightmare and had inadvertently kicked me.

The bag suddenly slipped again. It was done with deliberation. Abruptly the whole bag covering was roughly pulled away from my body. I felt a strong hand grasp my ankle. The fingers curled in an iron grip. I felt my heart skip a beat as a chill of fear raced up my spine. The hand touched the waist belt of my trousers. The breath went out of me as I felt the fingers twist around the band and pull the trousers down, hard. I grabbed out at the hand and felt a plastic *tekan* around the wrist beneath my fingers.

Aem!

I screamed.

Sjam woke up.

Aem escaped from the *uma*.

Mama Aem caught him in the courtyard.

(28)

I suddenly found myself in the position of plaintiff in a Dani court of justice.

Sjam was the co-plaintiff.

Aem was the defendant.

Kolo was the judge.

The Dani courts inherited their laws from their ancestors. The laws were accepted with the knowledge that everyone had to obey them or suffer punishment for breaking them. The laws dealt with life, property, manners, dishonesty, dishonor and misconduct.

The crimes that existed in the Baliem Valley were few. Killing was not considered a crime because it was a part of the Dani culture. If a woman ran off with another man, the problem was solved with the payment, or fine, of a pig. The theft of one pig was settled with the payment of two. The chief crime was against friendship and human feelings. This crime was an act of evil. The ordinances, due to ancestral origin, were not open to question.

Sjam and I were sitting in an abandoned *abiai* in Old Dialec's village, Analaga, when Kolo came in and asked me about the incident with Aem. Sjam told him about her mistreatment by Aem in Punycul and together we informed him about Aem's translation foul-up in Tumagonem. We could have mentioned Kitty's death, but we were without concrete proof.

Kolo listened to the complaints with delight. Little ripples of pleasure chased over his face. He turned the matter over and over in his mind until he was ecstatic with glee.

In the early evening, the trial began. The jury, lead by Old Dialec, solemnly filed into the tiny *abiai*. The jury was composed of the village elders. They would sit in judgment of Aem.

Old Dialec was still telling everyone he was afraid. He tilted his head back when he said it, to see who was listening to him.

When the defendant arrived, he was not allowed to come inside the *abiai*. Aem sat down outside the house, close enough to be heard but not seen. He had brought his "lawyer" with him, a friend from the neighboring compound. The lawyer sat in the doorway, half in and half out. Aem was not allowed to speak directly to Judge Kolo. The lawyer spoke for him.

Mi Hijo was the court translator. Considering that he was too young to understand the nature of the case, his translating hit notes of hilarity at times.

I was asked to relate the events of the night in question to the jury. Sjam was called upon to give her testimony of the incident in Punycul.

Kolo said a few words. Before he was finished, Aem's attorney entered a plea of guilty.

Kolo had smiled through the hearing of the whole case. The plea caused him to laugh out loud.

"Like my wife!" he said. I remembered Aem's accusation that Kolo's wife had sexually attacked him in his own compound.

Based on Aem's confessed guilt, Kolo's sentence struck me as strange: Aem was fined one, exceptionally large, pig. The pig was to be paid to Kolo!

Aem was formally denied entrance to Analaga. He was officially considered an outcast who had lost standing with both his family and friends until the fine was paid.

Later that night Sjam and I sneaked over to Abulakma to talk with Mama and Papa Aem. Before we returned to Analaga, I gave my piglet to Mama Aem.

I hoped it would make Papa Aem richer.

(29)

Kolo had changed from a snarling wildcat to a big, shaggy and nearly loveable bear. This new gaiety spread around over the village and even the pigs in the courtyard felt it. They quit fighting over the waterhole, and one great boar was reported to have given up his food to another.

Kolo had become nearly saintly in character. He even humbled himself a little toward others. On one occasion he was overheard boasting about some unexpected successes he had had with the ladies in the area. One of the women had even wanted to marry him. He said he didn't half try.

The change in Kolo's disposition was mostly due to his decision to build Sjam and me a house, himself, outside of Abulakma. Our friends were sad to see us leave the *uma*, especially Mama and Papa Aem, but they honored Kolo's decision because he was their chief and they were distrustful of Aem, anyhow.

As chief of the entire Analaga district, Kolo could build a house anywhere he wanted to. He chose his father's village, Analaga. He probably felt Old Dialec would keep his eye on us and we'd be safer there.

Kolo's joy in building the house became so general that he had a hard time keeping his mind on his objective.

In the interest of space the pigsty (*wamai*) next to Old Dialec's *pilai* was torn down. The manure was scraped out to make room for the new house. Kolo was seen working on the house himself. As a rule he abhorred the whole idea of working; he felt it was silly and gainless when others could do it just as well. Sjam and I looked at him in wonder.

The house was perhaps Kolo's most outlandish achievement. The plan was exactly like the *uma* in Abulakma. The walls were constructed with the same lumber that had been used in the pigsty. The wood had not been altered or disguised. This was confusing to the pigs in the compound, for they believed they should be permitted to enter the house, and often did.

When Kolo wasn't around, Sjam and I called the house *wamai* because the lumber was filled with pig fleas.

Kolo accepted the idea of our having a house in the north.

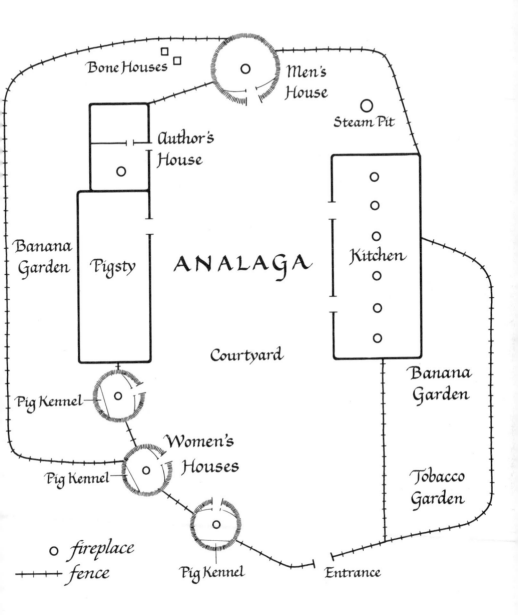

Bone Houses □ □

Men's House

Steam Pit

Author's House

Banana Garden

Pigsty

ANALAGA

Kitchen

Courtyard

Banana Garden

Pig Kennel

Women's Houses

Pig Kennel

Tobacco Garden

○ fireplace
+++++ fence

Pig Kennel

Entrance

He was overheard explaining to his people that we would be living in two houses. They were all invited to accompany us to the north, whenever they wanted to go. The people smiled and nodded in agreement.

Kelion, Asuan, Sike and the others were waiting for us in the north. Our house in Tumagonem was probably already finished and ready to occupy.

Fish, Man with Bow and Arrow, Portrait of Asuan DRAWINGS BY WALEK

CHAPTER THREE

Walek

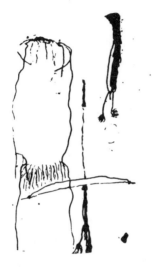

(1)

The house in Tumagonem wasn't finished; in fact, it hadn't even been begun.

"Asuan is too lazy," wailed Old Pum. "I have scolded him. He pays no attention! What to do about your new house?"

There were five posts leaning against the *thop* of Tumagonem. The posts were meant to be used in the new house. They had been carried to the site. That was all that had been done.

Kelion had sprained his ankle. At least he said he'd sprained it. He'd been gathering wood when a tree fell on his foot. He limped whenever he remembered it.

Kelion swung himself through the *thop*. He winced because he was certain we were all looking. With a wave of his big hand, he motioned us into the *pilai*.

"Asuan is too lazy," Kelion said. "He'll build the house but it will take a long time. I want to build you a house in my village."

"Where is your village?"

"Well, my village burned down. I'm living in Wiyagoba right now. I can build a house for you there. Chief Walek can help me."

"What do you mean, your village burned down?"

Kelion ducked his head between his shoulders in embarrassment. "I found some little sticks with fire on the ends of them. When I took the sticks into my *pilai,* they burned down my village."

That was probably true. If Kelion had been playing with matches in the *pilai* and a fire had started, it had only to run across the adjoining fences to the *abiais* and kitchen. The whole grass village would go up in smoke in a matter of minutes.

Kelion was inclined to be careless about almost everything he did. It was likely he'd burn down any house he built for us in Wiyagoba. But we agreed to talk to Chief Walek.

It was a thoughtful group of local men who agreed to go with us. The people of Tumagonem and Wiyagoba were subjects of a common war alliance, but they had never met one another. The footpath cut through the tall grasses of Mulima. Then it angled sharply northeast beneath a mountain whose long slope crept down onto the Valley floor by the Aikhe River. The sun was at our backs. It lighted up the world around us. I was struck by the serenity of the Valley landscape.

The path dipped abruptly into a gully in which a village was nearly hidden from view. On the other side of the village was the Lagora River.

Sjam and I found that no step could be taken on the path without someone's hand to steady us. Neither of us trusted

Kelion very much. He was too clumsy. I leaned on Mi Hijo. Sjam sought help from a young man named Noak.

Noak was older than Mi Hijo, with great ambition. He had taught himself the Indonesian language by hanging around the police post in Jiwika. Noak latched on to Sjam and me with the hopes that his newly acquired Indonesian would pay off.

The sun was just below the horizon when we came to the river crossing. There were mischievous winds playing through the trees lining the riverbank. The air was sweet with resin.

The water was not deep, perhaps eighteen inches. A twenty-foot log spanned the gorge. Sjam and I walked across the river bottom to the other side.

Beyond the river we could see a tiny village, with smoke rising from its center.

Kelion led us through the *thop* of Wiyagoba. We faced two *pilais*. They were standing side by side at the opposite end of the courtyard. Wiyagoba is probably the only village in the Valley that has two such structures. They had been created as a result of a distrust. One of the *pilais* belonged to Kelion, the other to Walek. Walek had allowed Kelion to move into his village provided he built his own house and promised never to smoke in it.

Kelion's *pilai* could be identified by the carelessness of its construction. Kelion was not known for dexterity; he had not even mastered Dani knot-tying. The *pilai* was loosely lashed together with gaping slots here and there. The whole structure had an air of impermanency about it.

Most of the material had been stolen. Kelion had made an attempt to disguise the stolen lumber by hacking at it; he'd wanted to destroy its identity in case the former owner looked in. He had made ample use of grass on the roof which he had found close at hand, in the neighboring village's lot. It was grass the villagers had never missed because they never knew about Kelion's taking it. Most of the grass had been tied onto the roof backward.

Inside the *pilai* Kelion tried to keep things neat, but his natural clumsiness sometimes defeated him. When we went in,

Kelion knocked over the water gourd. The water soaked the grass. In getting settled, Kelion leaned against the wall and crushed two *holims* he had left to dry. And then he pushed his tobacco into the fireplace with his foot. The *pilai* was messy but it functioned as a place for Kelion to sleep. As long as he didn't burn it down, Walek let him call it "home."

The Wiyagoba women slept in three *abiais* facing the kitchen. Walek's wife and his relatives were installed in two of them. Kelion had built one for Wenybake. It was pitifully tiny. Kelion had miscalculated its dimensions in the early stages of construction. When it was finished, the *abiai* was so small that no two people could be under its roof at the same time.

Walek arrived in the village. He had been stealing a small pig. When his garden work was finished, he'd found that luck was with him. He came across a small piglet which had wandered away from its owner. Walek grabbed the pig without even having to step too far off the footpath.

He'd run all the way home. He was breathless when he arrived. The pig's muffled screams came through teeth clamped shut by Walek's firm hand. Above the sounds of the animal we could hear Walek sneezing. He had been out too long in the damp grass in his bare feet.

Kelion had gone to sleep with his ears wide open. When he heard the sneezing and squealing, he rushed from the *pilai* into the courtyard. Kelion inspected the pig with the same objective care he lavished on all stolen goods. A wide grin spread over his face. He could find no fault with the pig.

Kelion wanted the pig for himself. He put his mind through a stunning method to get it. He intended to chisel the animal away from Walek by using a Dani legal system which Walek could not question.

The maneuver involved me.

I had crawled out of the *pilai* and was facing Walek. At the sight of a stranger in his village, Walek felt caught with the stolen pig tucked beneath his arm. He thrust the squealing piglet into my hands. Kelion began to chant, "Wa, wa, wa, wa, wa," to thank me for passing the pig to him, which I did.

If Walek realized he had been swindled, he made no sign of

it. The exchange of property had been too swift for his mind to follow. He shrugged his shoulders and lapsed into a happy incoherency. Whatever had happened had happened.

Chief Walek was a slightly crazy, lisping chief who spoke the whole Dani language without ever using the letter *s*. Walek didn't trust *talking* very much as a means of communication; he'd always felt that actions were stronger than words.

Walek was of average height. His face was sculptured from the materials of devils and rascals. His eyes were as bright as a peacock's, although a curious glint of madness shone in them. He was interested in everything, even though he didn't understand much of what went on around him.

Walek was left-handed, but he didn't know that. He knew ordinary men found their strength in their right hand, but his left hand was the strongest. He concluded that the gods had given him a supernatural power and appointed him to be chief. Walek had found the way to be noticed.

The people accepted him with respect because they feared his great left-handed strength, and because he was forever killing someone. Walek's mind was choked up with uncatalogued memories of enemies he had killed or of those he intended to kill. Sometimes he couldn't remember one from the other. He had found killing not only pleasant but highly interesting work. Once in a while he had a motive and at other times he did not. He thought everyone was that way.

Walek was related to nearly everybody in the northern part of the Valley through blood or love affairs. He had wives and children scattered from one end of the country to the other. They were families he longed to see again, but he knew it was impossible.

Walek's real name was Mabel. He and his older brother had been largely responsible for the attack of 1966 against the people with whom he was now living. When Walek found his compound burned to the ground by the enemy, he decided to live with those who fought better than he did. He moved out of his old alliance and founded the village of Wiyagoba in the enemy's territory.

Fortunately, Walek took a fancy to Sjam and me. He wanted us to live in his village.

"Tham! Mama Wyn! You live in Wiyagoba! I will build you a houth. A big houth. Big, big, big!"

Thoughts came rather slowly to Walek. A momentous question entered his mind: What *kind* of house should he build for a white person and a dark-skinned Indonesian?

Walek placed his hands in a manner of prayer and waited for inspiration. Kelion offered what his memory of our house in Abulakma could resurrect. The description made quite a struggle to get into Walek's mind, but it failed. Walek tried to grab hold of Kelion's information but each time he reached out, it slipped away from him.

There seemed to be a slight sizzling sound coming from Walek's brain. Then Walek said an astonishing thing: "The houth will be ath tall ath the talleth tree in Wiyagoba!" Walek looked appalled at his own daring.

Kelion sucked in his breath. Mi Hijo let out a soft "Whew!" Noak's eyes went blank with wonder.

Walek looked as though he'd approached a state of collapse. The strain of such intense concentration with such poor equipment had probably blistered his brain.

"Good idea! We can do it!" Kelion said.

Walek smiled weakly. He had never been accused of having a good idea before. He didn't know quite how to handle it.

"The girls can sleep in the spare kitchen meanwhile," he said. A gentle peacefulness settled over his face.

The spare kitchen was situated behind Walek's *pilai*, outside the courtyard, and it had an entrance of its own. It was a small structure, a rectangular boxlike affair with a dirt floor. The men brought in armloads of grass to cover the floor.

And then Sike showed up for the first time in Wiyagoba. He did not come alone. His friends from Punycul were with him.

To celebrate our arrival in Wiyagoba the men began to sing together. Walek tried to join in. He could not even come near imitating the men's voices. The sounds emitting from his throat put Sjam and me into hard labor to stifle the mirth we felt.

(2)

Early the following morning Sjam, Mi Hijo and I started out on the first of the many, many long trips we were to make between Wiyagoba and the *wamai* Kolo had built for us in Analaga.

When the path was dry, we could reach Analaga in about four and a half hours if we didn't stop too often to pass out medicine along the way. The Aikhe River slowed us down. It was a place to meet and talk with our friends from Tumagonem, Punycul and other villages. Occasionally we saw Obaharok there. Once we watched him fell a tree. It seemed rather menial work for a man of his distinction.

When we arrived in Analaga, Kolo was genuinely glad to see us. He was amazed that we hadn't been killed by his enemies, since we had walked right through their territory.

One day Kolo decided to initiate me into the membership of his own family. To create the union, Kolo was required to sacrifice a pig. Since he didn't have any pigs of his own, he asked Wimbilu, one of his neighbors, to offer a pig on his behalf. But the animal had to be paid for, and Kolo didn't have anything worthwhile to barter with. I ended up giving Wimbilu a large shovel for the pig which Kolo used to cement my relationship with his family.

The pig-killing ritual was without much fanfare. The importance in the affair was found in Kolo's influence to order the killing of a pig, and in my eating the meat. The result was a binding agreement in which Kolo would be responsible for any and all of my actions. It was a one-sided deal. The membership alliance benefited my position far more than it could ever work for Kolo. I didn't know it at the time, but the union was destined to come in extremely handy later.

When you are given a pig to eat in the Baliem Valley, you are expected to consume the entire animal, not just part of it. It's a task of enormous proportions.

"Kolo, why don't we share this meat with Walek and Kelion?" I suggested.

Kolo suddenly saw himself in the position of a man admired. Perhaps he would be envied if he divided his gift among two chiefs he regarded as lesser than himself.

"*Nen* ["Yes"], take the pork to them. Tell them it's from me!"

Later that night Kolo sang. Sjam and I recorded his voice to play for Walek. At the end of it, Kolo sent Walek a message: "Walek! Why don't you come see me?"

(3)

Armed with half a pig tied up in banana stalks and a tape of Kolo's voice, we struck off to begin the long trudge back to Wiyagoba.

Sjam's shoes were just about worn out. She had switched to wearing light tennis shoes. Now the big toe of her right foot stuck up through a hole in the canvas top. The sole on the other shoe had come loose at the front. It slapped the ground loudly with every step and slowed down her walking. In desperation, and to get her moving faster, Mi Hijo cut the sole loose at the heel with our kitchen knife.

Obaharok was waiting for us at the river. He wore a cloud of dark anxiety on his face.

"*Laok,*" he said, motioning us to sit under the trees.

Mi Hijo hung back. He looked at us sideways. When we were seated, he sat down on a rock some distance away.

"Are you afraid?" said Obaharok, waving his hand. "Come translate for us."

Mi Hijo approached warily and squatted behind Obaharok.

Very few things could happen in the Valley without Obaharok's knowledge. He had probably caught wind of the new house being built in Wiyagoba and of the recent family alliance made in Analaga.

"You see I carry the knife you gave me?" Obaharok said in a desire to make us happy.

"Obaharok, are you going to fine me for the house in Wiya-goba?"

"Why do you need two houses? Is one house not enough?"

"Well, we have many friends in two different places. We need two houses to be able to live near our friends."

"You have good friends in Analaga and in Wiyagoba. But you do not have friends in my Siepkosi territory in between. I would build you a house in Pabuma if you want."

I told Obaharok it was something I'd like to think about. Meanwhile he was invited, along with his people, to visit us in our Wiyagoba and Analaga houses.

"I cannot come to Wiyagoba. The people fight against me sometimes. I understand Kolo built you a new place since the trouble with Aem."

"Yes, in Analaga. Obaharok, I became part of Kolo's family during these past days."

Obaharok bent his head slightly forward and squinted at the ground in front of him.

"Yes, I know," he said in a whisper.

We left Obaharok sitting by the edge of the river. He did not look up as we crossed the log bridge to the other side of the river. We walked on to Wiyagoba.

(4)

The house in Wiyagoba was finished. We saw the top of the roof jutting up into the sky from the other side of the river.

As we approached the house our steps slowed down until we came to a frozen halt. We stood staring at the structure in disbelief.

"My God!" Sjam gasped.

The house was built to dazzle the eyes. It looked like an enormous cathedral. It was large enough to house a tank with its guns positioned.

Walek had brought ferocity into the building of the house. It spilled out of the compound and went on its own way right out into the jungle.

Walek must have had lots of help to build such a thing. He had probably threatened people into helping him build it.

"My God!" Sjam said again.

You would expect the entrance to this marvel to be found on one of the long sides. We circled the entire building before we discovered a door at the far end of it.

Inside the house was a partition with a door in it. On the other side was some kind of room. Beyond that room was another partition and still another door. Behind the last bamboo division was a raised platform. It was about waist-high, meant to be the sleeping quarters for Sjam and me. Even standing on the platform, you couldn't touch the ceiling.

"Tham, Mama Wyn!" Walek came panting in. "Do you like the houth?"

"Uh, it's a beautiful house, Walek. We like it. It's big, isn't it?"

"Yeth! Big, big, big!"

At night the house was drafty and cold. Walek loved to talk at great length in the evenings. Usually he could stick out almost anything, but now he found himself shivering with cold. He had to leave early. The house began to lose the delight it had given him; it was not the joy he thought it was going to be.

We sent for four more blankets from Wamena. They didn't help much. Mi Hijo built a fire in one of the rooms before he left to sleep in the warmth of Walek's *pilai*. We envied him. The house was filled with the roar of the fire but it did little to heat up the big structure.

In the middle of the night, strangers walked into the house. They did not mean to molest us, they meant to steal our goods. They came and went without our even knowing it. In the morning whole cases of cooking oil were missing. It was not an unusual theft; the oil would be useful for the Dani hairdo.

The following night our corned beef was looted. The Dani did not like the beef as much as the sharp metal in the can

The Dani drink water
by throwing it up into their
mouths with their hands.

Chief Sike talked Sjam
into buying an opossum fur
for her red fur hat.
He didn't have to do much talki
She thought the straggly fur
was beautiful.

The men saturate their hair
with pig fat and then pull
the long, kinky strands into
springlike coils that drip
over the head from the crow
The hairdos indicate the
elaborate and time-consumir
effort of the Dani men
to be gorgeous.

The Dani women are full-hipped,
big-bellied creatures.
When they get together they are a
robust, boisterous, rowdy bunch.
Their energy is volcanic.

Kelion did not abide by the principle of private ownership of property. He believed that "thinking honest" could strain the mind. He usually devoted all of his energies to making wide circles around that kind of stress.

Aem was a Dani.
Aem got by because people thought he was harmless, but he was unsafe to be around. Sjam and I were to become sorry victims of both his deadly thoughts and actions.

This male mummy is perhaps the most remarkable, if not the gaudiest, curiosity in the Dani culture. The people pray to the mummy, sacrifice pigs to it, and even rub its stony legs and arms with pig oil.

Sjam and I had to watch
ourselves when we were around
Old Pum. He was senile, but
he had moments of recovery.
During those lapses he loved
to pinch a girl on the hip.

———————

Sike was the new chief
of Punycul. He was a
very young handsome Dani
with wide, high cheekbones
and dazzling black eyes
that pinched shut
whenever he smiled.

I was presented
with a small, squealing piglet.
I was grateful for the past
experience of patting
Kelion's pig on the head,
but it did not fully prepare
me to hold such an animal
in my arms.

Sometimes, at funerals,
the men cut their ears and
fingers to show grief, if
their loss is of a very deep
and personal nature.
The amputator raps a sharp
blow to the "crazy bone"
to anesthetize the hand.
Then he chops off a single
finger joint with a stone adze.

———————

I was puzzled
by the injuries on one of
the young Dani men.
"What happened to you?"
"I was beaten."
"Who beat you?"
"The police at Jiwika."

Chief Kolo was the most difficult
man I had to work with in the Valley.
He had a sour eye for the whole world
and he took pride in showing it.
He believed his foul disposition was an asset.

I walked to the little
nest where the piglet
lay asleep and knelt to
touch Mi Hijo's hand.
"Ma," Mi Hijo said,
sobbing to break your heart,
"it's not good enough.
The pig is too small.
I'm so ashamed."

Chief Walek was
a slightly crazy, lisping
chief who spoke the whole Da
language without ever
using the letter *s*. His mind
was choked up with
uncatalogued memories of
enemies he had killed or
of those he intended to kill.
Sometimes he couldn't rememb
one from the other. He thoug
everyone was that way.

Obaharok: "I knew I was
meant to be a *kain*.
My father told me.
I have killed many, many
people. In the end I was
accepted by the people
as overlord. I am not
afraid of anybody."

Walek placed the pig's
tail and ear between
our wrists, explaining that
they made the ritual
stick better. He wrapped
a length of rattan around
our wrists and tied
a knot. Obaharok
(*standing*) was struck with
the giggles.

——————

→
Not to know Kelion
is to fail to know
that he was primarily
a man torn between
robbery and murder.
Mostly, he was a thief.

←

"Kelion! Kelion,
you stole my pig!
And now you're eating it!"
she screamed, pointing an
accusing finger at Kelion.

↑
To listen to a dying pig
is worse than looking at it,
although both are
frightening. The arrow punches
its way through
the pig's heart and a
sudden belch of blood
spews out. The animal's
screams split one's eardrums.

———————

←
It was a fine house.
The entrance was high,
and there was lots of room to
sit up straight inside it.
We decided to buy the house.
We bought it with salt, umbrellas,
flashlights and rupiahs.

———————

→
Kusupia had been badly
beaten and tortured.
His nose was broken
and his lip battered
and torn. His chest
and back had been burned
in ribbonlike patterns.

Obaharok climbed over the fence
between the *pilai*
and the kitchen and left.
When he returned, he stood
in the gateway, motionless.
I looked at Obaharok and Kolo.
None of us had the kind of
courage it takes to smile.

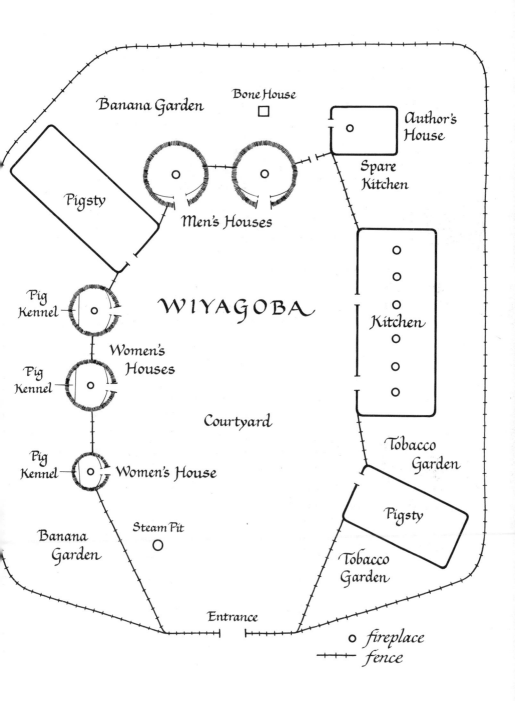

Banana Garden

Bone House

Author's House

Spare Kitchen

Pigsty

Men's Houses

Pig Kennel

WIYAGOBA

Kitchen

Women's Houses

Pig Kennel

Courtyard

Tobacco Garden

Pig Kennel — Women's House

Pigsty

Banana Garden

Steam Pit

Tobacco Garden

Entrance

o fireplace
+++ fence

around it, which could be put to all kinds of uses. And the key to the can could be smashed flat to form a long needle.

The house was vulnerable. It was too large. There was no fence around it. Walek had thrown up *silos* in the area, but no one paid any attention to them. It hurt Walek's feelings that his warning signals had been ignored.

One night Walek lay in wait to try to catch the thieves who had been disregarding his danger signs. He caught Noak with a can of corned beef in his hand. It was everything we could do to persuade Walek not to kill the boy on the spot.

Sjam and I moved back into the tiny kitchen behind Walek's *pilai* the day Obaharok came.

(5)

Obaharok had not ventured to Wiyagoba alone. With him was a grand and rather stately man whose name was Wali, chief of Opagima. Wali had been a great *kain* in his day. In 1966 the younger Obaharok had done Wali a favor. In gratitude, Wali gave one of his daughters to be Obaharok's wife.

Wali was a thin man, gray-bearded. He was old, but his eyes were young. Little wrinkles drew up around the corners whenever he smiled. He smiled quite often.

Obaharok and Wali had timed their visit. Walek and Kelion were working in the sweet-potato gardens. And Wali and Obaharok left before the men returned from their fields.

The children passed the word to Kelion and Walek that the two *kains* had been in Wiyagoba. Kelion lumbered into the kitchen with Walek at his heels. Both men looked angry.

"Why did Obaharok come here?" Kelion asked.

"Obaharok is my friend, Kelion. I made peace with him in Hiyasi."

"Who did you meet first? Me or Obaharok?"

"Why, I met you, of course. The first time I saw Obaharok

was in Tumagonem. You remember, he wanted to sell his stone axe."

Kelion and Walek stared with hatred in their eyes.

"Obaharok wants to be your friend," I said.

"Obaharok wanth to be my friend?" Walek suddenly grinned. He looked at the people around him. "Obaharok wanth to know me!" Walek felt flattered.

"Kolo wants to be your friend, too. He sent you some pork to eat."

"He thent me thome meat to eat? Will I die if I eat it?"

"No, we will eat it together. I'll show you."

Walek ate the pork and waited to die. Nothing happened. I switched on the tape recorder. Walek listened to Kolo's voice. At the end of the tape he received Kolo's message: "Walek! Why don't you come see me?"

"I will! I will!" Walek screamed and ran outside, to talk to the trees. He had a habit of doing that. He thought the trees understood what he was saying.

(6)

It was three-thirty in the morning. The women were screaming. The men were yelling bloody murder.

"Sjam! Wake up! Get Mi Hijo! Something terrible is happening out there!"

"Wyn! Sjam! Help!" It was Kelion's voice.

Kelion banged on the door until it came loose. He charged into the room. Mi Hijo followed him in. Walek arrived with more children than I had ever believed lived in Wiyagoba.

The courtyard was suddenly quiet.

"Ma," Mi Hijo said, "Ma, it was the schoolteacher. He wanted to take the children."

The story came out slowly. Everyone in the kitchen had something to contribute to it. This was not the first time Joseph

Tatoko from the St. Lucas school in Mulima had broken into the villages to force the children to attend his school. He was an old hand at it. He had been taught by the former schoolteacher, Bernard Mujakir.

This morning Tatoko, armed with a band of larger boys, had entered Thakulobok village and taken away two children. The parents were left crying and nearly hysterical.

When Tatoko went into the village of Wamhalilmo, he found that the children had mysteriously disappeared from the grounds. He felt sharply disappointed at being outmaneuvered, so he decided to make up for it in Wiyagoba. He broke through the boarded *thop*, entered the womens' *abiais* and grabbed whatever sleepy children he could lay his hands on.

"If they don't go, then he beats them," said Kelion. "Pituin was beaten on the head and there's still a big crack there."

"And when the girls reach the marriage age, they leave school and their parents have to give the teacher their pigs!" Mi Hijo added.

"Well, learning in school is usually a pretty good thing. Walek, have you ever thought of voluntarily sending your children to school?" I asked.

"I already thent four," Walek said.

"I've sent six," Kelion said, "but they can't all go! Some must stay and tend the pigs and work in the gardens with us."

"Thall we kill the teacher?" Walek asked, because he had nothing against murder.

"No, no. Wait a minute. Let me think."

Two dark lines appeared between Sjam's eyes. "They treat these people like animals," she said beneath her breath.

"I'll visit the teacher," I said. "Maybe we can reach an understanding."

The villagers left the kitchen, and the compound quieted down. Sjam and I couldn't sleep.

(7)

Joseph Tatoko was more savage than the people with whom I was living.

"I come from a cannibal family," he yelled. "I know all about cannibals! The only way to handle them is to beat some sense into them. I have the right to force the children to go to school. I'll continue to force them. If they don't come, I'll beat them and they know it. Not you or anybody else is going to stop me!"

Tatoko turned on his heel and stalked back into his half-filled classroom. Sjam and I left the grounds. We heard Tatoko screaming to his children in Indonesian.

"Wyn, do you know what he said? 'I would kill her with one finger and she would die at once!'"

"Let's get back to Wiyagoba, Sjam. I want to write a letter."

(8)

"Ma, they got your letter," said Mi Hijo.

"Who got it?"

"The police in Jiwika. The letter never reached Father De-Heinz in Wamena. Ma, when Tatoko tried to take the children away this morning, he didn't want to teach them anything. He needed them to help him raise his new house."

(9)

Sjam and I got mixed up in some Dani nonsense. We not only got mixed up in it, we contributed to it.

Walek, Kelion and Mi Hijo rapped on our door. It was a

quiet rapping, unusually quiet for men reputed to carry noise to its highest point.

Kelion and Walek looked like naughty boys who were happy about being bad. They were secretive and bashful. Both men glanced behind them. They wanted to be certain they hadn't been followed.

Mi Hijo shut the door and tied it closed with a length of rattan. Then he lighted another candle, the better to see the others.

Kelion and Walek crawled up onto the sleeping platform, smoothed out the blankets and sat down cross-legged. Mi Hijo came in on the side to translate.

Sjam and I waited for someone to say something. I felt we were about to be drawn into some kind of conspiracy.

"*An obeti,*" Walek whispered, "*an obeti warok kagimeke timeke thekop, karok, pthie, nait*" ("I want that medicine more than I want a spade, knife or parang").

"What medicine, Mi Hijo?"

"The woman-medicine."

"I want some, too," Kelion piped in a voice that was dry and hoarse.

Mi Hijo half recalled that *perhaps* he had told the men I had "woman-medicine," but it wasn't a certainty.

Woman-medicine was not a new thing to the Dani. They had been practicing it for a long time. If a Dani saw an odd-shaped berry, or a gnarled knot, or even something that smelled different than anything he'd ever smelled before, he kept the curiosity in the hopes he'd found the real thing. If he acquired a wife shortly after the discovery, the acquisition was credited to the odd object. The need for woman-medicine created it. Tales of good fortune presumed its existence.

Twentieth-century drugs, used on a people who had never been exposed to them, had produced some startling and dramatic miracles. The drugs had come from my medical kit. Now they put me into the curious position of being a possible possessor of love potions.

I have never believed in trying to fool anyone. I tried to

explain there was no such thing as woman-medicine. But I had to give it up. First Kelion was suspicious, then he became resentful. He was convinced I had the medicine but refused to share it. Walek thought I had criticized his beliefs. That was a dangerous thing to do to a man who talked to trees. He sat motionless, gritting his teeth, clenching his fists together.

"It's no use, Sjam. They're convinced I have it. The woman-medicine idea is a little like security, I guess. Those who don't have it feel the need for it. I'll have to give them something. Maybe it'll give them so much confidence in their own eyes, it'll make them desirable in the eyes of women."

I reached for the medical kit. A new respect showed in Walek's eyes. Kelion let out a deep sigh of relief. Mi Hijo was grinning broadly.

"Mi Hijo," whispered Walek, "make thure no one is outthide."

Mi Hijo tiptoed to the door. "There's no one there," he said, turning to join the group again.

Mi Hijo was almost as familiar with the drugs as I was. I had to be careful to select a pill he wouldn't recognize. We had dispensed nearly every kind of medicine in the kit, with the exception of laxatives. Constipation had not been a serious consideration in the Baliem Valley. I took out the little bottle of pink laxative pills. Mi Hijo's eyes shone with excitement. A tender tone came from his throat. "That's it!" he whispered.

Walek shivered. His lips moved but no words came out. Kelion's eyes brightened in ecstasy. Sjam looked at me speculatively.

"Now, there's a certain routine that goes with this medicine," I said, trying to explain something I didn't understand myself.

Walek and Kelion were singularly open to suggestions. They nodded their heads in furious agreement.

"The medicine should be tightly wrapped up in dry banana bark. Tie it with string and wear it beneath your *walimos*. The string should be long enough to drop the medicine next to the heart."

Our customers were wild-eyed with interest. Walek's mouth

had dropped open from furious concentration. His mind was unaccustomed to the trick of paying attention.

"Wear the medicine only when you want to attract a woman," I said.

"*An innagolukmo hareken uguwelagimeke nokologo bigima?*" ["When I drink water, do I take my medicine off?"], Walek asked.

"If you want to," I said. Sjam fought to keep a straight face. "You'll know when the medicine is working because your heart will become very warm. Smile at the woman."

"Oh, I'm good at that," Walek said, practicing.

"If the woman smiles back, then talk to her. When she sees your smile and hears your voice, she will probably find you irresistible."

Walek was apt to forget everything he had been told. He repeated the procedure to himself. When he thought he had it straight, he threw the routine into the box of his brain and slammed the lid down on it.

Kelion would probably forget part of the procedure. If he did, he'd make up something almost as good.

I unscrewed the lid of the bottle, took out two pills and put them on the blanket between Walek and Kelion. Both men leaned forward to study the pills. Mi Hijo brought the candle nearer. Walek reached down and picked up one pill. He felt it with his fingers. He carried it up to his nose to smell it. His chest was rustling with emotion. Abruptly he shook his head from side to side. He wanted to forget he had the woman-medicine lest the thought make him mad.

Kelion picked up the medicine shyly and put it in the palm of his right hand. He petted it with his left index finger.

"I want to use your mirror," he said.

Sjam handed him my mirror. Closing his fist around the medicine, Kelion put his hand beneath his *walimo*. He looked at himself in the mirror. It was a long, contemplative look.

"This medicine is very powerful," he whispered.

"Leth go," Walek said.

Walek and Kelion climbed off the platform. They put their heads down and hurried out into the black night.

(10)

The Dani have a limited knowledge of geography. They believe the land they live on is hemmed in by an imaginary dotted line beyond which lives the enemy. And they have learned, through rumors spread along the native trade routes, that there is a great body of water somewhere, but they have no idea where it is. Beyond the water there is probably nothing.

There is nothing nomadic about the Dani. The people are landowning farmers. They move when they are forced by wars or through disputes with their brothers. In the case of the latter, they do not move far away.

The Dani are curious about their world. They would like to go sightseeing once in a while, but their constant fear of ghosts and enemies keep most of them within the geographical boundaries of their own villages.

Walek had made a three-mile trip across the country when he moved out of his old territory. It was so long ago that Walek had forgotten nearly everything he saw on the way.

Kelion had expanded his geographical knowledge by walking into Wamena a couple of times. To ensure his safety he took several of his brothers with him. Nothing more serious happened to him than that he returned to his village with sore feet.

When Kelion visited us in Abulakma, he believed he had personally discovered a new world. He used this discovery to elevate himself in Walek's eyes; in fact, he never stopped talking about Abulakma. Walek was beside himself with envy. He was dying to visit Analaga.

"I'm not afraid," Walek said, unaware that he wouldn't have made such a statement if he was not afraid. Walek's fears were not without good reason: although Kolo would probably welcome him, there was uncertainty about the kind of reception Old Dialec would give him.

Women and sometimes older children are sent by their chiefs into unfriendly tribal areas, to pave the way for future war confederations. Sjam and I had slipped into this position without even realizing it. When we discovered it, we took advantage of the custom. We encouraged the children in Wiyagoba to follow us to Analaga. Noak was one of the first to go.

Our first attempt to bring these hostile people together was not without failure and not without moments of stark fear. One of the moments involved Old Dialec.

Noak and Mi Hijo were cooking dinner in the *wamai* in Analaga when Old Dialec entered and sat down by the fire. He peered around the room out of his good eye. He noticed that the boy in front of him was a stranger.

"Old Dialec," I said, "this is Noak. He's come to be your friend."

Old Dialec stood up, turned his back on the boy and hooked his index finger around his thumb, making a shooting gesture.

"He's the one who put out my eye!" he screamed, turned around and kicked the boy in the derrière.

Things got better when Abinyai dropped by. He announced to everyone that Noak was his nephew. Noak was so pleased that he tried to help Abinyai figure a way to be related to Kelion.

That night the whole end of the Valley was chattering about the stranger who had come to Analaga. The next morning nearly every child in Analaga wanted to follow us back to Wiyagoba. Many of them did.

(11)

Kaok was a young warrior. He was small and thin, but he was stalwart and strong. He lived in the compound next to ours in Wiyagoba. Each afternoon after work he dropped by our kitchen to get medicine for the skin rash on his forehead.

Kaok was in the kitchen the day Chief Thotnisi visited us. Thotnisi, a widower from Abolekdek village, had been left with two daughters. One of the girls had been forced to attend school. According to Thotnisi, the teacher was demanding the attendance of the other. He asked me to write a letter to the schoolteacher requesting the girl's exemption.

"Wouldn't it be a good idea for you to talk with the teacher yourself?"

Chief Thotnisi held up his left arm. There was a big knot on the wrist. "I'm afraid to talk to him. Last time, when I refused to send both children to school, the teacher, Donatus Iyai, broke my arm. He hit me with a steel rod."

I wrote the letter.

After Chief Thotnisi left, Kaok said, "Obaharok's holding a *kanake* ritual in Opagima village tomorrow. That's a religious ceremony. *Kanake* also refers to the group of religious stones and their ornaments. Are you going?"

(12)

"Walek, don't throw this chance away! Obaharok will be pleased to see you. Kelion's going! Nothing will happen to you. We'll go to the *kanake* together."

"I don't have a pig to take," Walek whined.

"Where's the one you stole?"

"Kelion'th going to take it."

"Here, here's some money. Buy a small pig. Pay for the pig, Walek."

(13)

It took about an hour to walk to Opagima from Wiyagoba if the path was fast and dry. This included the time required for Sjam and me to pull off our boots at the river and slosh across to the other side.

Kelion and Walek hung back. They hadn't crossed over the log bridge and they looked like they weren't going to. Apparently both men had lost their courage to attend Obaharok's *kanake*.

"I'll get them over here, one at a time," Mi Hijo said.

Mi Hijo ran to the center of the bridge. Kelion, his little pig tucked under his arm, had already stepped forward. In the middle of the log the two collided, and with arms flailing for balance, Kelion dropped the pig into the river.

Mi Hijo managed to turn a half circle and return to the bank. Kelion followed him at nearly a dead run. Walek in the meantime raced down the bank to the river to retrieve Kelion's fallen pig. On the riverbank, Kelion carefully examined the animal. It was wet but unharmed. The pig was probably tidier at that moment than it had been in its whole life. It would have been the cleanest pig at the *kanake* if Kelion hadn't accidentally dropped it again in the mud outside the village of Mapilakma.

Kelion's nerves were frayed. Mi Hijo dropped back to help him carry his pig. Walek had hung on to his pig but he had lost his daring. I took Walek's hand and pulled him along until we reached the *thop* of Opagima village.

"Sjam, take Kelion's hand and bring Mi Hijo in close. I'll hang on to Walek."

I climbed through the *thop* and dragged Walek in after me. Sjam pushed Kelion through from the other side of the entrance. Stumbling on a piece of tree stump in front of the *thop*, Kelion dropped his pig. The animal ran into the center of the courtyard, where a large group of warriors sat in stunned silence, staring. Sjam's red fur hat came through the *thop*, and then the rest of her popped through. Mi Hijo bounced from one side of the entrance to the other like a ping pong ball. He hid behind Kelion.

The warriors seated in front of the *pilai* were decorated in their party best—furs, shell necklaces and plumes. Their bodies were thickly greased, black and shining in the sunlight. Every head was turned our way. The warriors sat stock still. It was a suspenseful moment.

A few young boys stood by the *abiais*. There were no women

in the compound. Kelion's pig had joined the other pigs running about the grounds. Theirs was the only movement in the courtyard.

Obaharok was nowhere in sight.

I pushed Walek a little. We advanced in the direction of the *pilai*. There was a movement in the kitchen on the left. Obaharok stood in the doorway.

"*Laok*, Mama Wyn, Sjam," Obaharok said, smiling.

"*Laok*, Obaharok," I said. "Walek is here and— Sjam, where is Kelion?"

Sjam pointed to her right. Kelion had begun chasing his pig through the cluster of men, who were scrambling around on the ground trying to escape being stepped on.

Then, to my astonishment, Obaharok turned to his men and with great ceremony announced the presence of his "two *dear* friends, Walek and Kelion, chiefs of Wiyagoba."

Abruptly Chief Wali stood up in the group's center. The men began to chant, "*Wa, wa, wa, wa, wa*," to receive Walek's and Kelion's pigs into their *kanake* ritual.

Kelion was deeply touched. He quit chasing his pig. He lumbered over to shake Obaharok's hand. Obaharok spoke to Kelion with a kind of affectionate courtesy.

Obaharok shook Walek's limp hand and invited the men into the *pilai* to visit. The honor was singular. Only *kains* and the highest-ranking chiefs were allowed to enter the house during the *kanake* ritual.

I felt no harm would come to Walek and Kelion, but I couldn't imagine the two men alone inside the *pilai* with Obaharok and Wali. I was allowed to go into the *pilai* with them because the people had never quite got used to the idea that I was a woman. Sjam slid in beside me as my interpreter. Mi Hijo was denied entrance, even as my Dani translator.

The inside of the *pilai* looked exactly like the inside of all other *pilais* I'd ever been in. Nothing new had been added, nothing had been taken away.

The men spoke softly among themselves. Sjam and I didn't understand what they were saying. Walek's senses seemed to have returned, and so had his power of speech. He contributed words and sometimes gestures to the conversation. When he got stuck in expressing an idea, Kelion helped him. Obaharok smiled a good deal. So did Wali. The men seemed happy together.

The men cried in a funeral chant because the dead are remembered at all pig feasts. Each man remembered the person he mourned. Kelion couldn't think of anyone to cry for. In the end he wept for Walek's dead son, a boy whom he'd never known and hadn't even heard about until then.

My research of the religious architecture of the Dani world was extremely limited. Many things I learned seemed to be contradictory. There is a great need for study in this field.

As far as I could determine, the Dani have no name for their religion. Like many other people in history, the Dani carved their religion to fill a need. They had often found themselves subject to great emotional turmoil and physical danger. They reached outside themselves for comfort and protection.

Old Dialec had invented a god called *uwe namet mina pike.* This god was responsible for manipulating the darkness to daylight. He had also authored the Dani's original ancestors, Tabhe and Hesage. Old Dialec greatly respected this god but he did not worship him.

It is believed that most natives found in Southeast Asia are fundamentally animists. According to Old Dialec, Tabhe and Hesage were stone people whose spirits were later embodied in stone. I am uncertain if the northern Dani knew much about Tabhe and Hesage but they worshiped the ancestral spirits they believed were found in stone. Therefore, the Baliem Valley Dani might be considered animists. Contrary to the animist doctrine, however, the Dani do not believe all stones have spirits, nor do they worship the soul stuff supposedly found in the trees, rivers or hills.

If a Dani were asked if he worshiped stones, he would most likely say no. He kills pigs as sacrifice to appease the ancestral spirits he believes live within the stones. Sometimes those sacrifices are especially generous.

Through the ritualistic sacrifice of pigs at the *kanakes,* the Dani tries to please the spirits within the stones so that they will not harm him. Abinyai said he believed the spirits determined the health of his pigs, the happiness of his women and the abundance of his sweet-potato harvest each season. He believed that if his ancestral spirits became angry, the children, pigs and sweet potatoes would grow thin and perhaps even die.

According to Old Dialec, the stones are said to have the power to liberate the souls of Hesage and Tabhe at the marriage ritual. The souls supposedly give reproductive powers to the married Dani.

The Dani ancestral spirits are not ubiquitous. They live within the stones and they never leave. The spirits, however, often lose their strength to perform. When this happens, the stones, although still valuable, are no longer regarded as sacred. They become objects for exchange at funerals or they can be sold.

All Dani families possess a stone, or a group of stones. They are hidden in the *pilais* of the villages. One evening during a discussion of Dani religion, Old Dialec announced that the stones came from another world. When they arrived in the Baliem Valley, they split up into people. Abinyai said that the stones originally came from Galime, a five-day walk to the east.

It is this writer's opinion that the Dani's faith is not strong, but it is permanent. This impression came from Obaharok's statement, "I know, as all older people know, that God made us. We know humans come from other humans. But children do not know this. We have seen snakes come from other snakes and animals come from other animals." Obaharok also spoke of original sin. He believed that if people would stop fighting, it would pay for the sin. It was an unusual reflection for the *kain*.

Women are not allowed to come near the *kanake* ceremony. They visit relatives in other villages during the days of religious celebration. *Kanakes* are a man's business. The Dani believe that the women will misuse ritualistic information.

Feasting forms the center of every Dani ceremony. Pigs maintain an exalted place in the Dani culture. They figure in the social and economic status of the Dani men, and often they are considered more important than people. Pigs are regarded as a "living currency" and are used to buy almost anything a

Dani would want to own. A Dani pays for services and fines with pigs. He can use a pig as payment for a wife. Often the pig is more highly prized than the wife just purchased. Pigs are believed capable of performing magic and sometimes miracles. When slaughtered, the pig's death can appease the spirits of the Dani cult, placate ghosts and have even been known to exorcise disease.

The Dani women raise the pigs, although they are owned by the men. The men decide which pigs are to be killed at a funeral, wedding or religious ceremony.

The seven pigs in the courtyard of Opagima were running about in frantic activity. A few of the animals had been bitten by rats, and their sores were filled with pitch and ashes. One of the pigs in the group was considered sacred. Obaharok had brought it to the village. I supposed that's why it was "sacred."

Obaharok did not live in Opagima, but Wali had asked him to oversee the *kanake.* It was noon when Obaharok ordered the slaughter of the animals. The pigs were killed in the same manner as they had been in the funeral ceremony. The dead animals were placed in a row in front of the *pilai.* Obaharok shouted the names of the owners over the bodies. The pigs were then singed and butchered. The parts were carried to the Dani fire pit for cooking.

While the men were waiting for the meat to steam, they opened a Dani beauty parlor in the middle of the courtyard. The client lies on his stomach. Three or four Dani operators work on his hair at the same time. First some of the longer, uneven strands of hair are cut off with a sharp piece of bamboo. Then the hair is separated into patches and knotted into small balls. Gourds of pig fat and soot are brought from the *pilai.* Each patch is rubbed vigorously between the palms of the hands with fat and soot. When the hair is well saturated, the patches are separated into strands. Beginning at the nape of the neck, the strands are pulled out to their entire length and allowed to jump back into place through natural curl. Each strand looks like a soft spring. One spring is built on top of the other until the entire hairdo resembles a ballooned beehive.

Other Dani, while waiting for the pigs to cook, busy themselves making *yopos* from the strings of orchid fibers. The *yopos* are then rubbed with pig fat to give them magic powers.

Sjam and I moved around among the men. We were conspicuous in our Western dress but the Dani were at ease with us. They didn't care what we wore or even how we looked; they were happy because we were there and interested in them. Several of the men tried to share their *yopos* with us. One Dani gave Sjam a cheroot to smoke. It nearly strangled her.

During the course of the *kanake* pageant, the men sang. We'd been reluctant to sing along with the Dani people, for fear that our voices might offend them. Sjam, in a playful moment, threw back her head and yodeled with the men. Her notes were a little off key, but they were loud. The Dani thought she was marvelous. So did I.

When the pigs were cooked, Obaharok ordered the five most important chiefs to sit in the center of the courtyard. He selected Walek, much to his surprise, and Kelion, who took it for granted. The minor chiefs and their warriors circled around the five chiefs. A third circle, composed of young boys, sat around the entire group. Mi Hijo was among them. At the far end of the courtyard, near the *thop,* sat a committee of little children.

Obaharok cut the pork into small pieces and passed the servings to the five chiefs. The chiefs passed the meat through the various circles. The children were served last. Each received a generous share.

Large sweet potatoes (*hiperi kanake*), which had been grown especially for the *kanake* ritual, were brought in at this time. Some of them weighed seven or eight kilos. With them came a few extras such as spinach, cucumbers and a small roasted opossum.

The Dani, strangers to any kind of intoxicants, drink water with their meals. Some of the men had brought their water gourds. One Dani found something unexpected in the bottom of a gourd. The object got stuck in his throat. He coughed and spit it out on the ground. The men leaned forward to inspect it. Whatever it was, it caused the men to laugh out loud. They talked it over among themselves and decided it wouldn't kill anybody.

When the feasting was over, the *kanake* was closed for the day. Obaharok stood up and stretched his arms toward the sun. He crossed his right hand over his left and held the palms together. He threw back his head and howled—asking the sun to spread the news of the *kanake* to the ghosts roaming around the land.

The men began to leave the courtyard. They headed toward their own villages for the night. Tomorrow they would return to Opagima to continue the *kanake* and to feast on the leftovers from the slaughtered pigs.

Sjam and I hung back. We wanted to see the sacred stones (*wesas*) in Wali's *pilai*. Obaharok agreed to let us visit the stones. He said we could see them when the men in the compound were asleep. He was afraid the men might be angry with him if they knew Sjam and I were allowed to see the sacred stones.

Kelion assured us that he and Walek could find their way back to Wiyagoba. Mi Hijo would stay with Sjam and me.

Since Wali's wife was visiting her relatives in another village, Sjam and I were given the use of her *abiai*. Wali told us to slip inside when no one was looking. And then he boarded up the entrance to give the place a look of vacancy.

It was well after midnight when Obaharok came to get us. He looked worried. "Mi Hijo is in the kitchen. We had to wait until he was asleep. Wali is in the *pilai* with the *wesas*. Come quietly."

The moon was covered by heavy gray clouds, leaving the night in a muffled darkness. The night air was chilly. I was sorry I'd left my jacket in Analaga.

When we reached the *pilai*, Obaharok motioned for us to go on in. I got down on my hands and knees and crawled through the doorway. It was very dark inside. I placed my hand on something soft and wet. I couldn't see my hand, so I smelled it. I had touched a piece of pork.

When Sjam and Obaharok came through the doorway, I warned, "Be careful, Sjam. There's meat right in front of you."

Obaharok boarded up the doorway with wooden planks. As my eyes became accustomed to the darkness, I could see Wali's silhouette by the fireplace.

"*Laok*," he said softly. He placed a small log on the fire. The fresh log crackled and sent a little flame piercing upward to give more light to the interior of the *pilai*. I crawled over and sat down next to Wali.

The floor of the *pilai* was covered with pork meat. Near the fireplace were enormous sweet potatoes. The food represented an offering to the spirits and ghosts. It would be eaten later by the most important men in the territory.

"We don't offer food to the *stones*," Wali said. "We rub them with sacred pig oil to keep the spirits inside calm."

Wali touched my elbow. He pointed to a dark mass behind the fireplace. I moved a little closer. There was a jawbone of a human being lying next to the fire. It was half wrapped up in dried banana leaves. The jaw looked very old, and most of the teeth were missing. It was black from pig oil and soot. Behind the jawbone, wrapped in a *noken*, lay the *wesa* group of stones.

Wali gently uncovered the "head" of the largest stone. It looked like a piece of black slate. The stone was about eighteen inches long, six inches across and nearly half an inch thick. The top of the stone was rounded off. It came to a point. Wali lowered the *noken* a little. A miniature grass skirt was tied around the middle of the stone.

"This is a female *wesa*," Wali whispered.

Yopos were looped around the top of the grass skirt. Several tuffs of *cuscus* had been tied to the skirt. Scattered over the stone were circles of woven rattan, about an inch in diameter, several white boar's tusks, pigtails and a bunch of dried pig testicles. On both sides of the stone lay other, smaller stones similar in decoration to the large one. There was a tiny rock in the center of the group. Wali said this stone was the "heart."*

---

* The Dani believe in two forms of the souls of their ancestors, the *kanake* (which here refers to a group of sacred objects) and the *hariken*. The *hariken* is the group of decorations on the *wesa* stones. They have the power to begin the next feast. The *kanake* is meant to provide for the well-being of the pigs, gardens and women, and good fortune in war.

Some of the stones in this group had been brought to the *kanake* by other chiefs in the area. They were rubbed with pig oil by either Obaharok or Wali. For each stone in the *wesa* group, a pig had been slaughtered during the *kanake* ritual— seven pigs in all. I could see only five *wesas*. The bulky end of the *noken* indicated that there were more stones at the bottom of it. Wali made no attempt to remove the *noken*. It would leave the major stone uncovered. I had to swallow my curiosity.

"The *kanake* will last these days," Wali said, holding three fingers down in the palm of his hand. "On this day," he pointed to his index finger, "the *wesas* must be wrapped and tied in banana bark and hidden behind three wooden doors in the *pilai*."

"Where?"

"There," Obaharok said, pointing to the wall behind the fire-place.

Wali walked us back to the *abiai*. After Sjam and I crawled inside, Wali boarded up the entrance.

We climbed up into the sleeping loft to bed down for the rest of the night. We could have saved ourselves the trip up-stairs. Obaharok and Wali began shouting and yelling in the courtyard. Their voices were joined by Mi Hijo's. His voice was louder than theirs.

There was a crack in the boards covering the *abiai's* en-trance. I could see, with one eye, people running back and forth in the courtyard. I couldn't see where the figures went or where they came from.

Sjam and I guessed the men were chasing *mokats* (ghosts). It would be an insensitive Dani who didn't know the ghosts would walk tonight. We'd been told something about the Dani ghosts, so the men's activities didn't frighten us. But we were kept awake all night with their noisy pursuit of these illusive spooks.

The ghosts which make up the Dani cosmic world are both complicated and confusing. The more I learned about the ghosts, the less I felt I knew. The apparitions were a con-tinuously changing phenomenon.

The Dani people their world with ghosts because they need them in their personal environment. The ghosts belong to the Dani and they are theirs. Without them, the people would feel a sharp loss and their culture would be duller.

When a person dies and his body is cremated, a ghost emerges from the remains. The ghost is the same person he was when he was alive except that he is more demanding. He's cantankerous, and once in a while he's malicious.

Ghosts can do all kinds of things they were denied in life. They can fly, make rain and cause illness. They wander about the jungle because they refuse to stay put. They can be seen by the lights that glimmer from their invisible forms.

Ghosts are supposed to have long straight hair. They walk about with their tongues hanging out of their mouths. It's not that they are thirsty; the hanging tongue means that they are dead and, therefore, ghosts.

All ghosts take an active part in the lives of the living. They dictate what must be done and what must be avoided. If the people fail to heed their ghosts' wishes, they may expect to be pushed into a mud puddle, plagued with floods or struck down dead.

The Dani are uncertain how these vindictive acts are accomplished. A malaria-stricken Dani, for example, will claim he saw the ghost who gave him malaria. He knows the ghost was responsible for his sickness, but he cannot tell you how the ghost made him sick.

The Dani never know where they stand with the apparitions at any given time, regardless of their appeasements. The ghosts are highly unpredictable and selfish. The people are never certain whether they have wholly pleased their ghosts or not.

The main concern of the Dani is to get the ghosts to stay where they belong and not enter the villages, so they build tiny houses of sticks and grass for the ghosts on the outskirts of their villages. But the ghosts, much to the Dani's displeasure, are inquisitive phantoms who never stay put. They stray about, wandering here and there, creating mischief and deviltry wherever they go.

The Dani placate their ghosts at the funerals, religious and marriage pig-feast rituals. Pigs are sacrificed, important objects are brought together and there is a feasting together. The most important man in the village shouts to the ghosts that these things have been done. He asks the ghosts to be satisfied and to leave the people alone. The ghosts are able to hear human sounds because they have ears. They can understand human speech. The ghosts see the food with their eyes and symbolically eat with their mouths. If they are grateful, they leave peacefully.

Magic is often employed to send a ghost on its way. One of the methods used is to chant. A fire that suddenly burns brighter alerts the Dani that a ghost is nearby. The ghost will depart if the Dani simply chants, "*Yee, yee, yee, yee, yee, yee.*"

No Dani is afraid of a ghost. He fears its manifestations.

According to Obaharok and Wali, a whole fleet of ghosts paraded into Opagima the night of the *kanake* ritual. The men shouted at the ghosts, "Go home! Go to your home where you belong!"

They did not stop shouting until the sky turned blue with morning.

(14)

The Valley was beginning to come together.

Kolo had finally taken an interest in others. His sour eye for strangers had disappeared in the pure wonder of the strangers themselves. Kolo was currently interested in the two little strangers Sjam and I had brought to Analaga from the north. They were the daughters of Wali and Kaok.

Kolo even showed off for the girls. One time he leaped into the air, turned a half circle, danced a quick tap step and sat down again. The girls giggled. They loved him.

Even hard, mean, revengeful, unforgiving Old Dialec was

softening. He marched into the *wamai* and announced to everybody that the two children were his granddaughters!

The Valley was finally beginning to come together.

(15)

The exotic nature of the *wamai* in Analaga did not lend itself to privacy, neither from people nor from pigs. The people were better mannered than the pigs, however. The animals thought the house still belonged to them and wandered in and out all day long. Even the new door Wimbilu built to close up the entrance failed to keep them out. The pigs simply knocked it down whenever they wanted to get inside.

One day after a trip to the Huan River to wash our clothes, we returned to find a whole herd of pigs rooting around in the *wamai*. They had eaten just about everything within its walls. The sweet potatoes were gone. The rice and part of the bag it came in had been devoured. The pigs had also eaten half of Chapter Two of Hitt's *Cannibal Valley*.

Mi Hijo borrowed some potatoes from Abinyai for supper that night. Sjam and I were hungry and ate our potatoes wolfishly. Mi Hijo picked at his, seemingly without appetite. He placed his potatoes on the grass in front of him and stared at them for a while. Then he looked up at me.

"Is there something you want to tell me, Mi Hijo?" I asked.

Mi Hijo raised his knees to his chin, swung his arms around his knees and buried his face in his arms. He was itching with the shyness of whatever he had on his mind.

Sjam scraped the potato peelings together and threw them out the doorway for the pigs to eat. She turned, put her hands on her hips and remarked that the pigs had already had more than their share for the day.

Mi Hijo did not look up. His head was still buried in his arms. Sjam climbed through the doorway into the sleeping area. There was a tiny glow from the fire. The room was very quiet, filled with the stillness of suspense.

Mi Hijo raised his head slowly. He cleared his throat, licked his lips and drew a deep breath.

"Ma, Kelion wants me to tell you something," he whispered.

Mi Hijo curled his fingers into his palm and turned his hand upward to study his fingernails. They were dirty.

"My fingernails are dirty," he said. "They're never clean like yours. Ma, Kelion wants you to marry him." His brown eyes roamed over my face. His teeth flashed whitely in the firelight.

"Why would Kelion want to marry me?"

Mi Hijo's mouth dropped open. Then it snapped shut all at once. He was taken back a little. I supposed he thought I should know about such things by now.

"Because it would make him rich!" he squeaked. He spread his palms skyward and shrugged his shoulders in disgust. He shook his head from side to side. "Ma, wives make men rich!"

"Yes, I remember now, Mi Hijo. I'll talk to Kelion when we get back to Wiyagoba."

"Don't you want to give me a message for him? You're supposed to send a message when there's someone in the middle, like me."

"Well, you'll be translating for us. That way it only has to be told once. Go to the *pilai* now and get some sleep. I'll see you in the morning."

"Yes, all right. Good night."

Mi Hijo stood and walked slowly to the door. At the doorway he turned, glanced over his shoulder and smiled shyly.

"Ma, will you marry Kelion?"

(16)

"Kelion, how would you like to have a sister?" I asked.

"Who, me?" Kelion asked with innocent eyes.

"Yes, of course you! Would you like to have a sister? One with white skin maybe?"

Kelion's eyelids dropped sleepily. His interest in the subject was both passionate and profound.

"Kelion, if you had a sister with white skin who was tall and from America—well, it might make you rich. What do you think?"

Kelion's imagination began to work on the idea. His eyes narrowed. I supposed he thought if he had a sister he could make a racket out of it. Heaven knows what great actions might come about as a result of it.

"Would I be the only one in the Valley to have this kind of sister?" he asked.

"I would say so, yes."

"Would this sister give me pigs and money and other things?" he asked. There was a diabolical glint in Kelion's eyes.

"She might."

"When do I get this sister?"

"Tomorrow."

"Will she be here in Wiyagoba tomorrow?"

"Yes, I think so. Kelion, your new sister is going to be me."

"I know it."

(17)

A brother-sister kinship in the Baliem Valley could probably be formed with the slaughter of a pig; Dani became brothers through such rituals. As far as anyone knew, no sister-brother relationship had ever taken place before. No one knew how to do it.

Kelion asked how people became brothers in America. I mentioned that our American Indians became blood brothers by cutting and tying their wrists together. Kelion found the idea appealing. By morning he'd informed every village to the north, south, east and west of Wiyagoba that he was going to have his wrist cut. Even Obaharok and Wali heard about it. They were somewhere in Siepkosi district at the time.

Obaharok and Wali arrived in Wiyagoba about noon. Obaharok had dressed up for the occasion. White dog tails were tied to his upper arms. A *walimo* and a *mikak* hung around his neck. A white *cabanee* with three long feathers sticking out of it encircled his head. I scarcely recognized him.

Kelion was having difficulty getting dressed. He couldn't find his *holim*. He had loaned out his *walimo* to someone. He couldn't remember who had it. Walek gave him a *holim* to wear.

Half dressed, Kelion stumbled out of his *pilai*. In the courtyard he fell over a wood plank. He yelled at Wenybake to bring his dog tails. And then he went out of his way to kick a pig standing in the corner of the compound. Kelion had a flare for the dramatic on those days he thought were his.

The excitement of the event caused Walek to lisp more. He tried to welcome Wali and Obaharok to his village. The men shook hands and nodded politely to one another. Neither Obaharok or Wali understood what Walek had said.

Without a pig, a Dani ritual is not much of an occasion. I'd bought a small pig and given it to Kelion. It was supposed to be a remembrance of the brother-sister ceremony. Kelion gave the animal to Walek, who was motioning for us to sit cross-legged in front of the *pilai*. When we were settled, Walek called for a bamboo knife. Kaok gave him a knife. Walek handed the pig to Ilmunkuluk, who was squatting beside him. Without warning, Walek seized the animal's hindquarters and cut off its tail. The little pig kicked and screamed. Walek grabbed the pig's right ear and sliced off the top of it. The pig, still suffering from having lost its tail, did not have time to catch its breath before the loss of its ear. Its screams were one continuous noise. Ilmunkuluk put the screaming animal on the ground. The pig, having spent the night in Kelion's *pilai*, ran inside believing it was its home.

Balancing the pigtail and the piece of ear on his knee, Walek smoothed them out with his hand. The tail was bleeding a little. He pivoted on the balls of his feet and faced me, holding the bamboo knife in his strong left hand.

I shuddered.

Sjam, who must have been reading my mind, suggested that Walek use a razor blade. She gave it to him, warning him of its sharpness. Kelion persuaded Walek to practice his cutting on an unripe banana.

Obaharok and Wali offered advice about how my wrist should be cut. Their thoughts failed to get through; Walek was too busy concentrating. He took my right hand in his and poised the razor blade on top of my hand. Obaharok was struck with the giggles. It was the only time I ever heard Obaharok giggle.

I turned my wrist over and fought the temptation to close my eyes against whatever was about to take place. Walek lowered the blade and placed the tip on my wrist. He made a cutting movement about an inch long. Nothing happened; the skin wasn't even broken. Walek tried again, pressing harder. The result was not a deep cut, but there was plenty of blood.

"Why, your blood ith red, too!" Walek lisped in sheer surprise.

Everyone in the courtyard crowded around to see my blood. Kelion, who had been sitting next to me, was now leaning on me. He had been pushed by Kaok, who was being crowded in by Ilmunkuluk. Obaharok leaned over. He bumped heads with Walek. Wali stood up and announced to everyone that my blood was as red as theirs.

Walek's stylish handling of the razor blade had improved when he cut Kelion's wrist. Kelion was left with hardly any blood coming out at all. He looked a bit disappointed.

Walek placed the pig's tail and ear between our wrists, explaining that they made the ritual stick better. He wrapped a length of rattan around our wrists and tied a knot. Then he sat back to view his handiwork.

"Now, Kelion," I said, "while our wrists are tied up like this, we're supposed to promise each other certain things," remembering that eating our food was just one of the many things I meant to reform in Kelion. Kelion ate our food whenever Sjam and I were in Analaga. He did not eat just part of it; he ate all of it. He was especially fond of the hard candy and salt I'd bought from the Wamena government store. Those things were scarce and hard to come by.

"We must promise to be faithful to each other until we die. And you must stop eating my salt and candy."

Kelion listened with his mouth open as though he wanted to receive the words in his throat. He smiled and nodded in agreement.

"Is it my turn?" he asked and went right on talking. "*Nagot* [Sister], you are friends with the whole world in your heart."

I should have seen it coming right there, but I didn't.

"All of us know that you love us," he continued, "and I want you to buy me a big boar with teeth this long."

Kelion straightened his index fingers and placed one on either side of his mouth, pulling my arm up with his.

"There's a pig in Tulim that'll improve our animals in Wiya-goba. Walek and I want that boar, but it costs a lot of money. I can't steal the pig. We want everyone to know it belongs to us and to see the results of having such a fine animal in our village. Please buy me that pig."

I emerged from the brother-sister ceremony as the chief donor to a humanitarian animal-husbandry project. I contributed a little over eighty dollars to the cause. By giving Kelion the money to buy the boar, I figured he'd stop pilfering food from his new sister-benefactor. The savings in salt and candy would more than pay for the pig.

(18)

Walek and Kelion were sitting in our kitchen one afternoon when Obaharok and Wali came to visit us.

The two *kains* climbed up on the far end of the sleeping platform, sat down and crossed their legs. It was a matter of amazement to me that these men felt no hesitation to sit on what Sjam and I called, our bed. However, the floor and the platform were covered with grass and looked about the same. I supposed the men thought one place was as good as another to sit.

Obaharok waved Mi Hijo to join him on the platform. The posts beneath the structure creaked as Mi Hijo lifted himself up and sat down beside Wali. Mi Hijo was putting on weight.

"Mama Wyn," Obaharok began, "I want to have an *etai* at Haratsilimo."

Haratsilimo is the name of a piece of flat land between Silo Rock and the Aikhe River. I had no idea what *etai* meant.

"*Etai* is a victory dance," Obaharok explained. "Four of our enemies have died. We must celebrate!"

"Who are your enemies?"

"The people of Kurulu. Kurulu is the *kain* of Jiwika."

The name "Kurulu" made Walek cringe. He had belonged to the Kurulu Alliance at one time. Kelion's face remained blank. He had never belonged to anybody. Kelion fought on whatever side was winning at the time.

In the 1950s, Chief Wali was *kain* of the Wililhiman-Walilalua Confederation. His people fought with the tribes of Siepkosi, a large southern confederation under Chief Laokama's reign. The combined confederations fought Old Dialec when Kolo was still young. But the alliance didn't last very long. Old Dialec defeated Laokama and ran Wali's group back into the Mulima area, where he thought they belonged.

Sometime during the middle 1950s, Wali and the Wililhiman-Walilalua Confederation joined forces with Kurulu. They were tired of losing battles and wanted to win for a change. The Siepkosi Confederation and the Wililhiman-Walilalua Confederation maintained a friendly but distant relationship.

In the early 1960s, Kurulu became the most powerful *kain* in the entire Baliem Valley, and he remains highly respected today. As a young man he had inherited his chiefdom, which was unusual, from his *kain* father. It wasn't long before Kurulu surpassed his father's mighty reputation. Some of it was due, it was said, to the fact that Kurulu possessed supernatural powers over the elements. He also controlled the house where the sun "lived" in Wadlagu, near Jiwika.

Until 1966 Kurulu ruled over the area between the mountains north of Jiwika and the Aikhe River. There were five or six thousand Dani living in the land. These natives formed the many confederations which made up the powerful and fearsome Kurulu Alliance. Wali's confederation, the Wililhiman-Walilalua, was one of them. The confederation incorporated the fathers of Mi Hijo (Dokop), Sike (Lokop) and Asuan (Nilik).

When Laokama died of old age, Chief Pesimeken became *kain* of the Siepkosi Confederation. About the same time, Kolo became chief of Analaga. Kolo and Pesimeken fought each other. The battles were interesting but they were not very satisfactory. Pesimeken was getting too old to do well, and Kolo was too young to know much about warfare. Most of their energies ended in draws.

Meanwhile there was a young warrior running about Siepkosi trying to make a name for himself. He was the son of Laokama. His name was Obaharok.

"I knew I was meant to be a *kain*. My father told me. But everyone said I couldn't kill because I was too young," Obaharok said. He cleared his throat and continued, "I began by stealing a pig. I succeeded and so I stole again and again. Each time I succeeded. The braveness in my heart grew bigger. I felt myself a brave man. Quietly, I tried to kill a man. I returned home with that victory. I wanted to go to war and fight with the others, but they still considered me to be a child. I felt so angry. I went, anyway. With bows and arrows in my hand, I killed the enemy one by one. I killed and I killed until many enemy were dead. I have killed many, many people. In the end I was accepted by the people as overlord. I am not afraid of anybody."*

---

* This account was phonetically written from a tape recording of Obaharok's speech: "*An wal wanet palho logosak pakehesiq hagatlaga, an errabuankane uwal wathamonek dogosak nen an hagatomotogat dogosak. Arithogon hagaus ragasunen nebe kogasusak. Yimeke-timeke wamanke lagaimeke eloma, netage kogat asumonen nebe kainasusak. An limaro*

The room was very quiet. I looked at Sjam. She had paled a little beneath her brown skin. Walek and Kelion sat motionless. We had all felt the might of the man called Obaharok.

During my stay in the Baliem Valley, I would have liked to ask more questions concerning the war history of the Dani. But I felt uneasy about it. I thought that if I showed too much interest in their wars, they might mistake that interest for approval. There was always the chance, too, that through the recounting of wars, the Dani would feel desire to participate in battles again.

I would rather write out of knowledge than out of guesswork and therefore the war history of the Baliem Valley put down here is fragmentary. What I learned was volunteered by Abinyai, Old Dialec, Kolo and Obaharok. Their stories were consistent but they were incomplete. Through them Obaharok's name popped up with amazing frequency.

According to Old Dialec, Obaharok had scored his first major victory in the central mountains east of Siepkosi around 1962. A small group of Wililhiman-Walilalua Confederation natives were passing through the area on their way to trade goods in another part. They were killed by the resident tribe. Obaharok knew of his father's friendship with the Wililhiman-Walilalua Confederation. He staged a revenge attack on the tribe and wiped them out.

Inflamed with his success, Obaharok tested his strength on Kolo, in the south. Three years later he isolated Kolo in Analaga. He posted the retired *kain*, Pesimeken, in a village not more than five minutes from Analaga. Pesimeken's presence held the line.

When the Indonesian government came into the Valley, Kolo agreed never to fight again. The appearance of the government

---

akoniwarogo bisiki dogogin. An umaligin yimeke-timeke hagathelagimeke amanogolinom. An warok wim yabusak ap apurugi silimeke ninom. Mekere iren inaqla apegarek anebe yekeregat. An naqla age apik. Itinaba nelekan hisalokhat dogomo, an segelek sikelek warok silimeke agaike wasusagat, agaike watlugen agaikewatik hobugen motok apik inasusak. Apik apik motok an inyate. An nogonnenhe anebe kain hagat lagai. An nyukdek ap yoma thabokogoat."

did not deter Obaharok, however. As a matter of fact, he didn't know who the government was or why it was there. As long as the government didn't get in Obaharok's way, it didn't matter. Obaharok's sole objective was to be the *kain* his father had told him he was meant to be.

The Great War of 1966 gave Obaharok the *kain*ship he had always wanted. It was the most elaborate campaign of his career.

The events leading to the Great War are as varied as they are confusing. In the first place, there was unrest within the Kurulu Alliance itself. The Wililhiman-Walilalua Confederation became dissatisfied with Kur's decision to postpone the marriage pig feast in 1963. Kur was the only man able to initiate such an event, and the disappointment to the people in the southern part of the alliance was unbearable. Although Kur carried out the pig feast in 1964, the hurt feelings remained among the people.

Another contributing force which lead to the battle was the intrusion of the government. It had outlawed warfare and intended to enforce the law by establishing a police post in Mulima. The government believed that the threat of modern weapons would force the Dani to live together in peace. Mulima lies in the southern end of the Kur Alliance. When friction arose between the people, the police sided with those in the south. It created resentment in the north.

The forced pacification with guns and ammunition, the government's interference in internal Dani affairs, and the discontentment within the Kurulu Alliance itself channeled violence into the Great War of 1966.

Walek told me that he and his older brothers, all Mabels from the Dloko-Mabel clan in the Kurulu Alliance, had launched the surprise attack against the Wililhiman-Walilalua Confederation. It is possible that his statement is true.

The Mabels and Kurulu's warriors attacked the villages south of the Lagora River. It was the bloodiest massacre in the history of the Baliem Valley. They burned the compounds and killed the men, women and even the children. Silo, *kain* of Hipinima, joined the attacking warriors just for the fun of fighting. When they were finished, over one hundred and fifty people lay dead on the battlefield.

The natives of Opagima, Tumagonem and Punycul were stunned. They looked at their dead brothers, killed by those they had considered from a friendly alliance.

Kain Wali sent a desperate appeal for help to Obaharok. Obaharok did not need to be asked twice. Within hours he'd gathered his forces together and mapped out his strategy. He meant not only to revenge, but to defeat the whole Kurulu Alliance.

At dawn the following day Obaharok and his warriors attacked. By afternoon they had reached the Lagora River and were maneuvering themselves into position for the final kill. Kurulu, his empire crumbling, blew the whistle on Obaharok. When he called for help from the Indonesian military, the fighting stopped.

The Wililhiman-Walilalua Confederation merged with Obaharok to form a new alliance. Kurulu's powerful alliance collapsed, and he ceased to be the great overlord of the Baliem Valley he had been.

The new boundary line between the alliances of Kurulu and Obaharok was set at the Lagora River. The people south of the river moved from their burned-out compounds to build new villages closer to Mulima. Many moved farther south into Siepkosi to demonstrate their good faith in their new leader, *kain* Obaharok.

With the shifting population, young Mabel changed his name to Walek. He took a fast trip across the country and built the village of Wiyagoba. He hoped he wouldn't be recognized there.

A short era of peace entered the Valley. It lasted until February or March 1972, a few months prior to my arrival in Wamena. A handful of Kur's men staged a revenge attack on the village of Feratsilimo, near Wiyagoba. Some of the compounds were burned and a few people were killed. Obaharok and his warriors pushed in to counterattack. When the battle was over, the Indonesian police entered again. They captured Obaharok and seven of his chiefs: Wali, Pikale, Ukum, Tekan,

Hilikmo and Dokop, as well as Walek, who had fought because Feratsilimo bordered his own village of Wiyagoba.

The police marched the chiefs off to the police post in Jiwika. There they tied their hands behind their backs, strapped their ankles to wooden bars and tortured them by beating and burning their bodies for five days and five nights. The police did not give them food or even water. The local women brought sweet potatoes at night and fed the hungry chiefs when the guards were asleep. On the fifth day the police forced the chiefs, their hands still tied behind their backs, to walk beneath the water in a river so deep that they nearly drowned.

In the evening the police soaked the chiefs' hair with kerosene, then set it on fire. On the sixth day Obaharok managed to loosen his ties and he freed the others. The eight chiefs escaped from the Jiwika police post. The police, in pursuit, killed the pigs in the chiefs' various villages. But they were unable to recapture the chiefs.

In July 1972 the senseless robbing and beating of the Dani people by the Indonesian government officials incited Obaharok to attempt to overthrow the whole Indonesian government. Armed with bows and arrows and spears, Obaharok and his warriors marched to Wamena. But when he saw Indonesian guns and ammunition and the men who knew how to use them, realism moved into Obaharok's heart. He laid down his primitive weapons at the government's feet. For the first time in his life he had no way to fight back.

It must have been awful for him.

(19)

I've always believed that one of the most dangerous and ridiculous pastimes known to man is war. Now Sjam and I found ourselves living in a warrior society with professional fighters who had trained for such a thing all their lives.

War is a part of Dani culture, like eating sweet potatoes or roasted pork. It is challenging and exciting to them and a normal recreation, since they don't play football or compete in any other kind of sport. War puts a touch of exhilaration into their otherwise routine lives. From their battles new leaders emerge, new territories are absorbed into new confederations, and old alliances fracture and fade. These events warm the Dani souls and strengthen their spirits.

In the beginning it was the intention of the regional groups of Dani not to merge with one another. In their energy of independence, they turned their bows and arrows on anyone who came close to them.

Apart from their wishes to remain aloof from one another, the Dani fought because it was necessary. And the Dani were warriors because they wanted to be. Sometimes morals were involved, sometimes revenge, sometimes a desire just to be naughty. Sometimes it was a fusion of all of these things put together.

If one were to ask a Dani if he had fought over land, he would probably say no. And yet, many Dani have lost their lives on a battlefield because a neighboring tribe had extended its gardens into the other's territory. Obaharok had his eye on the whole Kurulu Alliance in 1966; surely this must be considered a desire to possess and rule. Old Dialec remarked that he had spent most of his youth fighting over the ownership of the Huan River, and in the end he got it. It seems obvious that the Dani fought, although infrequently, at one time or another to annex land for themselves.

To acquire land was not the primary reason for Dani wars, however. The Dani believed that through wars they were fulfilling their ancestral traditions. During the intervals between wars the Dani feared that their forefathers were unhappy with them. It left the ghosts unavenged, which created a feeling of disintegration among the tribes. The welfare and health of their society depended on the relentless aggression against the enemy to placate the ghosts.

Women sometimes figured as a cause of battles. They urged the men to revenge the deaths of their warrior husbands. When a discontented woman ran to the enemy to become one of them, her actions invariably had a retaliatory effect on the tribe she had left.

The theft of a pig brought down masses of warriors with bows and arrows on the suspected offender, to fight for satisfaction and payment. Sometimes, just to be mean, one tribe would uproot the sweet-potato vines of another. Then nothing short of killing could appease the injured tribe's feelings about the destroyed garden. All of these reasons were considered fair and within the natural framework of war promotion.

War, too, was a very personal and private affair to a Dani on the battlefield. It was there that he demonstrated his courage and won his manhood. The seeds of war were planted deeply in the soil of Dani culture. The people could not imagine an end to fighting. Like eating, war was never considered over once and for all.

When the government outlawed war, many Dani became quarrelsome and disgruntled; they felt their purpose in life was gone. The government gave the Dani no explanation of their laws; they thought that peace would naturally arise out of rules imposed by and maintained with guns.

According to Old Dialec, two kinds of war existed in the Baliem Valley. Sjam and I found them confusing. When Sjam thought of "war," it meant a revolution of some kind which eventually resulted in the overthrow of one government and its replacement by another. I found it difficult to grasp the concept of "regular war" as opposed to something called "ritualistic war."

Old Dialec explained the difference between *umain* (ritualistic, i.e., intertribal feudal war) and *wim* (regular war).

Wim might be compared to World War II when peoples armed themselves for survival, divided into two teams called "armies" and did everything they could to kill one another. *Umain* was a ritualistic type of warfare fought between tribes who shared a common culture. They were motivated into battle by similar considerations such as ghost placation, a stolen pig or an uprooted vine. *Umain* was fought with frequent regularity due to the pressures of cultural demands.

Wim and *umain* urged the Dani to live in a state of martial alertness. The people built *kayos* (watchtowers) and manned them with warrior guards. The Dani took their spears with them wherever they went and never ventured far from their villages without the companionship of others for protection, for the danger of ambush by the enemy was constant. The chiefs were permanently on duty in each village; they protected the families and compounds. When in deep trouble, they called upon the *kains,* who were the leaders of the confederations and who maintained authority in time of need.

The Dani fought their battles with only two weapons: the spear (*sege*), and the bow (*sike*) and arrow (*hete*). The length of the *seges* measured from six to fifteen feet. They were made from a hardwood called *yori.* On the battlefield the *seges* were aimed at the heart of the enemy from a distance of about fifty feet. If a *sege* killed a man, the spear was called an *abarek.* It was considered sacred and endowed with magic.

The arrows were made of strong bamboo with barbed hardwood tips tied to the ends. They were without feathers and therefore without straight flight. It was a rare occasion if an arrow connected and actually killed an enemy. Probably more died from infections left by the arrows' punctures.

Obaharok said he had killed most of his enemies with bow and arrow. When they were dead, he cut off their heads with a bamboo knife and left the head and body lying where they had fallen. He took the victim's weapons and a swatch of hair to present to the *kain* at the next war conference as proof of his kill.

As far as I know, Obaharok and the people living in the Siepkosi-Mulima, Wiyagoba and Analaga areas were not cannibals and never had been. Old Dialec said Obaharok's father had been a cannibal in his day, which Obaharok confirmed.

Many people who came into the land were killed, but there is no documentation that they were eaten. In other parts of the country, particularly in Oxibil and eastward, cannibalism was practiced in an effort to humiliate the enemy. Sometimes the big toe or some other part of the body was cut off a warrior fallen in enemy territory. The part was eaten in plain sight of the enemy tribe, standing on the nearby hilltop, crying and pleading for the return of the body.

In Agats and other regions on the west coast of West Irian I learned that cannibalism meant eating the palms of a man's hands and his brain. This was an attempt to transpose the victim's intelligence and strength to the diner.

It was said by many that Kurulu had eaten the hearts of some twenty men during the height of his empire. Whether true or not, this rumor of Kur's cannibalistic proclivities undoubtedly helped to inspire the fear and power he needed to hold his great alliance together.

Although the chiefs in the Siepkosi-Mulima, Wiyagoba and Analaga territories often referred to the methods of cutting up humans for cooking, Sjam and I saw no signs that cannibalism ever existed in this area. On the contrary, such an idea was disgusting to them.

What the Dani in the area lacked in cannibalism, they made up for in wars and *etais*. One was almost as good as the other. It had been a long time since either one had been performed in the Baliem Valley. With the exception of funerals and *kanakes*, the government forbid the Dani to congregate in groups larger than ten people at a time. An *etai* involved the massive gathering together of thousands.

"Mama Wyn, write a letter to the police," Obaharok pleaded. "Ask them to give us permission to have our *etai*."

I wrote the letter. The *etai* would provide the Dani with the opportunity to whoop it up with song and dance, to placate their ghosts, and they could let off steam at the same time.

"Can I come to the *etai*?" Walek asked excitedly.

Obaharok glanced at him. The memories of past wars and *etais* swept over him like a warm, consoling wind. "You will all come," he said.

"I was planning a *kanake* in Abukulmo," said Kelion.

"Put it off. Come to my *etai*! I will attend your *kanake* later," bargained Obaharok.

Kelion grinned. "I'll bring my *abarek!*" he said, pointing to a bark-wrapped rod half concealed in the crotch of the ceiling in the kitchen. Sjam and I exchanged glances. We didn't know that the weapon Kelion used to kill people with was in our house.

When we received permission from the Wamena police to stage the *etai* at Haratsilimo, the jungle echoed with bird calls for two days and two nights. This Dani communication system spread the news over the Valley within the first hour of the first day. But Obaharok ordered an additional day of chirping. He wanted to give the warriors plenty of time to prepare themselves for the event.

Two days is quite a length of time for people to spend decorating themselves. As a result, no army in history ever set forth to battle with more gaudy paint or garish gewgaws. Parrot feathers, colorful paradise plumes, furs, *mikaks* and *walimos* appeared on the heads and chests of Dani whom I'd never suspected of owning such things. Vanity set in on those Dani who had let themselves go during the past days. Their efforts gave them the appearance of garnished maypoles.

Sjam and I were involved, too. My hand mirror was in constant use. The Dani looked into it, admiring themselves with all the self-love of a newly elected beauty queen. When the warriors ran out of pig grease, then our cooking oil moved into demand. And when that gave out, the men painted "pants" on themselves with colored clay.

Walek was so excited he'd decorated himself with a clay mask. He had it on twenty-four hours in advance. He looked like a raccoon.

Kelion took his *abarek* out of our kitchen. He carried it down to the river to wash off the dried blood of the last man he'd killed. When it was clean, he rubbed the *abarek* with *pemut,* a white limestone chalk used on spears and arrows.

Obaharok had put immense thought into his costume. He wore one of everything. Each object was bigger and better than anybody else's: *walimo, mikak,* dog tails, *holim,* boar tusks and *cabanee.* There were yellow feathers covering his back. He'd wound a piece of old underwear around his hair. Riding on the top of the underwear was a furry *cuscus.* Above that waved the longest feather in the whole crowd. He carried the *thuelaga,* a stick filled with black cassowary bird feathers. The feathers encouraged the warriors in battle. In his left hand he held a wandlike whisk of yellow and white heron feathers, a symbol similar to the *thuelaga.*

By eight o'clock in the morning of the day of the event, the army was as well prepared as it was dressed. There were spears, *abareks,* throwing sticks, and bows and arrows. Each man carried as many weapons as his hands could hold. Kelion had the longest *abarek* of anyone; it measured nearly twenty feet. I supposed when Kelion killed a man, he wanted to be as far away from him as possible.

Walek was out of practice and had difficulty tightening his unused bow. Kelion helped him string the weapon to keep Walek from straining his imagination too much.

The warriors in the nearby confederations were supposed to rendezvous at a point called Kumina. From there everyone would go together to Haratsilimo for the *etai.* The men from the villages around Wiyagoba were supposed to join our group as we walked along toward the prearranged meeting place. Halfway down the path, Kelion tripped over his *abarek* and stubbed his toe. It kind of ruined the whole thing. We returned to Wiyagoba to tend Kelion's bloodied toe. The villagers were put out with us because we would be late in arriving.

We reached Kumina about noon. It was the same place Obaharok had gathered his warriors together in 1966. I was stunned at the size of the group that had already assembled there. The warriors numbered in the thousands. *Abareks* were stuck into the ground. They surrounded the group like huge porcupine quills. The men sat half hidden in the jungle grass; you could hardly see them at all. Obaharok stood in the middle of the group in the age-old posture of his war days.

When our party arrived, everyone began whooping and yelling. The men ran with all their might toward the warriors seated in the grass and stopped just short of knocking anyone over. They stuck their spears and *abareks* into the ground and sat down with the rest.

The men talked quietly among themselves. Others smoked or rested while they waited for additional fighting groups to arrive. By one o'clock there were more than three thousand warriors sitting in the jungle grass at Kumina.

Obaharok suddenly yelled something over the heads of the men. The warriors responded with an echoing "Woooooooooo!" Their cry announced the number of dead enemies. It was repeated four times.

Then Obaharok called for individual men to come forward. The men squatted in the grass, whispering. They showed Obaharok their war trophies: an arrow, a spear, a swatch of hair taken from their victims.

Sjam and I were unprepared for the event that followed. No one had apprised us in advance that the Dani were going to simulate a war prior to their *etai;* we thought we were seeing the real thing.

Three thousand warriors stood up all at once. They grabbed their spears and *abareks* and began singing the "kill song" (*wanepahut*). Some of the men jumped up and down, their feet creating little earthquakes on the ground. Above the thunderous noise Obaharok screeched like an outraged bird. Abruptly he darted out from the center of the group, ran past me and headed toward the open fields of Mulima.

The warriors pounded after him, three thousand of them, running and screaming at the same time. I have never heard such yelling in my life.

Ribbons of warriors ran after Obaharok. There were ribbons of running men and most of them ran beyond their ordinary ability.

Obaharok lead them like a giant. When he reached the open field he turned. He raced back through the threads of moving men. He cut in and out of the lines, yelling, running here and there, seeming to be in as many as four places at once. It was a wonder the man could cover so much ground so quickly.

Kelion charged by me like a giant plow horse, with Walek close on his heels. Mi Hijo ran along beside them, inflamed with the same passion that comes to all Dani during wartime. He looked nearly mad with it. It was frightening to see someone so young possess that kind of thirst.

Asuan appeared to be the only uninspired warrior in the crowd. He had taken a few steps forward but there was no other evidence that he was alive.

The men stampeded over the grasslands like a raging brush fire. Sjam and I trotted along beside the moving army, trying to figure out what was happening.

The Dani suddenly picked up speed. Every one of them tried to outrun us; it seemed they didn't want to have us along. I was able to keep up and I even passed a few, which surprised me more than it did them.

The warriors didn't stop running until they reached a flat piece of land outside of Wenebuborah. They divided into two teams and then sat down on opposite banks to rest after their exhausting method of arrival.

Obaharok paraded up and down the field, waving his *thuelaga*. Kelion rushed toward Obaharok from the undergrowth bordering the far side of the field. He fell down before he got halfway. There is one thing sure about Kelion when he falls: he doesn't fall just a little, he falls with all his might. Obaharok did him a favor. He penalized Kelion by placing him on the sidelines for the rest of the afternoon. Obaharok felt Kelion would kill himself through his own clumsiness.

Obaharok emitted a war cry. It was quick and it was real. The two armies stood up and faced each other. The battle began.

It was no start with bugles or bullets. The warriors jumped up and down. They shouted murderous challenges to each other. They pranced around on the balls of their feet, waving their bows and arrows, brandishing their spears. They cried like banshees. One side screamed venomous insults at the other. The insults, challenges and cries of defiance were exchanged between the two armies until the warriors were left shaking with emotion.

When they could take no more abuse from each other, a small squadron of men burst off the side of one of the armies. They raced across the battlefield. There were about one hundred warriors in the group. When the opposing side saw the men coming, they met them with a hundred men of their own.

The warriors roared toward each other, flailing spears as they ran. When they were within fifty feet of one another, they stopped running. They turned around and ran back to their own landbanks. More insults were belched out and the squadron sallied forth again. The men were swift and skillful runners, gifted with strong muscles and the knowledge of how to use them. The groups met, withdrew and charged again. I saw one man with a milky eye run by in the front line, like Old Dialec, who had lost his eye in battle.

Someone fired a spear over the heads of the opposing army. With that, a storm of violence spread over both groups. The Dani collided in combat, all mixed up together. There were bodies, arms, legs, arrows and spears rolling and tumbling around on the ground.

Suddenly it was all over. The two squadrons walked slowly back to their positions. The field was quiet. I looked around for dead warriors. There were none. Not even a wounded.

Without warning the men began screaming again. Their rage reached a new pitch. They were daring one another to do their worst.

The new groups raced out, withdrew as the others had done, and then charged again into one another's lines. Each man fought according to his own whim, as an individual, not as part of a team. A few spears were lobbed back and forth. They were always placed well above the heads of the opposing team.

The Dani, capable of extraordinary strength and endurance, played "war" for the remainder of the afternoon. When one set of warriors tired, a fresh team took its place. They ran around like children, having the time of their lives. Only when it began to rain did the warriors stop playing the game that fulfilled their need for grandeur. Or, at least, to satisfy the nostalgia that had settled over them.

(20)

At four o'clock the following morning, bird calls resounded through the jungle to announce the *etai*.

Walek was inconsolable. He'd lost his *cuscus* tail during yesterday's battle.

Kelion was grief-stricken. His woman-medicine had disappeared.

Sjam loaned Walek her *cuscus* from her red fur hat. I gave Kelion another laxative pill.

About noon the men and women of Wiyagoba went to the *etai*. The women had armed themselves with digging sticks. The men had spears and held bunches of arrows in their hands. They hit the arrows against their thighs.

The Dani ran nearly the whole way to Haratsilimo. They stopped running at intervals, jumped up and down and then ran again. They never ceased moving.

The women stopped at the clay pond to decorate their bodies with dots and stripes. A few of the men touched up their make-up. Walek painted on a pair of clay pants.

The footpath between Mulima and Haratsilimo was narrow. It was widened by the hundreds of Dani feet now racing over it. Walek and Kelion ran up and down on the sides of the moving mass of men and women. Obaharok and Wali charged back and forth in front of everyone. Sometimes the people stopped, jumped up and down, and then ran on again. The order was changeless.

There were groups of warriors stationed around on the mountaintops and hilly ridges. I saw Asuan on top of Silo Rock. He had given himself guard duty; as lookout he didn't have to move about very much.

When Obaharok arrived in Haratsilimo he placed his *abarek* upright in the center of a flat field. The women and children began running in a huge circle around the *abarek*. They went counterclockwise. They put their heads down and charged around the pole, singing and shouting and loving every minute of it.

Obaharok was standing at the south end of the running

women. He sent six chiefs to the north, east and west sides of the running circle (*dipik*). The chiefs ran back and forth (*hunike*) beside the circle. They held their *abareks* ready for thrusting.

The warriors joined the running women. They ran clockwise around the circle. The double circle never stopped revolving until dark.

Apart from being fun, the *etai* provided the Dani with the opportunity to tell their ghosts, through song and dance, that many enemies were dead. The songs, with the exception of the funeral chants, were the same songs I'd heard elsewhere in the Valley. The dance was simply running. There was no routine to it, and no steps. I'd never seen such a repetitious and monotonous event met with such enthusiasm and gusto as the Dani *etai*.

The Dani ran and shouted for two days straight. And they were still shouting when we left. They never wore out.

(21)

An *etai* usually lasts for two days. By stretching it out for another day, Obaharok missed going to Kelion's *kanake*.

Kelion's *kanake* at Abukulmo turned out to be the same as other religious rituals except for a curious incident which occurred during the feasting.

It had to do with a big black pig. The animal had grown to such enormous proportions that it was the only one of its kind in the whole Valley. The pig couldn't sit, stand or even lie down without getting up again right away. It was so fat that it couldn't get comfortable. It had made itself miserable with its own size. To this was added the influence of fatigue. The pig was tired and spent.

I was attracted to the pig in spite of the fact that I didn't understand it. Part of my feelings may have been due to Kelion's admiration of the animal. He referred to the pig with great affection. Once he walked over and petted it. The pig brought ecstasy bubbling in Kelion's blood.

Not to know Kelion is to fail to know that he was primarily a man torn between robbing and murder. Mostly, he was a thief. Kelion was a sure man when it came to stealing. He'd found cleverness in it, too. Some of the things he'd stolen he had hidden around in the Valley so adroitly that he never found them again.

Kelion regarded a man who didn't steal a dishonest man who was probably covering some less honorable occupation. Kelion not only loved another thief, he went further: he disliked anyone who was not exactly like himself. Everyone trusted Kelion until they were stolen from, then further trust became ridiculous.

If I'd remembered all these things about Kelion, I wouldn't have been so surprised at the events that ensued during the *kanake*.

Kelion saved the slaughter of the black pig for last. When its turn came, a strange thing happened. The pig rose up and challenged the Dani for one more day of its life. The animal displayed energies it didn't even know it had. It instantly became the most active animal in the compound, excelling in both speed and evasion. The Dani not only failed to catch the animal, they didn't come close to laying a hand on it. When four big men surrounded the pig in a corner, the animal miraculously disappeared, only to reappear on the other side of the compound. A few children threw themselves at the pig. No sooner did they arrive than the animal had left for another part of the yard. Some of the older men shouted advice and a few threw sticks. A handful of fresh Dani chased the animal, hurling themselves at the moving prize only to find their hands still empty.

An hour later the Dani were worn out, but the pig was still tearing around the grounds.

Kelion decided to kill the pig on the move. He called for his bow and arrows. He shot the bloodletting arrow into the animal's heart from mid-court while he was running alongside the pig. The pig stopped running. It was too stunned to scream for having been shot with an arrow. It plopped to the ground, rolled over and clawed at the air with its hoofs. It didn't die. Its eyes, which were staring wide open, had a pained look in them. That made Kelion angry. He didn't like the pig staring at him. And besides, he wanted his animals to be dead when he shot them. He pulled out another arrow and thrust it into the animal's heart. A great quantity of blood emerged from the pierced hole. The animal heaved a final breath, shut its pink eyes and died.

It took twelve men to haul the animal to the *pilai* and that many again to announce to the ghosts that the pig had been slaughtered.

The sun had turned the day hot. White cotton clouds drifted over the hilltops around the villages and hung about in the trees. The pork sputtered in the stone-filled oven. The smell of the cooking meat was delicious and penetrating.

It took longer than usual to cook the pigs. The black pig filled up so much space in the oven, it was a burden to time. Finally the oven was opened. The hot pork was placed on fresh banana leaves and spread about the courtyard. The men sat down to eat.

The men had their mouths chock-full of pork when the screaming woman came through the *thop*. She had covered her body with white clay as a sign of mourning, and she was crying her eyes out. She staggered half-way down the courtyard and stopped in front of the kitchen. Her body was trembling with sobs, shaking with uncontrollable sorrow.

"Kelion! Kelion, you stole my pig! And now you're eating it!" she screamed, pointing an accusing finger at Kelion.

Every eye in the crowd widened in astonishment. The men stopped chewing their pork and looked at Kelion. They turned their heads toward the crying woman and then back to Kelion again. Then, to my surprise, the Dani men pretended the woman was not there. They turned their backs on her, took fresh bites of pork and went right on with their dinner.

Lowering his eyelids a little, Kelion looked sleepily at his friends. He faced the clay-covered woman, resigned himself to the inevitable and waited.

The woman yelled bloody murder at Kelion. She kicked the ground, stamped her feet and threw her arms about, striking her fists against the sideboards of the kitchen. In her frenzy of sorrow and outrage she was a menace to anyone standing near.

Kelion had followed the woman's threats to a certain point, but now he quit. He began to search for a way to change the subject, then an inspired tranquillity shone from his eyes: he had stolen the pig as a beautiful and generous thing for his *kanake*. This thought would save him from being murdered. All he had to do was explain it.

"Dear woman, there is nothing nicer than to have a little pig," he began. "When the pig is young, you feed it and care for it. It becomes a member of the family and you can get to love it. But when the pig grows up, it becomes selfish and bad-tempered. It might even bite you. That would make your whole life miserable. I didn't want you to be bitten by your own pig. So I killed the pig and now we're eating it."

It was rather hard for me to believe that Kelion had been moved to stealing the pig for any moral considerations for the poor woman.

One of the older chiefs placed his pork on a banana leaf. He rose and advanced cautiously toward the stunned woman. With his arm around her shoulder, he gently lead her to the *thop* and on out of the village. Within a few minutes he returned to finish his meal.

The lady lived in the village of Tumagonem, about three miles from Abukulmo. While Tumagonem was on flat ground, Abukulmo was high on top of a mountain. I stared at Kelion in wonder. Although I was not impressed with his story, not even with the theft of an animal whose disappearance hadn't been discovered until after it had been slaughtered, cooked and partially eaten, I was overwhelmed by Kelion's ability to transport that huge black pig over the rocky mountain pass between Tumagonem and Abukulmo. It had taken Sjam and me nearly two hours to climb the steep, rugged path. It was like walking in the bottom of a rain gutter, for the great rocks rose in solid walls on both sides of the path. Often we shinnied our way through only by twisting our bodies sideways.

I don't know how Kelion ever negotiated that rocky pass with that giant of a pig, and kept it moving with its heart still pumping. But he did and had arrived with his loot in Abukulmo.

The robbery was a masterpiece of daring. From that day on, the Dani considered Kelion not only a pioneer in the field of larceny and successful transfer, they honored him as such.

(22)

The foundation of the Dani culture was built on the principle of simple survival. The people possessed a natural incentive to defend themselves against the enemy, against hunger and against the climate in which they lived. Their weapons, food and shelters provided the Dani with their tomorrows.

The Dani culture subsisted, grew and renewed itself exclusively on the fruit of its own labor. It was a healthy society. The Dani found life uncomplicated. They were simple people, at peace with their culture.

The missionaries have tried to bring a touch of the American and European cultures to the Dani, but for all their good intentions, they've met with little success. There was, and still is, a strong competition between the missions in the Baliem Valley. The Dani saw the missions set against each other. One was Catholic, one Protestant, both Christian, but each professed to be "better" than the other. The contest added confusion to the doctrine which preaches love and brotherhood.

The early missionaries asked the Dani to burn his trinkets and pray to a Christ who had been crucified a long time ago in a place where white men had lived. They asked the people to give up polygamy, which meant the destruction of the Dani economy. These things didn't make much sense to the Dani, and for the most part, still don't.

The military were harsh in their attitude toward the Dani. They meant to change the way the Dani looked, as well as their habits. The military bound up their hands and cut off their hair. They dumped them into a river and forced them to wash off the grease they'd spent hours applying. Then they put pants on them. It hurt the Dani's feelings. Sometimes self-righteousness tends to blind men to the sensibility of others.

The police fought the Dani too. And they made fun of them. They criticized their behavior, their morals and the way they looked. They presented a picture of them as dirty, ignorant savages who would kill you if you didn't kill them first. Much of this was motivated by the fact that the government knew the Dani did not want them there in the first place. When the Dani resisted the government's efforts to "civilize" them, they were simply shot down and killed. Police Chief Marpaung told us that the police march to "open a new territory" scheduled for February 1972 had to be postponed because of insufficient funds to support the marching troops. I understood the operation would begin somewhere east of Angrouk. The police meant to march for five days through the area in an effort to make friends with those Dani who were willing and to kill those who resisted. It seemed to me this was an intentional eradication of the indigenous people of West Irian. I was reminded that the United States took care of its original racial problem with the extermination of the indigenous Indians.

According to new statistics, the government had already reduced the underpopulated area of 800,000 natives to 600,000 by sending 200,000 children to Jakarta for schooling. The parents with whom we lived in the Baliem Valley had received no word from their children since their departure.

The Dani had been the majority racial group at one time, but now foreigners and the transmigrating Javanese were beginning to change that.

When Sjam and I arrived on the Baliem horizon, the Dani had already begun to fear and dislike strangers. They did not believe in golden promises. Sjam and I tried to work things out with the Dani through friendship, amity and good will. We began by accepting the Dani on their own terms. We ate the same food they ate. We lived in the same villages they did. We did not criticize the Dani, although we couldn't totally approve of some of the factions found in their culture. I am thinking primarily about warfare and killing. I suppose no one had ever loved the Dani as they were, nearly naked and non-Christian, and our affection must have been a surprise to them.

We found that the Dani desperately wanted to be liked. Through our acceptance of them, they wanted to know about us. When we sang their songs, they asked to learn ours. When medicines were introduced in the villages and the sick became well, nearly everyone wanted to learn "doctoring." We taught reading and writing to both young and old, simply because they asked us to. In the gardens we planted new seeds and gave out agricultural tools to help with the harvesting. I guess Sjam and I gave them just about everything we had, including clothes we could not spare.

Sometimes the Dani wanted to know how we thought about things. I was asked about the god I believed in. My Moslem friend, Sjam, who believes in God and concedes there may have been a Christ, allowed me to talk a little about religion as I knew it. It was interesting that the Dani understood it was God's love that drives people to help those who are hurting.

(23)

I suppose everyone, at one time or another during his lifetime, has asked himself the questions, "What makes me the way I am, what do I stand for and what do I stand against?"

Someone once asked me, "What makes Wyn Sargent Wyn Sargent?" And I thought it was a funny question. It was as though I'd been asked about a thing or a place rather than about a person. It indicated that maybe I was different from other human beings. That disturbed me. I couldn't answer the question because I had no idea how to reply to it.

I am a Quaker by choice, not by birth. I have also become a member of the Garden Grove Community Church because Dr. Robert Schuller convinced me I could belong to his church and still be a Quaker at the same time.

It meant a great deal to me to remain a Friend. When one is a Friend, then he is a friend to all people. Friendship has nothing to do with the color of a man's skin or the way a fellow sees something or even how he feels about it. You are his friend and that is all that matters.

It is no secret that my twin brother and I were adopted. Our natural mother died shortly after childbirth. Our foster mother was such a good mother to us that we never wanted to be reminded that we were not of her blood. Mother Sargent was the first humanitarian I ever knew. Through her undying generosity and great love for other people I learned something about trying to help those less fortunate. She taught me that man owes something to man.

I've found that when I look at baby birds above in their nest, I feel sorry for them. And I am moved to tears whenever I see a dog crushed to death on a highway. Certain flowers, especially the rose, bring my soul right down to its knees. I don't know why I feel this way about these things. But it has taught me that one must be careful with the handling of another's feelings.

The things I believe in have to do with love, friendship and humanitarianism.

(24)

When one becomes a part in the lives of other people, those people begin to play a role in his own life. Sjam and I had become nearly inseparable from the Dani and surely we loved them very much.

I don't know when a discontentment began to come over me. I suppose I was thinking about the time when I would have to leave the Baliem Valley and return to America. I wondered if Kelion's friendship with Obaharok would endure after I'd left. I found myself worried about the Dani and worried about their tomorrow.

The natives were becoming detribalized outcasts, patrolled by missionaries and police, living in the backwash of a civilization that was filled with the pale fancies of what used to be and the decaying dreams of what they could never become again. The flame of their culture had faded. When it was gone, only a smolder of the Dani greatness would remain.

I wondered how the Dani could travel on into a bright, livable future when they once realized they no longer had control over their own lives and that their tribal greatness had receded, withered and died. What would they do when they found that they must tolerate the coming changes and when the world would seem finished to them?

It occurred to me that the Dani might last longer if they stopped killing one another and became friends. It would not be impossible for the whole Valley to unite in an alliance dedicated to peace. The alliance could incorporate Kolo's territory in the southern end of the Valley and extend all the way north to Wenebuborah. But there was nothing stable about a confederation or an alliance. They emerged and faded according to whim, politics, economy or territorial fancy.

Nothing in the Dani world really counted unless there was a slaughter of pigs and a feasting together. The only events which allowed the massive killings of pigs were marriages, funerals and religious ceremonies.

Well, a funeral was out. Kolo would rejoice over such a thing. A *kanake* was no good, either. Kolo wouldn't bring his sacred stones into Obaharok's territory for anything in the whole world.

"Sjam, pack your things! We're going to Pabuma."

Sjam was peeling potatoes for supper. She put down her

knife, walked to the door and threw out the skins. She turned and patted the doorframe with her hand.

"Why?" she asked quizzically.

"I'm going to marry Chief Obaharok!"

(25)

Since Mi Hijo was sick—he was down with influenza—he would not be able to go with us to Pabuma. Sjam asked Talago to be a substitute interpreter. Talago lived in Wamhalilmo, but he hung out in our place most of the time. He had learned a little Bahasa Indonesia. Talago agreed to go with us. He accompanied us as far as Elima, then he got cold feet and fled.

Sjam and I went on alone. We knew enough of the Dani language between us to convey an idea. Sometimes we even understood what was said back.

When we arrived in Pabuma, the village was empty. The quickest way to get someone to come to a compound is to open the entrance of the warriors' *pilai*. I began to remove the boards. Before I unfastened the last plank a young boy came panting into the courtyard.

"No, Obaharok is not here," he said. "He is in Hiyasi. There is a *kanake* going on over there."

The boy volunteered to run to Hiyasi and tell Obaharok we were waiting for him in Pabuma.

The women of the village were beginning to come in from their gardens. They were corralling their pigs in the courtyard when Obaharok showed up. He was out of breath and he looked very tired. "*Laok,*" he said as he seated himself on the grass inside the *pilai*.

"Sjam, do you have a cigarette?" Obaharok asked, pressing his thumb and index finger into his closed eyes to remove the oil and perspiration that had collected there.

Sjam offered a crumpled pack of Kreteks from her shirt

pocket. In a few minutes the *pilai* was filled with the strong odor of the spicy cloves in the tobacco.

When two people come together from different cultural, intellectual and racial designs, and they want to communicate on a logical, coherent basis, they must start with factors which are familiar to both of them.

"Obaharok," I began testily, "your wealth is found in your pigs, gardens, women and in your *kain*ship, is this not true?"

"*Nen*, I have many pigs, gardens, women and warriors who follow me."

"The more wives and pigs you have, the wealthier you become?"

"You already know that, Mama Wyn."

"Well, yes. I wanted to be sure." I pushed on. "Obaharok, I wonder, would you marry me?"

A slightly shocked silence filled the air. Obaharok looked as though he were trying to absorb the thing, understand it. He scrutinized its meaning. It took several minutes before his gallantry awakened.

"It would be a great honor for me." His voice was dignified and kind. He reached over to shake my hand. "It's a bargain," he said softly.

Obaharok knew that according to Dani cultural laws, a wedding feast meant feasting with my friends and "family," who were: Kolo, Walek and Kelion. It implied the beginnings of new kinships and a new peace alliance. He knew that somehow he would be symbolically tied to a place called America and to a boy named Jmy.

"I will be returning to America soon."

"Will you come back someday?"

"Yes, I'd like to. I want to build a little hospital in one of the villages. Obaharok, I can't be like your other Dani wives. I couldn't work in the sweet-potato gardens or raise pigs. I have my own work I must do. Things after marriage would be the same as they are now."

"Mama Wyn, you are a white chief. I am a black chief. I feel ashamed to speak of such things."

It occurred to me that I should alert the Wamena government about the proposed wedding feast, since it would involve the getting together of thousands of warriors in the native villages.

"I'll write a letter to Police Chief Marpaung and to the district chief, Sunaryo."

"I'll go see Kolo first, about the pigs," Obaharok said before he left the compound.

Sjam looked happy. She was smiling. Obaharok and Kolo would be meeting for the first time.

"Everything came out fine," she said.

"He's a great chief, Sjam. I really must do something nice for him someday."

Face of a Warrior DRAWING BY OBAHAROK

CHAPTER FOUR

Obaharok

$2\sqrt{}$

(1)

When a man and woman get married in the Baliem Valley, they don't run off together and set up housekeeping in a little grass shack somewhere in the jungle. It's not the Dani way of doing things. To begin with, the Dani live in a warrior society, the men sleeping together in the *pilai* to protect their villages, the women, both married and unmarried, in the *abiais*.

There are no careers in the Dani culture for a bachelor girl. It is impressed upon a girl, nearly from birth, that one day she'll become a part of a very important group of married women. At a very early age she learns to plant and cultivate gardens, tend pigs and cook sweet potatoes to prepare herself to hold her position in that group.

Such a group of women, with their children and the women relatives who live with them, is the warrior's family. All the families in a single compound form a clan. The clans welcome new women into their midst because it means a sharing of the garden work and pig tending.

Marriage in the Dani world is only in terms of the pigs paid at the wedding ceremony (*maweh*). The *maweh* is held every four to six years. At the ritual every eligible girl in the Valley becomes a "married woman." A girl's eligibility is determined by her physical development and her ability to work. Most girls are married through parental arrangement and often before they reach puberty because they will mature before the next ceremony comes around.

At the *maweh* a girl will exchange her *thali* (grass skirt) for a *yokal* (married woman's skirt). At the close of the celebration, the girls are placed, according to prearranged agreement, in the various groups of women under the purchasing warrior's protection and ownership.

When a man grows a full beard and owns a few pigs, he's eligible to own a wife. He pays for her with pigs.

Sometimes an eight-year-old girl finds herself married to an old man of eighty. This does not mean she must stay in his group of older women. She can, and often does, run away to join another group more compatible with her own age. Since the girl has been paid for with pigs, the new warrior husband must give a pig to the former husband in return for the "divorce." Feelings are usually not involved and are rarely hurt.

The marriage ceremony provides for and takes care of all women in the Valley. Those physically handicapped or congenitally deformed are often married off to chiefs. Widows are usually taken in by their dead husband's brother.

"Romantic love," as known in the Western world, virtually does not exist in the Dani culture. The strongest affection is found between the members of the same sex. On occasion one sees a fondness between an older man and woman, but it is rare. A Dani wife, like a Dani pig, is "living currency" and a warrior's bankroll.

The most recent marriage ceremony took place in March 1972. No ceremony was scheduled for another four or five years. The *maweh* is initiated only by the most important man in the territory.

That man was Obaharok.

He had the authority to call for a *single* wedding, if he wanted to.

(2)

Early one morning Chief Hubi, Kelion and Walek came stumbling into our kitchen in Wiyagoba. They were crying. Sjam and I looked at each other and heaved a sigh almost at the same time. We had discovered that the arrival of tearful men meant lengthy letter writing or some financial loss to us. Usually it was both.

Chief Hubi was from Sekan village. He waved a letter in his hand, jerking it a little to give it additional importance. It was from the Yumugima schoolteacher and contained a threat. The teacher would take the chief's pigs if he didn't send his children to school.

Kelion was blubbering. He had lost his woman-medicine again. He had tied it beneath his *walimo* and had hung the shell necklace in his *pilai* for the night. That morning it was gone. He was certain a ghost had taken it.

Walek sobbed out his bitter story. He had managed to attract a woman with his woman-medicine, but he couldn't pay for her.

"Please write me a letter," begged Chief Hubi.

"If you give me more medicine, I promise to be more careful with it, Sister," pleaded Kelion.

"If only I had a thmall pig," wailed Walek.

Kelion stopped crying. Looking at Walek, he sat down on the floor, leaned against the wall and turned his face toward the ceiling. His eyes became narrow slits. Kelion's mind was spinning around as quietly as a well-greased machine. He was thinking that if I gave Walek a pig now, I would have to give him a pig, too, at the time of his success with the ladies.

"Kelion," I said, "if you can't hang on to the medicine, there's no sense in trying to use it. You must get the pig yourself, Walek. A pig from me wouldn't make the marriage worthwhile."

Walek let Kelion borrow his woman-medicine.

Kelion promised to find Walek a pig.

I wrote a letter for Chief Hubi.

(3)

There is a beautiful view from Wiyagoba in the morning. The sun rises behind the great eastern mountain and fires the sky into an orange blush. At the bottom of the mountain the green jungle grasses are wet with morning dew. The sun dries the water on the grasses, shakes the chill out of the air and begins to warm up the day with its golden heat.

Mi Hijo was well. He went with Sjam and me to Analaga. We met Obaharok at the Aikhe River.

"I haven't talked to Kolo about the pigs yet," he said. "I thought we could see him together."

Sjam put her tongue in her cheek. "He probably wasn't sure of his reception," she whispered.

We crossed the river and entered a grove of acacia trees. It was nice inside the grove, with a little pool in the middle of it. On the side of the pool was a shady spot where it was good to sit down and eat lunch. Mi Hijo gave us some sweet potatoes. He only had three. He gave his to Obaharok. Obaharok broke the potato into two pieces and handed a part back to Mi Hijo.

Mi Hijo did not eat his half until he was certain Obaharok didn't want any more.

"It's easier to peel a potato when it's hot," I said.

"It's harder on the hands. What if Kolo doesn't agree to come to the wedding?" Sjam asked.

"He has to attend, Sjam. He's my family."

"I'll bet Obaharok will have the wedding in his own territory."

"Maybe in Wiyagoba. Kolo'd have to walk the whole length of Obaharok's territory to get there."

Abruptly the sun dropped behind a cloud. The grove was enveloped in darkness. Within a few minutes the rain poured down. I looked at Obaharok and Mi Hijo. They'd flattened themselves against a tree trunk to get shelter from the limbs.

"Since they don't want clothes, let's buy them umbrellas!" I yelled at Sjam above the noise of the falling rain. And later, we did. We bought them in every color we could find. The Dani loved the umbrellas. Red proved to be their favorite color, with green running a close second. The Dani used the umbrellas because they were compact and could be taken anywhere. If you weren't prepared for it, however, it was a rather startling sight to suddenly come upon a naked man walking through the jungle beneath a red umbrella.

When the rain stopped, Obaharok and Mi Hijo rubbed the water off their bodies with their hands and we went on.

There was an irrigation ditch on the other side of the grove. The ditch had been abandoned but it was always filled with water. Now the rain had flooded its banks, and the log bridge floated on the water's surface. Obaharok caught hold of the log, pointed it toward the opposite bank and ran across it.

"Ma, you go next," Mi Hijo said.

I should take off my boots, I thought. But I didn't.

I took Mi Hijo's hand and began inching my way over the slippery log. A couple of steps out, the log began to sink beneath my weight. Suddenly the whole thing disappeared under the water. I couldn't see where to step any more. Obaharok was leaning toward me from the other side of the bank, with his hand outstretched. I still held Mi Hijo's hand. I grabbed

Obaharok's hand at about the same time I started to slip. All three of us fell into the water. Like Kelion, when I fall I don't fall just a little, I fall hard. And it's a long way down for me. The problem of falling into water is compounded: I don't know how to swim. I don't know why I didn't drown in the ditch. Panic-seized, I did nothing to help Mi Hijo and Obaharok save me from such a fate.

The men, neck-high in muddy water, helped Sjam across. She had removed her boots.

We walked on to Analaga, single file, and sometimes in mud up to our ankles. The Dani lookouts hooted our arrival. When we reached the outskirts of Analaga, the people ran out to meet us.

Kolo was not working in the garden—he was visiting a neighboring village—so he didn't see us walk into Analaga and enter the *wamai*.

On his way home Kolo dropped in to see Old Dialec. He noticed the door of the *wamai* slightly ajar. He guessed that Sjam, Mi Hijo and I had returned. He was unprepared to meet Obaharok.

Kolo came through the entrance of the *wamai*, bending low at the waist. He was smiling. When he saw Obaharok the smile froze on his face. He stood, half doubled-over, motionless.

"*Narak*," Obaharok said softly. He reached to shake Kolo's hand.

"*Narak*," Kolo said through his frozen smile. He shook Obaharok's hand from his bent-over position. Obaharok let go. Kolo's hand dropped limply in front of him.

"Please sit down," Obaharok said, patting the floor with his hand.

Kolo dropped down on the grass. He crossed his legs and looked at Obaharok. He was still smiling. The men had never seen each other at such close range. They began to study each other's face.

What followed was an attempt on the part of both men to make the other comfortable. They offered each other tobacco and tried to talk together. They began their discussion rather slowly, speaking so softly that you could barely hear them.

Even with a cigarette in his mouth, Kolo was still smiling. I felt a small distrust of Kolo, since his disposition was so unpredictable.

When Sjam and I were certain the men would not kill each other, we crawled onto the sleeping platform. We motioned Mi Hijo to follow us.

"Tell us what they're saying," Sjam whispered to Mi Hijo.

"Well, they're talking about pigs," Mi Hijo said. He was excited. He liked it when he could listen to the older men talk. They knew how to tell a story and make it good. It never came out all at once—that always sort of spoiled things for him. Older men let a story come out slowly. It gradually took its own shape and you never knew the ending until they were all finished talking.

"Kolo says he wants to bring a big pig. Uncle Abinyai will bring one, too," Mi Hijo continued his reporting. "They're talking about celebrating at Haratsilimo again. Obaharok says there was too much rain the last time." Mi Hijo's eyes suddenly widened. He began swallowing to clear the emotion of excitement from his throat.

"Ma, they're talking about a *maweh*. Who's getting married?"

"Well, Obaharok and I. . . ."

I suppose it was a mistake to tell Mi Hijo such a thing at this time. It caused him to miss the rest of the conversation between Obaharok and Kolo. You could see the excitement growing in Mi Hijo. His eyes began to sparkle with joy. He pinched them together to hold back the happiness he felt.

"Ma," he said huskily, "that would make Obaharok my father! And he's a *kain!*"

(4)

There was a scarcity of pigs in the Valley—the sacrifices at the *kanakes* had taken most of the animals—so it was strange when suddenly great herds of pigs began to invade the land. No one knew where they came from. They simply appeared.

When it comes to pig trading, it'd be nearly impossible for one Dani to cheat another. They know their pigs better than any other thing. When Kolo was gypped in a pig deal, it was a matter of astonishment to all of us. La Paloma sold him a sick pig for four thousand rupiahs (approximately ten dollars).

The pig looked healthy enough when La Paloma brought it into the courtyard. Its eyes were clear and its nose was not runny. As soon as La Paloma and the four thousand rupiahs left the compound, the pig's nose ran and its eyes fuzzed up. There was a death rattle in its lungs. The pig looked as though it were going to collapse and die any minute.

"I'll talk to Obaharok," I said. "He'll help straighten things out."

As it turned out, La Paloma bought a spade with his four thousand rupiahs. Obaharok pressed La Paloma to trade his spade for the sick pig he had sold Kolo, so Kolo became the owner of a spade he was too lazy to use. And La Paloma's pig died before he could get it back to his village in time to eat.

"Walek wants to give you a pig, Kolo," I said. "He wants to know if you want the pig killed or alive."

"Alive!" Kolo said.

I don't know where Walek got a pig. But you could predict what would happen. In kinship, Walek would give the live animal to Kolo. Kolo would take the pig, trade it for another, kill the new one and give the meat to Walek. Walek would be out one pig. Kolo would break even.

Mi Hijo had counted his money. He had enough to buy a pig for the *maweh*. It would be small but it would still count.

Kelion's mind combed through the possibilities of acquiring a pig. As a matter of fact, he had his eye on every pig in the neighborhood. I finally gave him enough money to buy the animal. I'm not certain he used the money to buy the pig he brought to the ceremony, however.

Sjam and I watched the pig trading go on in silent wonder. The animals were traded, bought, given, promised and some of them were stolen. They changed hands many times before the ceremony actually took place. Some of the pigs no sooner became accustomed to their new courtyards but what they were spirited away by some new owner through a spur of the moment negotiation. In Wiyagoba the animals came and went with such dispatch that they were left unnoticed by those of us who lived in the compound.

Sjam and I took Walek to Analaga to meet Kolo. The following day we went with the two chiefs to Opagima, where they talked with Obaharok and Kelion.

It was an incredible experience to see these former enemy tribesmen planning a pig feast together. Sjam and I wanted to stay and listen to the little committee of men. But we couldn't. We had to leave for Wamena. We were worried about the approaching expiration date on my three-month visa. It had been nearly a month since we sent my passport and request for visa extension to the Jayapura immigration office. So far we had heard nothing from them.

In Wamena we visited Police Chief Marpaung.

"Oh, don't worry!" he laughed. "We're not in America, you know! The Indonesian mail system is a little slow. The passport and visa extension will probably come along any day now. Anyway, the police have control over the people here whether they stay or not. Don't worry! I will support you!"

But I worried. I worried so much I forgot to write him a letter about the pig feast. Anyway, I didn't know where it was going to be held or even when.

(5)

Niren delivered the message to us before breakfast. Sike, he said, wanted to see me in Punycul.

We left Wamena and arrived in Punycul before noon. Sike was waiting for us in the *pilai*. He looked problem-burdened.

"Mi Hijo must return to Wenebuborah," he said. "There's too much work for the people right now. He has to help in the gardens."

"I don't want to go," Mi Hijo said, setting his jaw.

"Does Sike have the authority to order you back to Wenebuborah?" I asked.

"Yes. Sike is chief of both Punycul and Wenebuborah. There's nobody in Wenebuborah big enough to be chief right now."

"How long would he have to work?" I asked Sike.

Sike made two fists and then covered one of my hands with his own. Fifteen days.

"I think you'd better help your people, Mi Hijo. It's only for a little while."

Mi Hijo's jaw relaxed a bit. He looked down at his hands. He turned the palms over and studied the calluses lining the little hams beneath his thumbs.

"I'll go if you want me to. But, please, write a letter."

"What kind of letter?"

"They're cutting the trees. I want the letter to say they can't do that any more."

"Who's cutting the trees?"

"The police."

"Where?"

"On my property."

"On *your* property?"

"Yes. There are lots of trees growing on it."

"Does it have any houses on it?"

"Yes."

"Many houses? Like a village?"

"Yes."

"Does the village have a name, Mi Hijo?"

"Yes, it has a name."

"What's the name of the village?"

"Wenebuborah."

Sjam's mouth popped open. My mind bolted, turned and came back to examine the thing.

"Mi Hijo, are *you* the chief of Wenebuborah?"

Mi Hijo ducked his head in embarrassment.

"I guess so," he said shyly. "Only I haven't killed a man yet."

(6)

I understood there was a pig feasting connected with the *maweh* ritual. Old kinships would be reaffirmed and new ones formed. During the feasting there was a symbolic offering of food to the ghosts and the termination of certain funeral rituals. A *maweh* covered a multitude of pending tribalistic ritualism.

"Sjam, I'd better find out what's expected of me in this wedding ceremony. Ask Talago to get Kelion in here. He ought to be able to tell us something about the *maweh*."

Talago found Kelion asleep in the little ravine behind Wiyagoba. He had covered himself with jungle vines so Walek couldn't find him. Talago nearly missed seeing him at all.

Kelion drowsily staggered into our kitchen. He sat down heavily on the platform with half-shut eyes.

"Kelion, please wake up! Tell me about the *maweh*."

Kelion sighed deeply. Unless he could think of some kind of escape, he knew he was going to be stuck with me for the rest of the afternoon.

"Obaharok will kill a pig," Kelion yawned.

"He'll kill many, won't he?"

"Yes. All important chiefs will bring pigs to represent their people. There'll be many pigs."

"Then what happens?"

"The chiefs eat together. Then they go home."

"Don't the men and women eat together?"

"No, the women eat in the big kitchen with you."

Kelion's sleepy eyes roved around the room, taking inventory of the new supplies that had arrived from Wamena.

"Kelion, how do people know this is a *maweh* and not a *kanake*?"

"Because you get married at a *maweh!*"

"How do I get married?"

"You change your clothes."

"What do you mean, 'change your clothes'? Aren't these good enough?" I smoothed the wrinkles in my fading shirt and brushed a little at my trousers.

Kelion's brows knit together in a deep frown. "All girls," he said, "change from *thali* to *yokal* at *maweh*. This means they are married. What do you think *yokal* is for?"

Kelion swung his head to the left and pouted. I supposed I had hurt his feelings.

"*Yokal* means you're married," he said in a sweat of impatience. "Why? You want to cheat Obaharok? He kills pigs but you still dress in men's clothing. People think you not married at all."

The Dani may not read or write or use wedding rings, but they have worked out what they believed is a suitable method to document their marriages. At the same time, the women have a feeling of real participation in the *maweh* by wearing the *yokal*.

I thought about the yards and yards of *buen* fibers that go into the bands to make up a *yokal*. Men usually weave the fibers because their fingers are intact, but Sjam and I had seen many women, with nothing but finger stumps, quite capable of weaving the threads and lacing them with red and yellow orchid fibers (*urai*). The *yokal*, when finished, is a beautiful piece of craftsmanship. And the Dani women who wear them are quite as modest, in their own way, as other women of the twentieth century.

"Kelion, it seems like a lot of work. Can't we just tell everybody that I'm married, without going to all that effort?"

"If you marry Dani *kain* in Dani *maweh*, you must wear Dani *yokal*."

"There's nothing more to do? Nobody makes any speeches or anything like that?"

Kelion had stopped listening. His mind was wandering because he was tired of thinking. "I am hungry," he said lamely.

"We're going to invite you to lunch. You can have all the

food you want to eat. Kelion, what else do I have to do in the *maweh?*"

The thought that food was on its way boosted Kelion into thinking again. "You wear *yokal* and that is all. Marriage ceremony ends when women in Wiyagoba tie the last *yokal* knot on you."

So, putting on the *yokal* was the *marriage ceremony* and wearing it forever after was the *marriage document.*

"How long would I have to wear this dress?"

Kelion pinched the tops of his ring finger and little fingers with his right thumb and index finger. Two days.

"This day," he said, holding his ring finger, "you sing in the kitchen with the women. This day"—Kelion pressed his little finger—"you sing at Haratsilimo with the women."

"Can you imagine me in a *yokal*, Sjam?"

"No, I can't. I wonder how the women put it on you."

"Kelion, how do the women put the *yokal* on me?"

"Sister," he said with innocent eyes, "you must give me a piece of your old clothing. It is the Dani custom. Girls give their *thalis* to their families when they are put in *yokals*. You can give me your shirt."

This was not the first time Kelion had campaigned to acquire one of my two shirts. Once I'd caught him wearing the yellow one. It took nearly four washings before all the pig grease rinsed completely out of the sleeves. It would take a little checking to discover if Kelion's latest attempt to get my shirt was truly a custom or not. I decided to test him.

"Kelion, would you settle for my socks?"

"Yes. One pair."

It was probably a custom.

(7)

Sjam and I went to Wamena to get permission for Obaharok to hold another *etai* at Haratsilimo. We found Mr. Marpaung supervising the construction of his new jailhouse—a *pilai* which the local natives were building. It was surrounded by barbed wire nailed to six-foot posts.

The door to the old *pilai* was padlocked shut with a pair of police handcuffs. I asked Mr. Marpaung to let me visit the prisoners inside. He yelled in the direction of a whitewashed bunkhouse with a tin roof. An Indonesian attendant burst out of the house with the keys to the handcuffs in his hand. When he opened the door, I entered the *pilai* and heard the door close. The handcuffs clicked in the sound of locking.

The odor inside the jailhouse was strangling. The air was filled with the stink of refuse. The Dani are unusually clean housekeepers but have little chance to tidy a place in which they are confined. I saw the outline of a woman sitting in front of the fireplace in the dim interior. Her head was bowed. She did not move.

"Mama," I said, "*nocksu.*" I touched her hand.

"I am here because I had an abortion," she said softly.

"How many days have you been here?"

The woman did not look up. She showed me eight days on her hands.

There was a movement at the hole to the sleeping loft. Two young Dani men swept down into the room and crawled over to the fire. The woman turned her back to the men and began sobbing. It was against the Dani culture for men and women to be together in a *pilai*. She was overwhelmed with the shame of it. The men looked embarrassed for her.

"Mama," one of them said, "will they take us away?"

"What did you do?"

"We ate a man, but only a part of him."

"What village?"

"Oxibil. Do you know it? Mama, will they take us away?"

"*An nokodek.*" ("I don't know.")

I rapped on the door. The Indonesian attendant let me out. Marpaung was standing in front of me.

"A man's life doesn't mean a goddamn thing to these people," he said. "Not a goddamn thing!"

The look in the prisoners' eyes was a haunting one. They couldn't understand why they were being punished for something they had been taught to do.

"On the contrary. It's a matter of culture. Taking a man's life gives another his purpose in life."

"We'll punish them. Punish them good. Make examples of them. That ought to change their ways."

"Has it worked before?"

"Well, we don't know yet. These are the first half-tamed ones we've gotten our hands on."

"It's a challenge. I think Sjam and I are about to see a change in the people where we've been living. It looks like a new peace alliance will be made between the north and the south. If it comes off, the alliance will reduce killings to a minimum."

"Yeah? Well, good luck, lady! The whole thing turns me off. The only way to deal with them is to punish them. Make examples of them. Say, have any of these men married you yet?"

"No, not yet."

(8)

On January 9, 1973, at four o'clock in the morning, bird calls pierced through the Valley. It was mysterious to the point of witchcraft how the Dani communication system worked as effectively as it did in pitch-blackness. Within an hour the air was electric with whatever the message.

The bird calls were identical to those used to announce the *etai* at Haratsilimo. We listened to the calls for about an hour. Then Sjam lighted a candle. Further sleep in such a racket was impossible.

Kelion and Walek stumbled into the kitchen at five-thirty.

Kelion was still sleepy. He staggered a bit and accidentally fell against the door frame. The blow broke his *holim*. He turned and fled with a swiftness known to the speed of light.

Walek announced the meaning of the bird calls. "Today ith *maweh*," he lisped, smiling broadly.

"Where?"

"I don't know," Walek said and left the kitchen.

At seven-thirty a Dani warrior arrived in Wiyagoba to advise Walek that the *maweh* would be held in Feratsilimo.

"If the *maweh* is in Feratsilimo," Walek said, "then we'll have another feast here!"

At seven forty-five Mi Hijo showed up with a small pig under his arm.

At eight o'clock Obaharok and Wali arrived. They went into Walek's *pilai*.

At nine o'clock Kolo appeared.

At nine-fifteen it was announced that the *maweh* would take place right there in Wiyagoba.

Obaharok, Wali and Kolo left Wiyagoba together to inform the people where to meet. Walek and Kelion came into the kitchen. Both chiefs crawled up onto the sleeping platform.

Sick people poured into the kitchen for medical treatment. Between compresses and applications of medicine, Walek tried to explain the procedure for the day. The women, he said, would come from many villages. They would gather grass to be used in the *maweh* while the men searched for firewood. Meanwhile I was to wait in the kitchen. The women would come in to dress me when they were ready.

Mi Hijo rushed into the kitchen with a letter in his hand.

"Ma, here's a letter from the Jiwika police. It's for Mabel."

Mi Hijo handed the letter to Walek, who was afraid to touch it. Sjam took the letter, unfolded it and read it.

"You're supposed to report to the Jiwika police. Ibekene, Kurulu's son, has filed a complaint against you. He says he gave you a *wesa* stone at your mother's funeral and you haven't given him a pig in return."

Walek squinted his eyes and threw out his square jaw. "I won't go! My mother died a long time ago. I didn't athk

Ibekene to bring me anything. It ith our cuthtom to exchange a gift only if we want to. I don't want to!"

It looked as though the wedding day was not going to be dull.

It seemed that more people than usual came in for medicine. They came alone and they came in groups. One man was carried in by two others. His excessively high fever and shaking chills indicated he had malaria. I gave him chloroquine and asked Walek to keep an eye on him in his *pilai*.

It was nearly ten o'clock when the four women came to put the yokal on me. A few minutes later Sjam fainted. She did not lose consciousness completely. She had been standing near the fireplace in the center of the room. Suddenly she went limp and collapsed to the floor. Walek and Mi Hijo helped lift her onto the platform.

"I'm okay," she said weakly. "Just a little dizzy."

We hadn't been eating enough during the past few weeks. Each of us had lost more than ten pounds. We hadn't been resting enough, either. There was always too much to do.

"Mi Hijo, maybe there's a little fish in the river today. The children could try to catch it."

"I'll be fine," Sjam said. "I'll just lie here and watch the women put the *yokal* on you."

The women waved Walek out of the kitchen and shut the door. All four women took off the net on their head, then carefully placed the *nokens* on the floor by the fireplace. One by one the nets were opened. The *yokal* bands were reverently removed and laid out on the grass. They came in one design and two colors, red and yellow, and they were about ⅜-inch wide. The bands were wound up into five- or six-inch bundles and tied in the center with thread.

Then, to my surprise, the four women folded their hands in their laps and began to cry. They were not crying for the same reasons people weep at Western weddings. The Dani women were crying for their dead relatives.

I'd learned to fear the Dani women. The idea of being cooped up with four of these rowdy creatures in our small kitchen placed me near panic. Seeing them cry so, the women seemed gentle and nearly tender-hearted. I was tempted to trust them, which would have been a mistake.

Five minutes later they stopped crying. Smiles broke out on their faces. The smiles were replaced by boisterous laughter. One of the heftiest women grabbed at my trousers. It was only because of her unfamiliarity with zippers that she didn't yank the levi's off me. The kitchen began to take on an aura of a house for the mad.

"*Houtdogon!*" ["Wait!"], I yelled.

I took off my trousers and laid them on the sleeping platform, then tied my shirttail in a knot in the front. There was nothing to do but go ahead with it, so I turned around to face the music.

I was directed to put my hands on the rafters in the ceiling of the kitchen and to place my ankles together. And to stand straight.

Two of the women went to work on me. Strings of dried grass, as scratchy as steel wool, were wound around my waist. The strings were not wound around just once. They went around and around until a bundle built up to resemble a rope. It was an inch thick and the ladies were still going. The rope was tied in several places with little lengths of the same scratchy grass.

The other two women were sitting on the floor. They unraveled the *yokal* bands, the longest of which appeared to be about twelve feet in length. There was much haggling between these two women. They envisioned the placement of the bands on the skirt. They separated the bands into five or six piles. From the piles they took the bands and folded them into two-foot lengths.

The grass rope was getting thicker around my waist. I wondered how much more the ladies had to go.

Mi Hijo knocked at the door, but no one let him in. Talking through the door, he said he had caught a fish and had located some fresh beans. Sjam asked him to cook the food. One of the women ordered him to find a pole and some heavy stones.

When Mi Hijo returned shortly, the door was opened a crack and the pole slid through into the kitchen. The women put the pole across the ceiling and poked its ends into the kitchen walls. Mi Hijo tossed in several large stones and was told to bring more.

The women hung the bundles of *yokal* bands on the pole and placed a large rock in the bottom of each bundle.

"Those rocks are used to straighten the fibers," Sjam explained from the platform. "That's the way the Dani woman irons her dress. I wonder what the grass rope around your waist is for?"

"I think it's to hold the skirt up."

By eleven o'clock Sjam had eaten her fish, the *yokal* bands were hanging from the ceiling and I was still standing with a grass rope tied around my waist. That was all that had happened in one hour. The Dani women are not known for being brisk people. They have something against hurry.

The *yokal*, when worn by the Dani women, is quite low. The "waistband" is placed well below the waist because the naturally potbellied Dani woman's physique does not lend itself to a waistline. To accommodate my Western modesty, I wanted the *yokal* to be remodeled to improve its coverage and to get the waistband up where it belonged. I was afraid the innovation might outrage the Dani eye, but as it turned out, the people didn't care. Most of them didn't even notice.

Mi Hijo had already told the women I wanted my skirt "high and long" even though they wore their skirts "low and short." This extra costuming required an additional supply of *yokal* bands. The women didn't realize that. They thought it was because I was so tall that more bands were needed.

I discovered another reason why the women wear their skirts low when I was asked to take off the grassy rope around my waist. The Dani woman steps into her skirt and pulls it up in place. This rope around my waist would go neither up nor down. It was stuck around my middle. It refused to budge.

"Well, I'm in trouble already," I said to Sjam.

Sjam came over to help me. The women, who didn't want her to interfere, yelled at her and tried to keep her away from me, but she charged forward like a race horse, undaunted. Together we pulled and stretched the grass rope until it was inched painfully down and finally off. My skin looked as though it had been scraped with sandpaper where the rope had traveled over it.

The women passed the rope around between them. Each one scrutinized the work in it. They criticized it until all agreed that it was as nearly perfect as they could get it. Then they asked me to put it on again. Sjam and I struggled with it. Getting it on was no easier than getting it off. When it was back in place again, the raw places on my sides began to smart.

The compound was filled with the sounds of happy, excited voices. Sjam stepped outside to see what was happening. When she came back she said that an impressive group had gathered together in front of the *pilai*. Obaharok was there, Kolo and Abinyai, and many other chiefs she'd never seen before. There were violent preparations going on in the food line. Bushels of sweet potatoes, armloads of native vegetables and gallons of water were being brought in. And there were pigs running everywhere in the courtyard.

Mi Hijo knocked on the door. One of the women opened it and a handful of something that looked like pink snakes slipped through the narrow opening. The woman took them in her hand and turned around. She held about twelve feet of raw pig intestines. They were wet. With the help of another woman, she doubled the intestines together and wound them around my waist. They tied the ends in a sort of half knot in the front. I was allowed to sit down on the sleeping platform, provided the hanging lengths of intestines did not touch the grass. One of the women arranged the dripping ends on my legs.

The intestines had been taken from a *wesa* pig and were supposed to purify and sanctify the *yokal*. I'm not certain how this was done. The *yokal* bands were still hanging from the ceiling. Several minutes passed before the ladies decided that the consecration had taken place. They removed the intestines and handed them out through the doorway to Mi Hijo. I never saw them again.

It is a mystery to me how I survived the rest of the afternoon. Most of it has to be put down to magic. It took the four women nearly eight hours to wind the *yokal* on me. Each strand was wound around my waist and tied to the grass rope on the sides. The bands had to be perfectly laid, without twist or wrinkle, placed just so, turned just the right way. One woman held a strand while another ironed it with her fingers. A third tied it in place. The fourth woman was ready with another band in her hand, which usually provoked arguing because nobody thought it was good enough. There was hardly a time when all the women agreed on the placement of the bands at the same time. As the bands increased around the middle, they began to drop in the front and back in tight loops, like an apron. The loops swung upward at the sides and were tied to the grass rope. Some bands were tied onto other bands, near the waist. All this tying gave a final projection of three inches on each side of the top of the skirt.

When the last band was finally tied and knotted, the skirt weighed more than seven pounds. The bands had been bound around my middle with a ferocity that left me trussed into a stiff immobility known only to an Egyptian mummy and to the strait-jacketed insane. To walk anywhere was useless. I could not even raise my knee. To bend over, even a little, guaranteed cutting myself in half. Having stood up all day, I now found that I could not sit down.

Despite the protests of the screaming women, Sjam helped me. She backed me up against the sleeping platform, aimed and pushed me from the front. I fell over backward, half lying on the grass bed, my feet hanging in midair over the edge.

Lying there, I tried to review how I had arrived at this state. I vaguely recalled that the Dani social laws were based on kinship as well as patrilineal descent. Kinships were being formed between enemy tribes through pig feasting in the compound, which was the whole idea of my being in a *yokal*. I wondered if it was worth it. Well, yes, it was worth it. I would have been happier, though, if my legs and hips didn't hurt so much.

Chief Wamdierick burst into the kitchen with a piece of

charcoal in his hand. He started to come over to me. When he saw I couldn't sit up, he stopped. He talked to me from across the room.

"Many chiefs came here today," he said excitedly. "They came from Hela and Tulim. And Chief Maikmo was here!"

Maikmo's presence was an unexpected honor. At one time he had been a very powerful leader. After the battle of 1966 he and his warrior confederation went into hiding. Maikmo rarely left his *pilai* in the eastern mountains near the mouth of the Lagora River. His attendance and participation in the *maweh* pledged his confederation into the new peace alliance.

There was a tapping at the door. One of the women opened it. She was given two *nokens* full of cooked pork. She put the nets on the floor and faced Wamdierick.

"The chiefs have finished their feasting and all have left," Wamdierick said. "You must send meat, and don't forget the announcement letters, to Police Chief Marpaung, Sunaryo and the Jiwika police. Also, give your socks to Kelion."

I asked Sjam to stand me up. The women separated the meat into bundles. I wrote a few lines to everybody notifying them that I had participated in a *maweh*. I also gave up my socks.

The women dispatched the meat bundles and notes to the runners waiting outside the door.

Wamdierick held the piece of charcoal in front of me and began to chant. The chant sounded as if he were casting some kind of spell. When he was finished he said, "Now you are chief of people here, too."

When Chief Wamdierick left the kitchen, a rather violent madness followed. The women tied the door shut and took off my shirt, but they did not take off my underwear. As a matter of fact, they liked it, and it was responsible for the women's starting a rash of bra buying later at the Wamena market. The merchants couldn't fill their orders fast enough. The women splashed their fronts with twin circles of pink, blue and red; sometimes the circles came in purple. The ladies were charmed with the colorful apparel and the instant uplift it gave their appearance.

One of the women tied a wide *walimo* around my neck. The

owner of the *walimo* wore a smaller size than I did. Whenever I swallowed I had the feeling of acute strangulation.

When the women tried to saturate my long hair with sacred pig oil, Sjam and I fought them off. Soap and water were too hard to come by. Instead, my lipstick was replaced with pig oil. This compromise reassured the ladies that I would receive the proper blessings by their ghosts.

To all the other rewards of wearing this costume was added that of nets. The carrying nets had been made by the various chiefs' wives in the area. The women had been mindful that I was tall. The nets were longer and heavier than usual. The number of nets signified the importance of the occasion. The four Dani women heaped fifteen nets on my head, at two pounds each.

The accumulated bands from the fifteen nets built a pyramid of pressure on the top of my head. There are no words to describe the headache that began to develop, with utmost energy and vigor, and with such strength that no aspirin was ever able to reach it. I could not turn my head to the right or left. If I looked upward, the nets fell off. If I looked to the ground, the bands threatened to do permanent damage to the top of my head from pulling.

The chiefs had killed and eaten their pigs. The women had put me in a *yokal* and the *maweh* ritual part was officially over. To initiate the *maweh* celebration I was asked to eat and sing in the kitchen with the Dani women. I meant to see it through.

Walking from our kitchen to their kitchen was done more in the nature of shuffling than anything else. I was encouraged by the four Dani women, a thick stick to lean against, and Sjam's strong hand to steer me. I was amazed how the *yokal* impaired my maneuverability. The skirt was not only constricting, it was lacerating. Each step was murderously painful, physically torturous. Sjam looked at me with tears in her eyes. She felt so sorry for my personal misery that she'd lost her sense of humor. I felt that if I could only live through the night, why, I'd need never again fear anything in the whole world.

It was no small job to transport me from one kitchen to the other. As we neared the courtyard I was happy to see that it was empty. When we reached the kitchen door, I found that I couldn't get through it. The baseboard across the entrance was about a foot and a half high. I couldn't raise my leg to step over it. I told Sjam I intended to back into the kitchen. She ran around through the other door and got ready to receive me from the other side. I bent my right knee. I put my foot over the board and leaned backward. When my foot arrived on the other side, I realized I had no room to bend the left knee. The problem was worsened when the three-inch projections on the *yokal* got caught on the side boards of the doorway. I was stuck, half in and half out.

Sjam held me under the armpits and pulled. The women tucked in the trapped *yokal* bands. They pushed from the front. I leaned against Sjam and hopped backward on my bent right leg, holding my left leg straight out in front of me. My entry was ungraceful, but at least I was inside the kitchen.

There were about one hundred women in the kitchen. A pandemonium of excitement ripped through the crowd. The women started shouting and shrieking. The general turmoil indicated that it was not going to be a quiet evening. I was steered into the center of the kitchen. The rafters in the ceiling, draped with drying pig meat, hit me just about in the middle of the face. Having clung to rafters all day, I now clung to them again.

A magnificent madness followed. The women began to sing, and their singing was explosive. To this they added dancing; sometimes they jumped on each other's feet. They jumped up and down on the dirt floor, their feet packing the earth to a new firmness. In a soft spot, the floor gave way to a hole.

The women roared through the celebration, singing to themselves, to each other, to the moon and to the mountaintops. They bellowed their way through songs they probably doubted they were capable of singing. Some of the women didn't know the middle part of the songs, but they invariably hit the end on a final shrieking note.

The celebration was one continuing song and dance without end. When some of the women began to wilt, their vocal chords burned to a whisper, they moved out of the kitchen and other women came in. They came and went so the singing and dancing never collapsed.

About nine o'clock in the evening, the men in the village of Wiyagoba ran up and down in front of the kitchen with their *abareks* and spears. They sang their own songs, running back and forth. After an hour of it, with voices nearly gone for good, they retired.

The fifteen nets over my back and shoulders had heated me to the point of perspiring profusely. The moisture stretched the orchid fibers in the *yokal* just enough to allow me to get off my feet. The Dani women permitted me only two resting positions: sitting with my legs straight out in front, which I couldn't do, or getting down on my knees. It would have been a relief if the bands of the skirt hadn't cut into my skin.

The headache was worsening. I asked Sjam for an aspirin and remembered the malaria patient in Walek's *pilai*. I backed out of the kitchen the same way I had backed in. One hundred women went with me. I inquired about the sick man and found that he was on the way to good recovery.

In the courtyard one of the women said that I would be accompanied out into the jungle if I wanted to go there. Holding firmly onto Sjam's hand, twenty-five women escorted us outside. Two Dani women sprinkled white ashes on the path to discourage *mokats* from coming too near. When we arrived at an area half concealed from the village, I hardly knew how to cope with such an emergency. Twenty-five onlookers stood silently staring at me. They were waiting for me to do something. One chance would probably be all I would get; there was no time for experimentation.

"Sjam, I'm open for any kind of suggestions."

Sjam put her resources to work. She took off her jacket. She armed herself with a slender water gourd and moved in. We were cheered on by twenty-five women, encouraged by the multitude of women still singing in the kitchen, and scared to death that the men would come out of the *pilai* if we took too long.

Back in the kitchen we listened to the thundering of the women's feet and the chanting of their voices for hour after hour. At three o'clock in the morning we begged to retire. Although it was strictly against the rules, the women let us leave. Five of them half carried me back to our own kitchen-home.

It seemed odd to me that I had lived through such a day and night. I could find no reasonable explanation for it.

Sjam carefully removed the fifteen carrying nets from my head.

I slept in the *yokal.*

I couldn't get it off.

(9)

The bird calls began again at four o'clock in the morning. The women in the kitchen were still singing and dancing. We heard the calls between their gasps of breath.

"*Etai* at Haratsilimo," Sjam whispered and went back to sleep.

The *yokal* had cut off the circulation from my waist down. There was a decided advantage to it: the costume was less painful when my legs were numb.

At ten o'clock in the morning Mi Hijo banged on the kitchen door. He told us to get ready to leave for the *etai* at Haratsilimo.

Sjam pulled me up to a standing position. The sharp fibers of the skirt had cut my thighs. There was not just one cut— there were hundreds of cuts, crisscrossing and zigzagging over the flesh. We managed to pull the skirt up a little and wrap bandages around my legs. I swallowed some aspirins because the circulation was returning.

A patch of hair on the top of my head was gone, rubbed off by the nets. Sjam discovered a small goose egg of a bump on my head. We reduced the fifteen nets to three.

Thus far only the women had seen me in this getup. At

Haratsilimo the warriors would get a chance. The *yokal* would justify the slaughter of their pigs.

At eleven o'clock the women came to get me. The skirt had loosened up to the point that it allowed walking, even though each step meant agony and produced holes in my underclothing and bandages.

We left the kitchen and shuffled into the courtyard. Kelion and Walek came out of their *pilais*. I tried to look cheerful. Both men stopped dead in their tracks at the sight of me. Walek bit his finger. Kelion tapped his *holim* in surprise and took a retreating step backward. Walek followed him.

Kaok came running into the courtyard. He skidded to a stop when he saw me and his mouth dropped open. He turned and ran out as fast as he had come in.

Mi Hijo returned from the river with a bucket of water in his hand. When he saw me, he dropped the bucket. Standing motionless, he looked as though he was barely breathing.

"Sjam, let's ask Mi Hijo why all this reaction."

It was several minutes before Mi Hijo could find his voice. His explanation was direct. The warriors, he said, were frankly shocked that I appeared to be a woman. To this was added the confusion that they regarded me as a chief but I was dressed like a Dani woman.

Kaok popped back through the *thop*. He was joined by ten or more warriors, who carried bows and arrows and spears. They began running up and down the courtyard singing. The women ran in a circle around Sjam and me, singing and shaking their digging sticks.

When the warriors left the compound, the women nudged us outward to follow them. The men ran down the footpath toward Mulima, singing and jumping up and down at intervals.

Walking down to the river and wading across the water was much easier than climbing the bank on the other side. Sjam pushed from behind and Wenybake pulled from above. Between the two of them, they raised me and the thirteen-pound costume to the top.

The men and women jumped all the way to Haratsilimo.

They never stopped. Sjam let go of my hand and jumped with the women. She also sang. I tried to jump, but the skirt pinched so I had to give it up.

At Haratsilimo the women ran in a circle around us, singing in high falsetto voices. I thought it strange that we had replaced the *abarek* as their centerpiece.

Large groups of warriors rushed onto the field from all sides, the Analaga forces joining the Mulima warriors. They massed themselves around Obaharok, Kelion and Walek. The warriors numbered about six thousand. There were that many again of women and children.

The revolving circle of women around Sjam and me moved toward the edge of the field. The warriors entered the center and ran in a circle around an *abarek*. The *etai* appeared to be exactly like the other one. The only difference was that the women ran in a circle around Sjam and me.

I'm afraid I was a bit of a disappointment to the ladies. I couldn't jump up and down. I bounced a little but it wasn't like a good, faithful jump. And I didn't sing very much. I tried, but my voice was too low.

At two o'clock I had a fever. Sjam and I asked permission to return to Wiyagoba. By the time we reached home, Sjam also had a temperature. The women who had seen us to our kitchen left and returned to the *etai*. They would dance and sing until dark.

It was only three o'clock in the afternoon. I had been in the *yokal* twenty-two long hours. There had been moments of ungracefulness, but hopefully I was able to give the *yokal* at least part of the dignity and respect it rightfully deserved.

"I'll help you get it off," Sjam said.

"We'll use a knife. I can cut it off," I told her.

"No! We'll unwind it."

Together, weak with rising fevers, Sjam and I unwound the torturous dress. When we got down to the grass rope I cut it in half with the kitchen knife. We left the *yokal* bands heaped in piles on the floor where they had fallen, and I redressed the wounds on my legs. We took aspirins and collapsed on the platform. Within minutes, we were asleep.

We were awakened momentarily when the singing started up again in the kitchen. The people sang all night, but Sjam and I were only faintly aware of it.

(10)

The *maweh* in which I participated was the only one of its kind in the history of the Baliem Valley. It involved, directly or indirectly, nearly ten thousand people. The pig feasting, singing and dancing continued for almost a month.

At an orthodox *maweh* the celebration is officially closed when the warriors take the tails of the slaughtered pigs to a secret hiding place in the jungle, where a pig sacrifice is performed. The newly married girls are placed in various women's groups. They are expected to stay in their new groups and houses, at least for a little while.

I was not placed in a women's group. I did not tend pigs nor work in a sweet-potato garden. It was, therefore, interesting to learn that many rich chiefs wanted to buy a tall white-skinned woman. They came to me to place their orders. They were willing to buy girls, sight unseen.

Kelion was the only chief to display a bit of prudence. He wanted to be shown a photograph first.

(11)

Sjam and I were sick for two days. Talago cooked our food and brought it in to us. Mi Hijo had returned to work in the gardens at Wenebuborah.

Meanwhile the living stream of people flowing into Wiya-goba continued. They never stopped coming. The men feasted in the courtyard, and the women sang in the kitchen all night. Sjam and I wished our kitchen was a little farther from theirs.

On the evening of the third day we had recovered enough to think about walking to Wamena. The following morning, still weak, we left Wiyagoba.

Asuan met us on the footpath outside Tumagonem. He had received a letter from the police in Jiwika—they wanted timber.

"Please write me a letter," Asuan pleaded. "The Wamena police have taken all my wood. I don't have any more."

I wrote the letter.

Niren came running up to us. Large tears were rolling down his cheeks. The boy's tears increased as he told us his story. After he caught some fish in the Aikhe River, he had taken them to the military in Wamena. He asked one of the soldiers for enough money to buy a flashlight in return for his fish. The soldier took the fish, gave Niren ten rupiahs (about two cents) and told him it was enough to buy the largest flashlight in Wamena.

This kind of swindling is not found in the Dani culture. Niren, lacking experience in such a thing, could not understand he had been cheated. He was crying because the merchant in Wamena had not given him a flashlight for the bill he held in his hand.

Sjam and I tried to get the description of the soldier, but it was useless. All the boy remembered was that the man wore a uniform and had a big gun.

We asked Niren to go with us to Wamena. At the market-place I gave him a little money and told him to try again.

"And don't forget the batteries that go inside it," Sjam yelled.

The Sumitros were glad to see us. They had been told about the *maweh* and could scarcely wait to hear the details of it.

(12)

Sjam and I didn't feel well in the morning, but we could not rest. There was a representative from the military waiting in the living room. He wanted to talk to me.

"I am here, Miss Sargent," the soldier said, "to obtain a statement from you concerning the reasons for your marriage. I must make out a full report for the military commander before he returns from Jayapura."

I explained that the ritual had been performed to establish friendship between hostile tribes, but I could have saved myself the trouble. The man did not understand what I was talking about.

Most of the officials of Wamena were in Jayapura for the Moslem holidays. Sjam walked to the police post and sent Mr. Marpaung a cable. She asked him to get my passport and visa from Jayapura immigration. I spent the rest of the afternoon writing the following letter:

DEAR SIR:

On January 9, 1973, in the village of Wiyagoba, I was "married" to Obaharok, Chief of Siepkosi-Mulima. Because of the obvious, unusual nature of this marriage I feel a letter of explanation is in order. Kindly accept this letter as a statement for clarity. The marriage was performed for the following reasons: to unify three enemy tribes in peace and friendship; to create a greater understanding between the Baliem people and the Central Wamena Government and as a representation of good will between the countries of America and Indonesia.

I sent copies to the offices of Mr. Marpaung and Bupati (Regent) Andres Karma. I held on to the one I had written to Sunaryo, who was still in town.

(13)

Please come to the KPS office for a visit at 9:00 A.M.

The letter was addressed to me. It was signed "Sunaryo."

"I remember now where I've seen Sunaryo!" Sjam said. "It's been bugging me for a long time. Sunaryo used to work in the same tour office I did! Nitour fired him because of some crooked deals he'd pulled off with the customers."

At eight-thirty Sjam and I walked to the KPS office. The Indonesian clerks seated behind their desks stared at us out of the corners of their eyes. One of them said, "Mr. Sunaryo is not here." That was all he said, but he gave us a feeling that we had done something wrong.

Sunaryo arrived at nine-fifteen. He was wearing a gray Mao-styled uniform. There was a gold star pinned on the left side of the front.

"Miss Wyn!" he said loudly, smiling broadly enough to show his gold-crowned cuspid. "So! You have married a Baliem man!"

I cringed. Sunaryo's voice was noisy. The clerks looked up from their desks, smiled at their boss and winked at one another.

We shook hands with Sunaryo, then he put his arm around me and said, "We will not talk about such an occasion here in this dull office! This visit is not official business, you realize. We'll go to my home and have tea and cookies to celebrate your marriage!"

Sunaryo motioned Sjam to go first. He hung back, his arm still around my waist. He watched her walk down the road. We followed Sjam, rather slowly, I thought. I tried to quicken my step but found it was impossible. Sunaryo had hooked his fingers in the belt loops of my trousers. I felt uneasy. It was as though Sunaryo wanted everyone in town to see him with his arm around me. When one of his assistants trotted up to join us, Sunaryo ordered him to walk with Sjam.

"So, you have really married one of those people, eh?"

"I realize it's an unusual circumstance, Mr. Sunaryo. Here is a letter of explanation I have written for you. Copies of the letter have already been delivered to Marpaung's office and to the Bupati's headquarters."

"Oh, it doesn't matter, Miss Wyn!" Sunaryo said, waving my letter aside. "The important thing is that you have actually married one of *those* people!"

"They're considered Indonesians, aren't they?" I should have kept my mouth shut but I couldn't help it.

"Yes, of course. Tell me, what is it like to love one of those people?"

"I beg your pardon?"

I couldn't believe what I heard. Sunaryo was leaning heavily against me, his face touching my left shoulder. I backed away. The movement nearly put me in the ditch on the side of the road.

"I mean, how can a white-skinned person love one of those people? I don't understand it."

"What kind of love are you talking about, Mr. Sunaryo? Do you mean romantic love? Christian love? Humanitarian love?"

Sjam was turning the corner into Sunaryo's house. She was shaking her hands up and down in an effort to make some kind of point while talking to the assistant walking beside her.

"Sjam! Wait for us!" I yelled.

Sunaryo stopped walking. He tiptoed a little and put his face very close to mine. After unhooking his fingers from my belt loops, he squeezed my arm and placed his lips near my ear. "Please, Miss Wyn, tell me what it is like to have a sexual experience with a black man," he rasped.

The moment was horrible. I was speechless with shock and hurt. Then I began shaking with anger. I pressed my fingers against my eyelids until specks of white danced on my vision. I reached back, caught Sunaryo's wrist and pushed him with all my might. He stumbled backward and fell to the ground. Sjam came running up at the sight of the scuffle and shouted, "Wyn, what's happened?"

Sunaryo picked himself up off the ground.

"Mr. Sunaryo is confused about the Dani marriage," I said,

sick with pain. "Mr. Sunaryo, I have not seen Chief Obaharok since long before the *maweh* ritual. I believe you should read this letter before we continue talking."

"I will read it later," Sunaryo sniffed. "Here, give it to me."

He stuffed the letter into his pocket, then ran his finger around his tight coat collar and said, "Please, we will go inside my house for tea."

An imposing group of people had gathered inside. There were representatives present from nearly every government department in Wamena. The absence of the top officials left Sunaryo in command. He had the whole town of Wamena at his disposal and he was going to make the most of it.

Sjam was asked to sit at one end of the library table in the middle of the room, and I was seated on the side. A plate of cookies had been placed on the table, and the tea was brought in by Mrs. Sunaryo, whom Sjam and I met for the first time. Sunaryo indicated to the people in the room to sit down on chairs that had been brought in for the meeting. This was supposed to be an informal visit, but someone had done some planning.

Sunaryo sat down at the end of the table, facing Sjam. He brought the meeting to order by congratulating me on my "marriage." He expressed his happiness that Obaharok had married me. He said that, indeed, the whole Wamena government was happy about the occasion. The officials, he reported, wanted to celebrate the event by giving a party in the marketplace. The representatives nodded their heads in silent agreement.

I stated the reasons for the *maweh* and explained a little about the social structure of the Dani people. Sunaryo left the room. When he returned he was wearing his official khaki uniform with the gold buttons and badges.

There was a rapping on the windowpane behind me. I turned around. Obaharok and Wali were standing outside, their faces framed by the steel window casing.

"Trouble is not far behind," I whispered to Sjam.

"Who's that?" Sunaryo asked.

"Chief Obaharok and Chief Wali," I said.

Sunaryo bolted from his chair and flung open the door. He picked the man he guessed was Obaharok and wrapped his arms around him. He was careful to place his sleeves low enough to avoid Obaharok's greasy shoulders.

Chief Wali was not allowed to enter the house, but Sunaryo placed a chair next to mine and asked Obaharok to sit in it. The placement violated Obaharok's *kain*ship; he never sat to the *side* of anyone, unless he wanted to.

Sunaryo sent for a Dani police interpreter. When the man arrived, Obaharok said he'd been summoned by letter to the police post in Wamena for questioning. He gave the letter to Sunaryo, who held it for a moment and then put it on the table without reading it.

Sunaryo offered cookies to Obaharok by passing the plate to him. Sjam and I exchanged a glance of amusement, for Sunaryo didn't know how to offer food to a Dani. Obaharok ate the entire plate of cookies.

"And—do you love Miss Wyn?" Sunaryo began questioning Obaharok.

The interpreter used the word *warok,* which is as close as possible to the Dani equivalent for "love."

Sjam's face drew up into a tight frown. She opened her mouth to say something, but Obaharok spoke first.

"All people in the Valley love Mama Wyn. That is why so many pigs were killed. They were not just my pigs. The pigs were brought from many other villages. We must kill more pigs tomorrow. The people are still feasting. We have run out of meat."

"A pig feast, tomorrow? Would you invite me?" Sunaryo asked.

"Yes," Obaharok said.

"And what about all these people," Sunaryo said, "can they be invited, too?"

Obaharok looked around at the people. "Yes, of course," he said.

"Miss Wyn, write an invitation, please! Now, let's see. We'll send it to the Bupati's office, *Dandin* [army], *Danres* [police], the Information Service, and of course, me!" Sunaryo looked over the room. "And let's include some of the missionary priests. Father Camps and Father Urbanos would probably come."

I wrote the invitation. At Sunaryo's suggestion, Obaharok put his fingerprint beneath my signature.

"Here," Sunaryo said, turning to a policeman with the name Marsatyo written on his shirt, "fix this!" He handed him the police summons. Mr. Marsatyo wrote on the back of the note: "Please dismiss case due to party tomorrow."

Sunaryo leaned on his elbows on the table. He tried to look casual. "Obaharok, according to the tradition in Wiyagoba, is this marriage legal?"

Obaharok, without changing expression, said, "According to the tradition in any village, the marriage is legal."

"I see. Obaharok, would you be willing to go to Jakarta?"

"No."

Sunaryo sensed the edge of firmness in Obaharok's voice. He turned to me. "Tell us, Miss Wyn, how many children do you plan on having?"

"That's enough!" Sjam said. She stood up and walked around the table toward the door. I got up and followed her. Sunaryo rose so quickly that his chair fell over backward.

"I'm sorry," he panted after us. "Sorry! Please, we must take your photographs here in the garden." He motioned at a man holding a camera to take some pictures. The photographer fiddled with his light meter and then snapped a few pictures of all of us together. Then Sunaryo asked for a picture to be taken of Obaharok and me alone. Obaharok posed for a couple of shots and then lost patience. He remarked that "Mama Wyn did not take so long when she took pictures." He signaled Wali and the two chiefs left to return to their villages.

Sjam and I returned to the Sumitros' house.

An hour later Sunaryo showed up. "We have been discussing, Miss Wyn, about the possibilities of your becoming an Indonesian citizen. Now that you are married, it would be the right thing to do."

"I hadn't considered it," I replied, somewhat astonished.

"I see," Sunaryo said. "Well, would you like the Indonesian government to register your marriage?"

"I hadn't considered that, either."

"Miss Wyn, may I be frank? I want you to help me. As you know, the Koteka Operation has not been exactly successful. The people are quite belligerent. Now, with your cooperation we could make an example of Obaharok. You're his wife and you can demand that he wear clothes. We'll have photographs taken of him here in Wamena and send them to Jakarta."

"I couldn't promise you such a thing, Mr. Sunaryo. I really don't know him very well."

"Could you dress Obaharok's wives in blouses, then? Bring them to Wamena?"

"I couldn't promise you that, either."

"I see." Sunaryo squinted his eyes. He rubbed his hand over his lips and spoke through his fingers. "The wives must come to Wamena and fingerprint a document stating they agreed to your marriage. Miss Wyn, you help me, I will help you. I want to be sure everything is all right. You are an American!" He smiled with insincere courtesy.

"What does my being an American have to do with it?"

"Well, we must be very careful. We've never had this problem before."

"What problem, Mr. Sunaryo?"

"The problem of a white woman marrying a black man!"

"Oh, for pity's sake! The 'marriage,' as you call it, was a traditional village ritual meant to create a new peace alliance in the north and south of the Valley. It was not, and is not, in any sense, like a Western marriage!"

"Yes, well, that brings up something else." Sunaryo took a deep breath to give himself time to think. "I personally have no objections, but my superiors disagree. Our government is good, but there are a few officials who can't think straight. The Bupati and the military commander have mixed Dani traditions with their own customs and they are confused."

"That's contradictory to your statement about their wanting to give a party to celebrate the event."

"Yes, well, they want to, but they are confused."

"What does that mean?"

Sunaryo's smile was deadly. "It means that they have forbidden the killing of pigs until your marriage is registered with the Indonesian government."

"How can that be?" I asked. "They're out of town, you learned of the continuing pig feast but an hour ago, and there's no communication to Jayapura!"

Sunaryo pretended not to hear me. He folded his arms across his chest, turned his head and gazed at the ceiling.

Sjam suddenly stood up. She walked around behind Sunaryo and looked at me. Fear registered in her eyes. She put her hand up as a signal to proceed with caution.

I looked from Sjam's face to Sunaryo's profile. The man was unstable and untrustworthy. He did not have the thought, reasoning or discipline of learned men. He wanted to exploit this "marriage" for his own benefit.

I could not predict the reaction of a people deprived of killing animals they believed were their own, nor could I predict what would happen to Sjam and me as long as Sunaryo was in charge of running the town.

An ugly thought passed through my mind—blackmail.

"Then I understand, Mr. Sunaryo, that you forbid the Dani to kill their pigs until I have registered the marriage under Indonesian law?"

"That is correct." Sunaryo smiled.

I wrote the letter requesting the registration. Sunaryo took it from my hand.

"Thank you, Miss Wyn. It will take about ten days to process."

He got up and left the room.

(14)

Sjam and I walked back to Wiyagoba in the afternoon. We told everyone we met on the footpath not to slaughter any pigs for a while. We asked the people to send the message to Obaharok.

The bird calls sounded through the jungle. They finally stopped around midnight. Wherever he was, Obaharok had received the news.

The following morning Obaharok sent me a message. Mi Hijo brought it. He'd finished his work in Wenebuborah. He was walking to Wiyagoba when someone stopped him.

"Ma, the police are on their way to Opagima," Mi Hijo panted. "They've already been to Pabuma. They're looking for Obaharok."

"Where is Obaharok?"

"He's waiting in Mapilakma. He wants you to go to Opagima and talk to the police. He'll meet you there."

"Tell him I'm on my way. Come on, Sjam, let's go."

The footpath was muddy and difficult to negotiate. Walek and Kelion joined Sjam and me on the outskirts of Wiyagoba. They helped steady us over the slippery path. It took more than an hour to reach Opagima. Looking through the *thop*, we saw that the courtyard was abandoned. The village had an aura of deadness about it.

"Where is everyone?" Sjam asked.

Kelion raised his head and cocked an ear to one side. "There are many people in the *hunila*," he said.

I went through the *thop*, walked to the kitchen door and looked in. Obaharok's face stared back at me. He was sitting against the far wall, facing the entrance. He made no sign he had seen me.

I entered the kitchen. Sjam, Walek and Kelion followed. There were nearly fifty chiefs sitting in the two ends of the *hunila*. They sat still, wide-eyed, fear-filled. Four policemen lay sprawled on the dirt floor in the center of the kitchen. Three rifles and a machine gun were lying in a neat row between their feet. To the side of the guns was a stack of banana skins. Flies were feasting on what the policemen had failed to eat.

Walek and Kelion seated themselves in the corner of the kitchen, and Sjam sat down in the doorway. I stood in the middle of the kitchen and faced the four policemen.

"*Selamat pagi*" ["Good morning"], I said.

The policemen sat up. They leaned against the center poles of the kitchen for support.

"What can we do to help you?" I went on.

"We have an order to arrest Obaharok if any pigs have been killed today," said the policeman with the name Samsone printed on his uniform pocket.

"Is this a joke?" I asked.

"It's no joke. Here's the order."

The letter was handed to Sjam. She read the paper, nodded her head and passed it back to the policeman.

"What is your name?" I asked the policeman nearest me.

"Aruam."

"Who sent you here, Mr. Aruam?"

"Sunaryo ordered out the patrol early this morning," he said.

"Have you asked Chief Obaharok if he's killed any pigs?" I asked.

"No, we didn't bring the interpreter." The policeman's voice fell off in the middle.

"Do you want Sjam and me to ask these chiefs if they've killed any pigs today?"

"Yes," Samsone said.

It took about ten minutes to ask the fifty chiefs in the kitchen if they had killed any pigs. One by one they muttered "*Nayit*" ("No").

"Are you satisfied?"

Aruam looked at his three companions. They agreed they were satisfied that no pigs had been killed.

"Now, I want to send a message to Mr. Sunaryo," I said. "I promised him there would be no pig feasting in the Valley until the arrangement we discussed had been carried out. It's insulting that he's sent you here to check on me. I want to ask Mr. Sunaryo to send me a letter of apology."

The policemen drew themselves up a bit.

"I'm not through. I'm wondering if any of you are familiar with the Universal Declaration of Human Rights? There're about thirty articles in the declaration, and since I've been here, I've seen about half of those articles violated. We're going to talk about one of those articles right now. It has to do with a man's right to *own* property and to do whatever he wants with it. And it's up to you, as policemen, to protect that right by rule of law. I would assume, by reason of your presence here, you fellas are fighting on the illegal side of the fence!"

The faces of the policemen showed emotions of suspicion and anger.

"*Selamat jalan*" ["Good day"], I said and walked out of the kitchen.

Sjam followed me. We climbed through the *thop* and started up the footpath toward Wiyagoba.

"Wyn, you spoke too strongly to them," Sjam said.

"Are you afraid?"

"I don't trust them. I don't trust Sunaryo."

"I'm sorry, Sjam. But somebody's got to do something. The worst they can do is to kick me out of the country."

(15)

Barnabas Nussy and Nicanor Himan arrived in Wiyagoba the following day to check on the pig killings. They were from the Department of Internal Affairs. Sunaryo had sent them.

Apparently Sunaryo would stop at nothing. As a counter-threat I wrote him a letter, which notified him of my intent to sue him in the courts of Jakarta in March 1973 for the violation of Article 16 of the Universal Declaration of Human Rights.* I sent copies of the letter to President Suharto, Brigadier General M. Hasan, Brigadier General Panggabean in Jakarta and to Police Chief Marpaung in Wamena. I also sent a copy of the letter to Sunaryo's superior, Brigadier General Acub Zainal, in Jayapura.

---

* Article 16 (2) "Marriage shall be entered into only with the free and full consent of the intending spouses."

(16)

It was a smart, snappy-looking little committee of Dani men who accompanied Sjam and me to Analaga. Walek walked beneath his new red umbrella, Mi Hijo wore Sjam's dark glasses, Ilmunkuluk had hung one of my cameras around his neck, Kaok had covered his greasy hair with a banana leaf and wore Sjam's red fur hat on top of it, and Niren carried a small dog under one arm and a walking stick under the other. Why, anyone coming across the group would have mistaken us for tourists!

We met Obaharok by the pool in the acacia grove on the other side of the Aikhe River. He was sitting by the edge of the water with two warriors. They were smoking cheroots.

There was a vague sorrow about Obaharok. We sat down on the soft bank and waited for him to say something.

"Mama, why can't we kill our pigs?"

"Mr. Sunaryo has insisted we register the *maweh*," I said. "It takes a little time. Sunaryo thinks it's best if no pigs are killed until after the registration."

Mi Hijo translated. Obaharok listened carefully and nodded from time to time. There was a problem with the word "registration." There was no Dani equivalent.

"What is '*registration*'?" Obaharok asked in a soft, controlled voice.

"Well, in this case, the *maweh* and our names have to be written on a piece of paper and put in a government book."

"Why? You have worn the *yokal*, I have killed the pigs. Why is this paper necessary?"

How does one explain a culture of paper and printing to a man who lives in a culture of *yokals* and pigs? And how does one explain blackmail to a man whose dimensions do not encompass it?

"Tell me," Obaharok said, "what is a *maweh* in Wamena like?"

"Well, the man and woman ask for a piece of paper. The paper gives them permission to get married. Then, uh, a sort of chief tells them they are married. The marriage is registered on another piece of paper. Something like that."

"How many pigs does the man give for the woman?"

"He doesn't give any pigs."

"He doesn't pay anything for the woman? She's *free*?"

"Yes."

Obaharok's appraisal was instantaneous. "Something free is usually not very valuable," he said.

We left the men by the pool and walked on to Analaga. Kolo was enthralled at the sight of us. Just before supper, he presented his shovel to Walek, who was thrilled to have the spade. Kolo was relieved to get rid of it; he abhorred the whole idea of shoveling. Kolo could never understand the gain in moving dirt from one place to another.

"Your hair ith very thort," Walek said.

"The military cut it off," Kolo said, rubbing the palms of his hands over his head. "They cut the hair of all the chiefs in Analaga. And yours? You wear a net!"

"Polith burned it off," Walek said, bowing his head.

Kolo reached over and gently patted Walek on the forearm. "The military threw some of my men in the river not long ago," he whispered. "Forced them to take a bath. Then they put short pants on them. I have forbidden my people to sell their vegetables to the people in Wamena for a while. When they leave us alone, we'll sell again."

I looked at Sjam. "I have a surprise!" she said, changing the subject. "Mrs. Sumitro gave me some flour. I'm going to make some doughnuts!"

"*Doughnuts* in the jungle?" I could hardly remember what they looked like. "Don't you need an egg?" I'd nearly forgotten what an egg looked like, too.

"Going to try without eggs," she said. "Can't have everything."

Everyone pitched in and helped. The men sifted the flour through a bamboo screen. Sjam made the dough and formed the balls from the mixture. I dropped the spongy masses into a pot of hot cooking oil. By midnight the last doughnut had sizzled itself brown in the grease. We had made nearly two hundred doughnuts in four hours.

Sjam passed out equal portions to everyone. The absence of yeast and eggs left the doughnuts without much flavor or shape, but they were delicious. There were about fifty left on the wooden plank. The conversation had stopped, for everyone was thinking about stealing them. The doughnuts brought out the very worst in all of us; each person devised his own little plan for larceny. Before morning, the fifty doughnuts had disappeared. And one of us, perhaps the one who should have shown the most control, hid a whole handful in bed and ate them in darkness. We knew we had to stop making doughnuts in the jungle. They were making thieves of us all.

(17)

"Ma, do you think my beard is very thick?" Mi Hijo brushed his chin whiskers with his fingertips to fluff them up a bit.

"I think it's coming along—why?"

Mi Hijo sat on the floor. He bent forward and touched the ashes in the fireplace with his finger. He smoothed them out. Then he drew little designs in the white dust. "Well, if my beard is thick enough, then I should be thinking about girls," he said shyly.

Mi Hijo had matured markedly over the few months he had been with us. His beard had filled in enough so that his face looked dark, up close.

"Well, it might be a good idea to start thinking about girls," I said.

Mi Hijo smiled and his big white teeth flashed brightly. "Ma, could you give me some woman-medicine? I mean, I think I may need some help. This is new to me."

I wrapped a quinine tablet in tin foil and held it out to him. I tried to give the occasion a professorial air. Mi Hijo was delighted. He spent the rest of the day smiling. And he was still smiling when we left for Wiyagoba the following morning.

Kolo and Abinyai went with us. We passed Pabuma around noon and heard singing in the village. The people were celebrating the *maweh*. We entered the village. No pigs had been killed.

There were two policemen walking on the footpath near Elima. They were dressed in civilian clothes but rifles were slung over their shoulders. One of the policemen told us that Police Chief Marpaung had returned from Jayapura and was back at work in Wamena.

The following day Sjam and I left for Wamena. I wanted to pick up my passport from Mr. Marpaung. Mi Hijo went with us. It was a good day for walking: the sun was warm, and the path was dry and fast.

We arrived in Wamena about noon. Mr. Marpaung greeted us in the garden in front of his house. Policeman Samsone poked his head out through the front door. When he saw us, he withdrew it and disappeared into the interior of the house.

Sjam and I went into the living room with Mr. Marpaung. Samsone was nowhere in sight.

"Were you able to pick up my passport?" I asked Mr. Marpaung.

"Passport?"

"Didn't you receive the cable Sjam sent to Jayapura?"

"No, no cable."

Mr. Marpaung's face was convincing. I looked at Sjam. Her face was blank, expressionless.

"Well, we'll fly to Jayapura as soon as we can get a plane out," I said.

"Tell me, Miss Sargent, about this letter you have written to Mr. Sunaryo."

I told Mr. Marpaung that I thought things had gotten out of hand during his absence from Wamena. I recounted Sunaryo's questions and demands. I asked Mr. Marpaung for his opinion.

"Oh, I think he was overacting," he laughed. "Sunaryo is in Jayapura right now. He goes on to Biak from there."

"Did he have the authority to dispatch a police patrol to arrest Obaharok if he'd killed his own pigs?"

"I don't know anything about that," Marpaung said.

He snapped his fingers. The sharp report brought Samsone through the kitchen door into the living room. He avoided looking at Sjam and me. He stood at attention, his boot heels held tightly together. He appeared as though he weren't breathing. His face had the whiteness of a ghost.

Marpaung threw his head back. He asked Samsone for the dispatch order. Samsone, who had the paper in his pocket, took it out, unfolded it and handed it to Mr. Marpaung.

"Well, as you can see, there's nothing in this order to indicate that Obaharok was to be arrested for anything! It states 'routine patrol,' that's all."

Mr. Marpaung handed the dispatch to Sjam. She read the paper, looked at the back of it and passed it to me. Her face registered no emotion, but her eyes were deep and penetrating. I read the dispatch. There was a prickly chill moving up my spine. I placed the paper on the table between us.

"Fine," I said.

Sjam let out a nearly inaudible sigh of relief. "We have to be going," she said, "if we want to get lined up for a plane to Jayapura."

"Good luck!" Marpaung said from his front door.

When we were out of sight of Marpaung's house I turned to Sjam.

"What do you think?" I asked.

"It's a fake. That document is not the same paper Samsone and those other three policemen brought to Opagima."

"You mean, Marpaung would actually *change* official government documents?"

"Why not, if changing them protects his job. Look, Wyn— when Marpaung got back from Jayapura, he found your letter threatening to sue Sunaryo. He started asking questions and it all came out. When Marpaung learned that Sunaryo had used *policemen* to enforce his illegal demand, Marpaung didn't want any part of it. In order to protect his policemen, his police post and his own job, Marpaung destroyed that document I saw in Opagima and he's replaced it with another."

(18)

We told Mi Hijo we were going to a place called Jayapura and that we hoped to return within the week.

Sjam and I stayed at the Sumitros' while we waited for the Merpati plane to arrive. After waiting for four days, we finally gave up on Merpati. Instead, we walked to the airstrip, where the missionary planes were flying regularly. Although it was expensive, we chartered a plane to Jayapura.

After checking into the Hotel Pautan, we walked across the street to the immigration office. Sjam spoke to the clerk at the front desk, who said that the immigration officer was eating lunch. Meanwhile we should have our papers checked at the police station. He handed me my passport and visa. We walked the several blocks to the station, where the police checked us into Jayapura and reminded us to check out when we left the city.

When we returned to Immigration, the officer was waiting for us. He asked Sjam into his office. I sat in the lobby of the building and waited. When Sjam came out she said, "It's all fixed. The immigration officer wrote 'Visa in arrangement' on the back of your papers. Let's go eat. I'm starved."

After lunch we shopped. We bought candy, salt, flashlights and a harmonica. We bought seeds we were sure would grow, and some we were uncertain about. We bought spades, knives, fishing lines, notebooks, pencils, sunglasses, umbrellas, clothing for children. We bought aspirins, rubbing alcohol and sulfa powder. And we had as much fun buying these things as we did in giving them away later.

We bought so many things that we also had to buy suitcases and crates to put them in. And then we worried about how to get the crates and cases to Wamena. As it turned out, they were flown in two shipments. But they did arrive.

With passport in hand, Sjam and I left Jayapura feeling fortunate we hadn't run into Sunaryo. We hadn't asked for his whereabouts.

We chartered the same missionary plane to fly us back to Wamena. The pilot was interested to learn that we were the proprietors of the grass shacks in the Valley. When we entered the pass into the valley, we flew low and hunted for them. Sjam thought she could see Wiyagoba. The pilot banked left and we turned toward the mountain. We circled again, swooped down and the village came into view. The pilot banked and followed the mountain ridge, flying southward to Analaga. We could see some of the natives in the fields. They'd stopped work and were looking up at us. I wanted to yell or drop a note to tell them it was us. As we passed Opagima we noticed a new house going up in Wali's compound. When we reached Analaga we were flying very low. We saw Old Dialec running around the courtyard, shaking his fist at the airplanes. The noise had upset his pigs.

In Wamena we thanked the pilot for much more than we'd paid for. We left our extra baggage at the airfield and walked to Mr. Marpaung's house.

Mr. Marpaung asked to see my visa papers. He studied them at some length. "Oh! I forgot to congratulate you on your marriage!" he laughed, returning the papers to me. "And thank you for the pork! Tell Obaharok to drop in and see me. No hurry, just drop in."

We told Mr. Marpaung we planned to return to Wiyagoba in the afternoon.

An hour later a hundred Dani poured into the Sumitros' backyard. Kolo, Obaharok, Kelion and Walek had sent their men to give us whatever help we needed. Mi Hijo was among them.

"Mi Hijo! How did you know we were in Wamena?"

"No airplane ever drove around like that before!"

(19)

The people in Wiyagoba were still singing. Sjam and I had forgotten how loud and monotonous it could be at times.

There was a knock on the kitchen door. When Sjam opened the door, a man walked in whom we didn't recognize. His face was swollen. There was dried blood on his lips, and fresh blood still trickled from his nostrils.

Sike followed the man into the kitchen. They sat down by the fire.

"It's Inyomosi," Sike whispered.

I looked a little closer. Inyomosi's nose was broken. His lower teeth were loose and his gums were bleeding. His hair was dry. There was no grease on his body. Little blisters had formed on his shoulders.

"What happened?"

"The police beat me," Inyomosi said. His voice was just above a whisper; it was painful for him to talk. A native named Wamerago, he said, had stolen two *nokens* full of sweet potatoes from his garden. He notified Sike, and together they went to the Jiwika police post to register a complaint against Wamerago. The policeman, whom I shall call Basri, listened to the complaint. Basri asked Wamerago to pay a fine of "a few sweet potatoes" to Inyomosi, who refused the sweet potatoes. (According to Dani justice, the theft could be righted only with the payment of one small pig.) Outraged at the refusal, Basri picked up a board and hit Inyomosi in the face. The blow broke his nose. Basri threw the board down. He hit Inyomosi again, this time across the mouth with his hand. Inyomosi's lip split open and bloodied Basri's hand. Basri washed his hands in a bucket of water. He added scalding water to the bucket and poured it over Inyomosi's head. Then he arrested Inyomosi and put him in jail.

Sike left the post to fetch Asuan. Together the two chiefs confronted Basri. Asuan said, "Inyomosi is my brother. I have medicine for him. Set him free!" Basri released Inyomosi after warning him to say nothing about the incident to the Wamena police.

I treated Inyomosi's wounds and asked him to return to Wiyagoba in the morning. I wanted to photograph him.

(20)

"Ma," Mi Hijo said, "Obaharok wants to know if you've seen the new *pilai* in Opagima?"

"Sjam and I saw a new house going up the day we came in on the airplane. Why?"

"Well, the *pilai* is for us. Obaharok wants to know if it's good enough, so far."

"A *pilai*—a warrior's house? Let's go see it!"

Sjam, Mi Hijo and I tried to outrun each other to Opagima. We were out of breath when we reached the village.

The courtyard was filled with people. All of them were busy. Women were bringing in huge bundles of grass. The children helped the women. Men from every part of the Valley were working on the actual construction on the house. The wall planks were up and the sleeping floor had been installed. It was almost finished.

Wali's *pilai* faced the *thop* of the village. The new *pilai* faced the entrance of Wali's house.

The ground had been cleared with digging sticks. A large circle, fifteen feet in diameter, had been laid out on the ground with vines, and a trench had been dug around the circle. Planks, lashed together with rattan, had been placed vertically in the trench. When the structure was strong enough, a cane ceiling was anchored on top of the planks. The doorway already had a sill and a frame around it. There were four posts centered around the fireplace.

We arrived as the men were placing young saplings at spaced intervals around the planks. We watched them bend the long poles and tie them together at the top to form the dome-shaped roof. When they were finished, the roof would be thatched with long grass. The grasses would be laid on and pounded into place from the bottom up. Then the men would dig a fireplace and plaster the hearth with wet clay. The final work would be the bringing of clean, sweet grass to carpet the two-storied abode.

It was a fine house. The entrance was high, and there was lots of room to sit up straight inside it. We wanted Obaharok

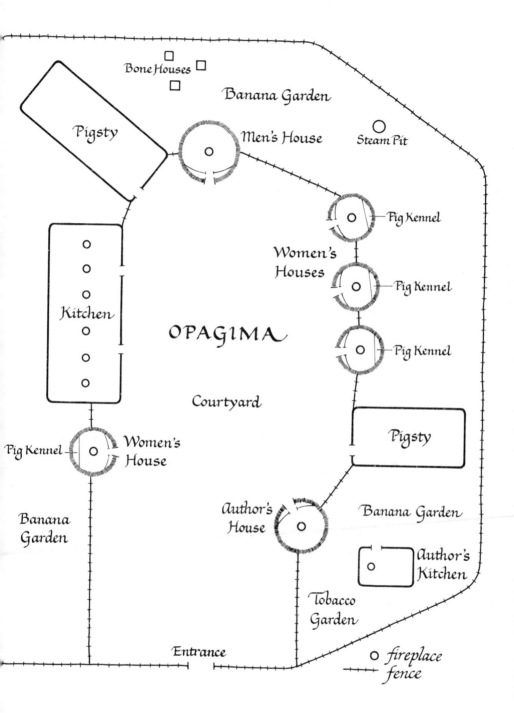

Bone Houses

Banana Garden

Pigsty

Men's House

Steam Pit

Pig Kennel

Women's
Houses

Pig Kennel

Kitchen

OPAGIMA

Pig Kennel

Courtyard

Pigsty

Pig Kennel — Women's
House

Banana Garden

Banana
Garden

Author's
House

Author's
Kitchen

Tobacco
Garden

Entrance

○ fireplace
╀┼┼ fence

to know we were delighted with the new house. We decided
to *buy* the house. We bought it with salt, umbrellas, flashlights
and rupiahs .

(21)

There are geographical parts in the world that offer four
varieties of malaria to the inhabitants. I had reason to suspect,
in Borneo, that two different kinds of malaria-carrying mosquitoes had gone to work on me. Once you've had malaria, you
may count on its returning unless it's *Plasmodium falciparum*
malaria, in which case you stand a good chance to kill the
disease if it doesn't kill you first.

Sjam and I were in Wiyagoba, ready to walk to Analaga,
when the pains took hold of my shoulders. I had just enough
time to grab the chloroquine and place the tablets in Sjam's
trusty hand before I went under.

It's difficult to describe the shaking chills, with teeth rattling,
muscle spasms and pulling pain, the hot and cold that sweep
through your body prior to arriving at the state of semicon-
sciousness that usually comes after such an attack. You have to
experience it yourself to fully appreciate the drama of the event
and the destruction to the body it leaves behind.

With drugs and the passing of time, the fever is discouraged
and you're liberated from bed, only to find that there's no
strength in your body to carry you through a day. Apart from
the debilitation, something called the "malaria headache" con-
tinues for days. There's no relief from it, not even when you're
sleeping.

On the second day of sickness, Kelion and Walek came plowing into the kitchen, mad as hornets. I raised an interested ear
off my pillow.

"Sister," Kelion began, his lips set in a firm line, "do you
remember giving Walek and me money to buy a big boar?"

"Vividly."

Walek stood with his hands on his hips, bottom lip stuck out and his eyes squinting darkly. "The polithman took our money!" he spat out.

"We were in Mapilakma," Kelion said, "and that policeman Basri sold us a pig he didn't have! We gave him all the money [about eighty dollars] and he promised to deliver the boar the next day."

"He thaid the pig had teeth like thith," Walek chimed in. He placed his index fingers on his cheeks so that the tips reached his temples. Kelion improved on the description of the pig. He presented an animal that was beautifully irresistible, magically exciting and glamorous beyond words. It was a description that had probably been exaggerated by Kelion's hope.

"And you gave Basri all the money you had without even seeing this pig?"

"Nen, because he promised to give it to us the next day," Kelion whined.

"When did all this happen?" I asked.

Kelion made a fist. Five days ago.

"What have you done since?"

"Every day I've gone to the police post in Jiwika. Basri refuses to see me," Kelion said. "That man is a crook, Sister! He stole our money. He's a thief!"

"Well, coming from you, Kelion, I'd say that was expert testimony. What do you want me to do?"

"Write uth a letter," Walek begged.

I wrote the letter. Kelion signed it with his fingerprint. The letter asked for the delivery of a large pig, as promised, or the return of the money. I sent a copy of the letter to Mr. Marpaung in Wamena.

Kelion took the letter to Jiwika. In the evening he returned with a letter signed by Basri and addressed, surprisingly enough, to Sjam:

Miss Sjam:

Herewith I, Basri, greatly apologize for I did not cheat Kelion and Walek but, as you know, that I'm not like the other men who wear *holim* who only eat and sleep, but I am a man who is responsible for the law, police, who is posted in Jiwika in order to keep peace and security for the people here.

Therefore, I apologize for the past days, until today, I'm still busy to settle the cases of the people here and therefore I got no time to pay the pig to both brothers, stated above and until I receive the letter from Miss Sjam then I felt that you're forcing me to pay it. But you did not think that I'm busy or not, but in order not to disappoint you and especially those who give the money to me, so right now I give to Kelion one pig and hoping that tomorrow Walek will come to take his part. I don't want to deliver it to anyone else except that person to take it. To close this letter I beg you to forgive me again because of the delay of the payment.

"He tried to give me a *baby* pig," wailed Kelion.

(22)

Sjam didn't have time to answer Basri's letter right away. There was too much going on. Obaharok began killing pigs, again, in Opagima.

Sjam, Mi Hijo and I arrived in Opagima about the same time that two policemen showed up. One of the men had a piece of paper in his hand. He looked around for someone to give it to.

"Tell him to bring it here," I whispered to Sjam. My heart felt as though it had stopped beating.

The letter was a police order for the natives to build bridges and to repair the roads around Wamena.

"Does the government pay these people for their road work?" I asked.

"No. It's their duty to keep the roads and bridges in good condition," said Policeman Karl Huriager.

"Why? They don't use them."

The policemen left. The following day another patrol arrived. They had an order for the people to cut their trees and transport the timber to Wamena. The wood was to be used in the new jailhouse.

"Does the government pay these people for their work? Even for the lumber?" I asked.

"No, it's their duty to give the lumber because it's their jail," said Policeman Mapini.

I didn't pursue the conversation. We were ahead. So far no one had arrested Obaharok for killing his pigs.

Sjam finally got around to answering Basri's letter:

DEAR MR. BASRI:

Thank you for your letter. It is my understanding that on January 21, 1973, 31,000 rupiahs were given to you by Walek and Kelion for the purchase of one large pig. Kelion tells me that you stated to him of your intent to deliver a small pig to those concerned. Under the circumstances, Walek and Kelion hereby demand the return of their money upon receipt of this letter.

She sent a copy of the letter to Marpaung.

Kelion took the letter to Jiwika, but Basri had left Jiwika for Wamena. The following day Kelion walked to Wamena. When Basri saw Kelion sauntering down the road, he ran inside his house, locked the door and pulled down the blinds. Kelion banged on the door and tried to peek through the shaded windows. Then Kelion slipped the letter beneath the door and sat down on the porch.

At noon Basri still hadn't come out of his house. Kelion began to get hungry. Abinyai and a few Dani from Analaga were passing through town and saw Kelion sitting on Basri's front porch. They had sweet potatoes with them. Kelion talked Abinyai out of his lunch.

In the afternoon Kelion stretched out on the porch and went to sleep. He began to snore. Basri poked his head out, saw Kelion fast asleep, stepped over him and disappeared into the Wamena crowd.

It was nearly dark when Kelion awoke and left Wamena.

"Don't worry, Kelion. I'll talk with Mr. Marpaung."

It was an effort to cheer Kelion. But I felt a false confidence in what I'd said.

(23)

The events which ensued from the *maweh* ran ocean-deep. They began a turn in history. Notoriously famous enemy chiefs from far away places walked unexpectedly into the Valley to feast with Obaharok.

Sjam and I did not meet all of the visiting chiefs, but we met many. Silo was among them. Chief Silo was a mighty man and the vicious ruler of a tribe who had venomously fought Obaharok for years. In the wake of the continuing *maweh*, Silo trudged for two days and two nights to pledge peace to a man he had formerly fought in war.

Another chief of notable reputation arrived by walking through a narrow mountain pass for five days. His name was Sinuk. He was the cannibal chief from Jagarekabaga.

We met Chief Asualeak from Hugusilimo. He came with two of his warriors. Walek was so thrilled to see the strangers that he put them up in his own *pilai*. That was after Walek had studied the scar on Asualeak's thigh. It was a scar caused by one of Walek's arrows shot in an old war.

(24)

A malaria headache causes one's vision to become myopic at times. I thought the two men walking into the kitchen were Walek and Kelion. But the man accompanying Kelion was Chief Kusupia from Pumo.

Kusupia was splendidly attired. His white *walimo* was admirable. There were fluffy white dog tails around his upper arms. A beautiful feathered *cabanee* encircled his elaborately greased hair. The man had presence about him.

"I guard many of Obaharok's *wesas*," Kusupia said as a point of reference.

Mi Hijo gave the men some coffee to drink. The Dani loved coffee, especially if it was loaded with sugar.

Kusupia unfolded his story. "A long time ago my wife, Haliale, performed an abortion on herself. It made me very angry. I hit her on the leg with a fistful of arrows. She left me. Later she married Mukoko, a man from a neighboring village. Mukoko mistreated her, maybe worse than I did. She returned to me. Mukoko wanted payment for Haliale. I gave him one large pig in settlement. The police have called me to report the affair to them. I want you to write a letter explaining that everything has already been settled."

"Why don't you go to the police and tell them?"

"They'll beat me," Kusupia said. There was real fear in his eyes.

I'd begun to feel a bit uncomfortable about the number of letters I'd written to the government people protesting and complaining. The officials needed a vacation from me and my letter writing.

"They won't beat you," I said. "There's no reason for such a thing."

"If it's safe, I'll go," Kusupia said.

"Fine. Let me know how it comes out."

Kelion and Kusupia left.

Sjam, Mi Hijo and I closed up the kitchen. We wanted to spend the night in the new *pilai* in Opagima. And the next day we'd go on to Analaga to see Kolo and our friends in the south.

When we arrived in Opagima we found Chief Wali clenching his fists. He was frustrated. He had a letter he couldn't read and there was no one around to help him. Sjam took the letter. It was from the schoolteacher Tatoko. The letter ordered Wali to send children to the school to build a new fence.

Mi Hijo built a fire to smoke out the insects in the new

pilai. The wood was damp and the smoke got out of control. Sjam and I fled the house with teary eyes while Mi Hijo battled with the stinging cloud inside.

We were in the courtyard when a Dani named Huseroba was lifted through the *thop* of the village and carried into Wali's *pilai.* Huseroba's body was coursed with black bruises, blood and burns. His left leg was hugely swollen. Mi Hijo brought the medical kit. Wali motioned us into the *pilai.*

"What happened?"

Mi Hijo translated. There had been a fistfight between Huseroba and Wamerago. Whatever the men were fighting over resulted in a loss to Wamerago, who went to the police and filed a complaint against Huseroba. Huseroba was fined a pig. When he offered it to Wamerago, the animal was refused. The attending policeman turned on Huseroba, told him the pig was too small and began to beat him. He picked up a steel bar and hit Huseroba across the thigh. The blow felled Huseroba and he lost consciousness. The policeman took a hot coal from the fire, placed it between Huseroba's buttocks and left the police post.

"What was the policeman's name?"

"Basri."

Outside the *thop* came the wailing of women. Their cries were pitiful. One woman, her body covered with red clay, staggered into the courtyard leaning on the shoulder of another and went into the kitchen.

Wali and Mi Hijo left the *pilai* to console the women. Sjam and I stepped outside.

"Ma," Mi Hijo said from the kitchen door, "that woman is Kusupia's wife, Haliale. She's been raped."

"Who raped her?"

"Basri."

I grabbed the medical kit and ducked into the kitchen, where Haliale was babbling hysterically to Mi Hijo.

"She says that Basri got Kusupia, beat him and stole his pigs," Mi Hijo said.

I looked at Sjam. It seemed like a nightmare.

"Mi Hijo, get a message to Obaharok. Tell him to come to Opagima. Tell him it's urgent."

Mi Hijo left the compound. Within a few minutes we heard the bird calls echoing through the Valley. I asked Wali to leave the kitchen while I examined Haliale. The attack had been vicious.

Sjam and I walked back to Wali's *pilai*. We improvised a splint for Huseroba's broken leg. Opagima was taking on the personality of a camp for disasters.

Sjam and I had our own kitchen in Opagima. It was built directly behind our *pilai* and surrounded by a fence. The kitchen was divided into two parts; one for cooking and the other for the storage of supplies. We crawled into the store-room, where we could be alone. It was dark in there but I could see Sjam very well. When one sees horror, it is reflected in the eyes. There were deep wells of it in Sjam's eyes.

We listened to the bird calls. I wondered where Obaharok was and how long it would take for him to reach Opagima.

"What are you going to do, Wyn?" Sjam whispered.

"Build a case against Basri," I said. "I want Obaharok to use his influence to get Kelion, Walek, Inyomosi, Huseroba and Kusupia to testify in Wamena. What's the worst I stand to lose?"

"Deportment."

I didn't really believe it. Sjam didn't either. Both of us were convinced that justice prevailed somewhere.

Mi Hijo came into the kitchen. His eyes were very sad. "The message has been sent, Ma," he said.

It was about seven o'clock in the evening when we heard sobs. Sjam and I were sitting in our *pilai*. Mi Hijo stuck his head through the entrance.

"Ma, it's Kusupia," he whispered.

Kusupia's daughter helped him in. He struggled painfully to get through the doorway of the *pilai*. He pulled himself along on his elbows, crawling across the grass. He sat up near the fire. The light flashed over his face and body. Kusupia had been badly beaten and tortured. His body was covered with clay as a sign of shame and humiliation. His nose was broken and his lip battered and torn. His chest and back had been burned in ribbonlike patterns. Kusupia wrapped his arms around his stomach to cover the pain that lived there. He began to cry in a funeral chant. Sjam wept. I felt hot tears flush up behind my eyes. I took Kusupia in my arms and rocked him as a mother would a child.

Haliale came in. Mi Hijo asked her for the details. She said three policemen, one of them Basri, were waiting for Kusupia when he arrived in his village of Pumo this morning. Basri asked Kusupia where he had been. Kusupia said he'd been talking to the "white woman chief." The two policemen held Kusupia at gunpoint while Basri tied his hands behind his back. And then the brutal, torturous beatings began. Basri whipped, kicked and beat the man into senselessness. He went into Kusupia's *pilai*, took a hot coal from the fire, returned and spread Kusupia's buttocks. He placed the coal on his anus. Basri loaded his rifle, held the barrel alongside Kusupia's head and fired twice. The explosion left Kusupia deaf and unconscious. Basri turned his gun on the sacred *kanake* stones in Kusupia's *pilai* and destroyed them with bullets. Then he helped himself to the tobacco, *holims* and shell necklaces he found there.

Outside, Basri rounded up eight large pigs and herded them out of the village. The other two policemen tended the pigs while Basri returned to Kusupia's *pilai*. He deposited two bullets on the grass near the entrance and went out into the courtyard. He stepped over Kusupia's nearly lifeless body. Dragging Haliale and her daughter from their *abiai*, he told the daughter there were two bullets in the *pilai* which would be used to kill Kusupia if he did not have two more pigs to give him when he returned. Basri tied Haliale's hands behind her back and prodded her out of the village with the barrel of his rifle.

Somewhere on the footpath between Pumo and Jiwika, Basri raped Haliale. Having used her, he left her in the ditch where she had fallen.

"Where is Basri now?" I asked.

"We think he's in Tumagonem. The stolen pigs are there," Mi Hijo said.

Kusupia handed something to Mi Hijo, who turned the objects over in his hand and said, "These are the bullets Basri left in Kusupia's *pilai*." Mi Hijo dropped the shells in my hand. They were about three inches long, and on the bottom of one was stamped "WRA 303 BRITISH," on the other, "K50-7."

Sjam stared with unbelieving eyes at the bullets.

I looked at the man whom I had told the police would not hurt, the man who had been robbed and beaten because he had talked to me, the man who came to the *pilai* in Opagima now, despite the brutal treatment he had suffered as a result of my advice. It felt as if a great iron hand had grasped and twisted my heart. I was seized by an overwhelming desire to do something to restore dignity to a people meant to live as the human beings they are.

Sjam read my thoughts. "When do you want to go to Wamena?" she asked.

"After I talk with Obaharok."

"Mama Wyn," Kusupia said through torn lips, "Basri swears he's going to kill you. His gun shoots very far."

Wali, who had been sitting in the doorway, said, "Mi Hijo, run up to Wiyagoba and get Kelion and Walek. Ask Waikimo to go to Punycul and get Sike, Inyomosi and Yoli over here. The men can sleep in my *pilai*. Don't worry, we'll protect you."

I had confidence in the men. But bows and arrows were useless against a madman with a gun.

(25)

Obaharok arrived in Opagima at six o'clock in the morning. He looked very tired.

"Yes," he said, "the men will go with you to Wamena. Someone will have to carry Huseroba. Haliale will go, but she won't testify. She's too ashamed. Basri is in Tumagonem. You have to pass by the village on your way to Wamena. Be careful."

We left Opagima an hour later. Kelion, Walek and Inyomosi took turns carrying Huseroba. Kusupia was supported by his wife and daughter. In the distance we saw smoke rising from the kitchen in Tumagonem. I wondered about the safety of Old Pum and Asuan. We worried about our own safety, too. We made excellent targets for a long-range rifle as we moved slowly across the horizon.

We arrived in Wamena about noon. Mr. Marpaung was in Jayapura, again. The attendant at the police post told us that Mr. Dharta, the second man in command, was "in conference." We asked directions to Policeman Marsatyo's house.

When we reached the house, Marsatyo was still in bed. We sat down on the front porch and waited. A few minutes passed. A remarkably well dressed young man walked up to us.

"My name is August Parengkuan. Here's my card. I'm a reporter from *Kompas* newspaper in Jakarta. You're Wyn Sargent, aren't you? I've traveled over thirty-five hundred miles to get an interview with you concerning your marriage."

"*That* news has reached Jakarta?" I was astonished.

"Well, yes," he said, studying the wounded Dani men sitting on the porch. "What's happened to them?"

Mr. Marsatyo came to the front door. "Come on in," he said, which did not mean he was inviting *everyone* into his house.

Sjam and I reported the complaints against Basri. I gave Mr. Marsatyo the two bullets Basri had left in Kusupia's *pilai*.

Mr. Marsatyo listened with apparent interest. When we were finished, he stepped outside on the porch. He looked each man over, shook his head from side to side and clicked his tongue against his cheek. August Parengkuan jumped up, readied his camera and shot a series of pictures of the men, Marsatyo, Sjam and me.

At one-thirty Mr. Marsatyo excused himself. He said he wanted to make a report of what he had been told to Mr. Dharta. Thirty minutes later he returned and told us we could go back to the villages.

"I'd like to talk to Mr. Dharta myself," I said. "And he should see these men!"

"Very well, come along," Marsatyo said.

August Parengkuan followed us.

At the police post Sjam and I met Mr. Dharta. We were taken into his office, where we made formal charges against Basri. We put down the various complaints on paper, dated and signed them. Dharta left the office, looked in the direction of the wounded Dani and ordered the police attendant to lock them up in the jailhouse.

I couldn't believe it!

"We want to give them medical treatment," Dharta said, smiling, "and listen to more of their stories."

"How long do they have to stay there?" I asked.

"Well, this afternoon is a Moslem holiday. Then comes the weekend. I think Monday or Tuesday they can go home."

I looked at Sjam. She had paled. I felt nausea in the pit of my stomach. I wondered if the miracle of simple justice was ever going to happen.

"Now, what else can I do for you, Miss Sargent?" Dharta asked.

"Mr. Dharta," I said, "would you please pick up Basri before he kills somebody? And give me a police escort back to the villages."

Dharta ordered out a police patrol to accompany us. We waited nearly an hour before two policemen showed up.

August Parengkuan went with us. We met Basri on the outskirts of Pikke. Sjam and I hung back. We watched the patrol shake Basri's hand. They jokingly told him they'd been sent to advise him he was needed at the Wamena post. Basri was herding eight of the pigs he had stolen. They were very large pigs, worth about eight hundred dollars.

"I'll take those pigs," I said. "They belong to Kusupia."

"No," said one of the policemen in the patrol. "They can go on to Wamena. They'll be taken care of there."

Wali and Obaharok met us at the *thop* when we reached Opagima. They were dark with despair.

"Kadir was here," Obaharok said. "He threatened Wali and

me with a gun. He wanted to know what right I had to marry a white woman. I felt very ashamed. He wanted to know where you were. I told him you were in Wamena. He said he would return this evening."

"Who is Kadir?" I asked.

"He's a policeman."

In the courtyard the people were gathering for medicine. Mi Hijo carried out the medical bag. We were working on the last patient when an explosion blasted through the air.

"That was a rifle shot!" I gasped.

Another shot rang out. I dropped the bottle of sulfa powder and ran for the *pilai*. Mi Hijo followed. Sjam and August Parengkuan were already inside. I looked through the doorway of Wali's *pilai*. I could see Obaharok sitting in the entrance; he motioned with his hand for us to stay inside the house.

The jungle was silent. The birds had stopped singing. There was no movement of any kind. We sat huddled in the *pilai*, waiting.

"Kadir," Mi Hijo whispered, "Kadir has returned."

"Is the *thop* closed?" I asked.

Mi Hijo shook his head. Sjam was breathing lightly through her mouth in very fast, shallow breaths. I glanced at August Parengkuan; he was looking down at his hands.

A half-hour later Sike came into the *pilai*.

"That was Kadir," he said. "He stood outside and shot twice through the *thop* of the village. There was another policeman with him, Sitmoran. They're gone now."

I wrote Mr. Marsatyo a letter. I told him Kadir fired his gun at Opagima village, and asked him to question Kadir as to his intent. August Parengkuan promised to deliver the letter to Marsatyo in the morning. He had more news and pictures than he'd ever bargained for. He was also a witness to the Dani's struggle to gain recourse.

August Parengkuan slept in our kitchen in Opagima that night. The following morning, before anyone else got up, he was gone. His stories were never published, and as far as I know, no one seems to know of his whereabouts.

Sometime during the night, Kelion escaped from the Wamena jail. He hid in the jungle grass near Pikke until dawn. Then he ran all the way to Opagima.

"They don't give you anything to eat!" he said.

"How do you know? You didn't stay long enough to find out."

"If they don't give you supper, you're not going to get breakfast!" he reasoned.

"Did they give the others medicine?"

"*Nayit!*"

A Dani named Lebarek came into Opagima about noon. He said Basri had beaten him in Ikenkuka village more than a week before. Basri had taken seven of his pigs. I wrote Mr. Dharta a letter stating the names, the date and the place of the event.

Sike arrived while I was writing the letter. He had a police order in his hand which instructed him to transport timber from the Aikhe River to the Wamena police post immediately. Sike said that Kadir and Sitmoran were on their way to Opagima. Both of them had rifles.

Sjam and I went with Kelion to Wiyagoba; it seemed safer there. Maybe Kadir and Sitmoran didn't know where Wiyagoba was located. Sike and Asuan came in later that night to guard the village.

The following morning Mi Hijo told us the men were still in jail. They had had no food and no medicine. Asuan rounded up a team of women to take sweet potatoes to them. The women could poke the potatoes through the fence to the men at night.

The following day Sjam and I returned to Opagima. I wanted to know if Kadir and Sitmoran had been in the village and if they had hurt any of the natives. There was a chance, too, that reason had returned to the men. If they were in Opagima, perhaps I could talk to them.

When we arrived the *thop* was boarded closed. The village was deserted.

Mi Hijo opened the *thop*. Sjam and I went into the kitchen and roasted sweet potatoes for lunch. After we'd eaten, Mi Hijo opened our *pilai*. We went inside to wait for someone to show up.

It was a strange day, the kind that had a quality of lifelessness about it. Gray clouds hung in the sky. They covered the sun and they wouldn't go away.

At sunset the people began to return to Opagima. The men, women and children crawled in through the narrow entrance of the house to sit with us. We shared our food but no one ate very much; in fact, none of us had any appetite.

It was dark when Walek and Kelion walked into Opagima. Walek had also broken out of jail. He'd made a hole in the side of the jailhouse and crawled through it. When he was outside, he tore down just enough fence to let himself out, then he walked away. Apparently no one noticed him, which was just as well. If anyone had tried to stop him, he probably would have killed them.

There was a bird call outside the village. It sounded quite near. Mi Hijo cocked his ear and exchanged glances with Wali. They left the *pilai* together. When they returned, Mi Hijo had two letters in his hand. They had been given to him by a Dani man from a neighboring village. The letters were addressed to me.

Mi Hijo placed the letters in my hand, face down. There was a blue envelope and a white one. I turned them over and read the return address. One letter was from the Bupati's office in Wamena, the other from the immigration office in Jayapura.

"Let's go to the kitchen, Sjam. We can be alone there."

Inside the storeroom of the kitchen, by the light of a candle, Sjam read aloud the letter from Immigration:

> "We would like to inform you that your application for four months visa prolongation could not be given. Prepare your departure for Jakarta and then straight abroad.
>
> "(*signed*) Ngamino Woeriohatmodjo"

Sjam ripped open the envelope on the other letter and read:

> "Based on the news sent to the Governor of West Irian in Jayapura, on February 5, 1973, we would like to request Miss Wyn Sargent to visit the Immigration office in Jayapura.
>
> "(*signed*) Acting Bupati S. H. Gultom"

"That's funny," Sjam said. "The immigration letter asking you to get out immediately is dated *before* the Bupati's letter where he asks you to chat."

"Maybe they've had a change of heart."

"No," Sjam said, rubbing the corners of her mouth with her thumb and index finger. "They want to cover something up."

One letter contradicted the other.

"How much do you think the government knows, Sjam?"

"Well, everyone in the Baliem Valley has received letters from you."

"Do you think the government knows we've been photographing the evidence of their brutality?"

"God only knows, Wyn."

"I'll tell Mi Hijo to send for Obaharok," I said.

The *pilai* was filled with people. I asked Mi Hijo to come out into the courtyard.

"Mi Hijo, please get a message to Obaharok to come to Opagima. It's urgent."

Mi Hijo stepped outside the *thop.* I waited until the bird calls began and then I returned to the kitchen.

"Wyn," Sjam said without looking up, "if they know about the photography, we're dead."

"We'll play dumb, then." I felt the blood pounding in my temples.

Sjam threw her head back. "That won't help," she said, half laughing. "Don't you understand the government by now?"

Mi Hijo stuck his head into the kitchen and looked up into the storeroom. "What's the matter, Ma?"

"Mi Hijo," I said, "the government wants to talk to me in Jayapura."

"Will you come back?"

"I don't know, my son."

(26)

Obaharok arrived in Opagima at six o'clock in the morning.

Kolo was with him. Both chiefs had heard the bird calls and had responded to them. They'd met each other on the footpath and walked to Opagima together.

"When do you leave?" Obaharok asked.

"As soon as I get my things packed."

"Will you take everything with you?"

"No, only my personal things. Everything else, the sleeping bags, blankets, food and supplies can stay in the houses."

"We'll bring everything to Opagima. I want to close up the *pilai*. No one will be allowed to enter it until you return. Wali can guard it."

Kolo left to supervise the emptying of the Analaga house. Kelion and Walek, who had spent the night in Wali's *pilai*, left with Mi Hijo to pack up the Wiyagoba house.

"I need clean clothes," I said to Sjam. "My other shirt and pants are in Wiyagoba.

"I think they're clean," Sjam said. "Talago has probably washed them."

"I've got a pack of exposed film and one camera in Analaga. I hope they bring everything."

In trying to get things together, everything suddenly seemed terribly strewn out. When our goods came in from Wiyagoba we tried to give them away. The people refused to take anything. Even the children could not be talked into accepting a flashlight or a lump of sugar.

Kolo and his men returned from Analaga about four o'clock. Sjam and I dug into the boxes, found the camera and film and repacked the cartons. Then we opened them again and looked at the things one more time, just to have something to do. We worked to escape thinking. We worked until after dark. And finally we could work no more.

Exhausted, Sjam and I crawled into the *pilai*. The house was filled with people. They moved a little to make room for us. I looked at the Dani faces around me. Kelion, Kolo, Walek, Obaharok, Mi Hijo, Sike, Osuan, Wali, Abinyai, Ilumunkuluk.

Wimbilu, Talago, Wagaga, Niren, Kaok. They were all there.

"Mama Wyn," Obaharok said, holding a handful of pigtails in front of me, "these are from the pigs that were killed to honor the *maweh*. Please count them and write down the names of the chiefs who gave the pigs."

Obaharok lined up the little tails, side by side, on the floor. I counted them. Twenty-five. Twenty-five pigs slaughtered by people who'd accepted me into their society. I felt tears coming and fought to choke them back. I yearned to do some tremendous thing for them, something to let them know how much they meant to me.

"Obaharok, if I don't return by this day"—I bent my fingers to indicate nine days—"please give everything in this *pilai* to your people. Then remain in the jungle for a while. You will not be safe here."

Obaharok looked at me with eyes that were rimmed red with fatigue. He was a man who knew better than to talk about miracles, but he wanted to believe we would return within the week.

"I have made a pig sacrifice in Hiyasi. Nothing can stop your feet from returning!" he said.

Obaharok bowed his head in deep thought. When he raised his face, a look of anguish had stolen over it.

"There is a traitor among us," he said softly.

Sjam and I looked at each other. Neither of us knew whom Obaharok meant. I wondered if he knew about Sunaryo.

An enormous wave of sadness washed over the room and the Dani began to cry. Each man cried alone, individually. I'd never seen that before.

Kolo wept openly, unashamedly. Sometimes his shoulders jerked up and down at the end of a sob.

Kelion held up his head, looking straight ahead, the tears rolling down his black cheeks.

Mi Hijo was whimpering in the corner. He sounded like a puppy that had been badly hurt.

Obaharok sat like a half-melted man in the crowd of weeping Dani. He remained motionless through the night, his head bent forward, staring down.

(27)

With the coming of morning, light entered the doorway of the *pilai*. I looked at the Dani faces around me and saw the hundreds of cigarette stubs that lined the fireplace. We filed out of the *pilai* into a day that felt dead.

"Seal up the *pilai*," Obaharok said.

Sike and Mi Hijo boarded the entrance together.

Kolo sat down on a log near one of the *abiais*, trying to get used to the thing. Obaharok climbed over the fence between the *pilai* and the kitchen and left. When he returned, he stood in the gateway, motionless. Some of the men started off in the direction of the river. Mi Hijo said they were going to cover their bodies with clay.

"If you can't stay, then take us with you!" Kelion said.

I promised them I would come back.

I looked at Obaharok and Kolo. None of us had the kind of courage it takes to smile. Walek and Kelion were standing together in the middle of the courtyard, and I looked at them. I looked at Mi Hijo standing at the *thop* with the other Dani who were waiting to walk to Wamena with us. And I took a long, last look at the village.

I turned and climbed through the entrance.

Opagima looked after us and watched us go.

I felt like a stiff mechanical person and I couldn't feel my feet touch the ground. There was a salty taste in my mouth and a hard knot in my stomach.

When we made the first turn in the path, we stopped and looked back. Opagima was gone from sight.

Ear-splitting screams suddenly ripped through the jungle air. The screams came from the men and women in Opagima. I closed my eyes and envisioned the people cutting their ears and fingers.

"Oh God, they don't have any medicine! We've got to go back and stop that!" I cried. Sjam and Mi Hijo threw their arms around me.

"Ma, they'd only do it later. You can't stop them," Mi Hijo said.

The world whirled dizzily. I closed my eyes.

Chief Hulolik was standing where the footpaths intersected near Aikima. His head was bent down and his hands hung at his sides. Sjam took off her red fur hat and placed it on his head. Hulolik never looked up. We left him standing there, his head bowed.

(28)

An attendant at the police post checked us out of Wamena. There were no officials around. Sunaryo, Marpaung, the Bupati and the military commander were in Jayapura.

Kusupia, Inyomosi and Huseroba were still locked up in the jailhouse. We asked to see them. The attendant said he didn't have a key.

"The Merpati plane is waiting for you at the airfield," the attendant muttered and walked away. That was unusual. Merpati never waited for anyone.

At the airstrip we gave the copilot our tickets and climbed aboard. We were the only passengers on the plane. We fastened our seat belts and listened to the engines whoop up a bronchial clatter, then clear and catch. The twin propellers spun and we lifted off the runway. Clouds moved over the Valley. We circled up and through the fleecy puffs into the blue above.

The pilot looked back through the cockpit door and smiled. It was not a friendly smile.

We disembarked at Sentani Airport and walked into the ticket office. Everyone stared at us. I looked down at my clothes. My trousers and shirt seemed a little worn but they were clean. Sjam was dressed in clothes like mine.

We caught a taxi into Jayapura and arrived at the Hotel Pautan at about four o'clock in the afternoon. The clerk at the desk informed us there were no vacancies. No one was in the lobby; the dining room was empty. Sjam and I exchanged glances but said nothing.

Trouble wears the clothes no one ever mistakes. There was plenty of it in Jayapura.

"Something's going on," Sjam said. "Come on, let's get this cab."

The driver drove us down the main street of Jayapura without receiving directions from either of us.

"Look," he said, "there's only one place you girls can get a place to stay. It's down this road a bit. It's not much, but at least it's a room."

"What's going on?" Sjam asked.

"Well, there's been a lot of publicity about you." The driver nodded in my direction. "They say you're a spy. Is that true?"

"A spy for *whom*?"

"For the United Nations!" the man said, peeking at me out of the corner of his eye.

The cabdriver let us out in front of a dingy waterfront rooming house. We walked up a flight of stairs and found the manager sweeping out one of the tiny rooms. He let us have it for twenty dollars a day, in advance. He said the bathroom was at the end of the hall.

·We went downstairs, found a restaurant and walked in. It was like facing a jury. The place was crowded with people and all of them were staring at us. Seated at a corner table was a young couple. When we entered they put down their rice spoons and walked out of the restaurant.

We sat down at the first unoccupied table we came to. The waiter, speaking to us at a distance, said the restaurant was closing; there would be no more food service until tomorrow. Sjam and I left the restaurant. Three men passed us and went in to sit down at the same table we'd left. We stood outside and watched them place their orders for dinner.

"Go on back to the room, Wyn. I'll buy some bread or something."

That night I wrote a letter to Jmy. It was nearly four months since I'd written him. I wrote two more letters to friends back home.

In the morning I stood on the streetcorner while Sjam went inside the post office. She had a feeling the letters would be confiscated if the authorities knew they were from me. She was right; they were confiscated.

At eight-thirty in the morning we walked to the immigration office. We arrived before the building opened its door. We hung around and waited for something to happen. At nine o'clock a janitor unlocked the front door. We went into the lobby and sat down by a table loaded with old Indonesian newspapers.

Sjam picked up *General Cendrawasih,* a newspaper published in Jayapura. There was a picture of me and Obaharok on the front page. It had been taken the day we met with Sunaryo. We were standing in front of Sunaryo's house. Obaharok looked terribly naked and I appeared rather overdressed.

"My God!" Sjam exclaimed. "This is awful! This paper says you're an *anthropologist,* running *naked* in the jungle and performing a *sexual* survey on the primitive Stone Age people of the Baliem Valley!"

"Please come in." The immigration officer was holding the door open for us. He was wearing a gray Mao-styled uniform. He was very thin.

We sat around a table that had been placed to one side of the room. The officer leaned back and tipped his chair against the wall, hooking the heels of his shoes over the lower rung. He pressed his fingertips together, took a deep breath and spoke the piece he'd memorized. He stared directly at Sjam the whole time. He never looked at me, not even once.

"I apologize for the news articles," he began. "We must forgive each other after we solve this misunderstanding. You will please write a report which shall include three points. First, your purpose for being in West Irian. Second, your method of research. Third, the purpose of your marriage. Deliver the report to me tomorrow. That's all. Good day."

Sjam and I walked out of his office. The officer yelled at us before we reached the outside door.

"I would strongly advise you not to talk to the press," he said and disappeared into his office.

Sjam grabbed some of the newspapers on the table before we left the building. On the way back we bought a loaf of bread and some strawberry jam. Inside the room, Sjam read some of the news articles aloud. They described me as a highly undesirable person, one who had married Obaharok for the sole purpose of sexual research.

"I liked it better when they accused me of being a spy," I said. "Sjam, August Perangkuan knew this gossip was going on and he never said a word about it to us. I wonder why?"

"Wyn, what day did you write that letter to Sunaryo?"

"To sue him for trying to force me to register the *maweh* marriage? January seventeenth."

"What day did Sunaryo come to Jayapura?"

"January nineteenth."

"The date on this Jayapura newspaper is January twenty-first. That was nearly three weeks ago."

"Let's get the editor of that newspaper and set the record straight," I said.

Sjam called the editor of *General Cendrawasih*. She also called Antara, the Indonesian internal wire service. We talked to both of them in the afternoon. We asked them why they had published stories without checking their sources. Neither of the men had an answer.

General Cendrawasih never published our story. We were to learn the results of our interview with Antara later.

I wanted to talk to Brigadier General Acub Zainal, who had enthusiastically supported our expedition from the start. I thought maybe he could help us. He was out of town.

Then we went to the Governor's Palace. The governor was "not in." We left a written request for an audience with him.

Back in the room I wrote the report requested by the immigration officer:

My purpose in West Irian, as a photojournalist, is to photograph and write a book about the customs, traditions, arts and culture of the Baliem Valley people. My method of survey is to gather information by living with the people in their villages and to observe, photograph and record their culture as it transpires. Hopefully the final work will be an important contribution to the country of Indonesia by providing the citizens with a better understanding of her primitive people. The marriage to Obaharok'was performed for the express purpose of uniting three enemy tribes in peace and friendship; to create a greater friendship between America and Indonesia; to bring the primitive mountain people into Wamena to learn about the economy, the educational opportunities and to acquaint them with the local Government structure. The marriage is non-functional.

February 9, 1973

There was a knock on the door. Sjam opened it. A tall man stuck his head inside and looked around.

"Is everything all right, Miss Sargent?"

I nodded.

The man shut the door and left.

"Who was that?"

"*Intelligence*," Sjam said. "There's more involved here than just the bad stories Sunaryo's spread around."

We choked down a strawberry-jam sandwich and tried to sleep, but without much success.

(29)

The intelligence officer was standing outside the rooming house in the morning. He followed us all the way to the immigration office.

Inside I gave the immigration officer my report. He received it without looking at me.

"Miss Sargent," he said, his eyes again fixed on Sjam, "I talked with the acting governor last night. I will see him again this morning. Marriage in the Baliem Valley is new to us and we must study it further. We hope for a good result. Please meet me at the police station this afternoon at one o'clock. Good day."

The intelligence man followed us as we trudged back to our

room. At noon a letter from the Governor's Palace was delivered. It was brought by the intelligence man. The letter stated the acting governor's refusal to see me.

At one o'clock we met the immigration officer at the police station. We also met the commander in chief of police. I was so upset at being in such a place that I scarcely remember what the man looked like.

The commander said there could be no prolongation of my visa because I did not have a letter from LIPI (Indonesian Institute for Scientific Research) to support the "scientific research" I was doing. The letter of support could be obtained only in Jakarta, and a cable or telephone call to the institute would not do. I would have to go to Jakarta and arrange for the letter myself. The commander dismissed the meeting and left the room. The immigration officer said he would arrange our departure for Monday morning.

Sjam and I walked back to our room.

"Well, the police have asked me to apply to an institution to which I'm not eligible for a letter they know I can't get. What are we going to do?"

Sjam left the room. She returned with more newspapers and said she'd been talking to some of the local people. It didn't take her long to figure out what had happened.

After Sunaryo tried to force me to register the traditional village wedding with the Indonesian government and I threatened to sue him, he had flown to Jayapura, where he cooked up detrimental stories about me. He released them to the newspapers in the hope that he could avoid the lawsuit. Sunaryo intended to have me declared a *persona non grata* who would subsequently be asked to leave the country. When the stories were published, Antara sent them on to Jakarta.

The central government in Jakarta, however, was suspicious of the stories. On January 25 the Department of Social Affairs ordered an investigation to get at the truth of the situation. The Jakarta police advised the police chief in Jayapura to alert Police Chief Marpaung in Wamena to conduct the investigation.

Meanwhile Marpaung had found himself embarrassed by the

presence of Kusupia, Inyomosi and Huseroba in his Wamena jailhouse, proof of the existing police brutality in the Baliem Valley. Marpaung, in order to cover up the horrendous torturing inflicted upon the Dani people by his policemen, had no choice but to support Sunaryo's untrue stories.

The presence of the intelligence officer in Jayapura, however, gave Sjam and me reason enough to believe that the Jakarta central government had remained unconvinced about the truth of the police report.

"When that investigation order came through," Sjam said, "Marpaung must have been scared. It wouldn't surprise me if he'd ordered Kadir and Sitmoran to kill you, just to get rid of the whole problem."

Sjam pulled at a frayed corner of the handkerchief she held in her hands. "Wyn," she whispered, leaning forward a little, "if Intelligence learns that you've photographed and documented any evidence *against* the government, we'll both be arrested."

(30)

Sunday came, and with it our flight reservations.

Early Monday morning the immigration officer arrived in his green truck. He took us to Sentani Airport.

When we landed on the Biak airstrip, Immigration put us on a connecting flight to Jakarta. It was a flight no one even knew existed.

As soon as we touched down in Jakarta the police surrounded the airplane. They were dressed in plain clothes. The police took us to a little room behind "baggage." They said the airport was jammed with members of the press.

The police asked me where we wanted to spend the night. They put us into an unpainted car and gave the driver the address. The reporters and journalists tore after us in a mad chase through the Jakarta streets. When we arrived, the police told us to "hide tomorrow" and report to Immigration on the morning of the following day.

In the morning a friend brought us three weeks of newspaper clippings.

"Do you want to hear what Antara wired from Jayapura after our interview?" Sjam asked. "Antara reported from Jayapura recently that the denial of Miss Sargent's visa was mainly based on the consideration that her activities in West Irian would be harmful to the implementation of central and regional government schemes for the civilization of isolated tribes."

I hardly heard what Sjam said. I was thinking about Jmy. "I'd like to telephone Jmy. I wonder what time it is in America."

"It's yesterday. I'll place an order for the call," Sjam said.

I picked up a stack of clippings and began to read through them. The papers carried the same picture of Obaharok and me in front of Sunaryo's house.

"They'll call back when they get the line through. Be careful what you say on the phone. I think it's bugged." Sjam's voice had lowered to a nearly inaudible whisper. "I wonder if this room's bugged, too," she said, looking around at the furniture and at the sideboards of the wall.

Sjam sat down on the sofa and picked up a newspaper. "Good God!" she said. "Reuter, UPI and AP have translated all this crap and sent it out over the world wires! A reporter has interviewed Jmy. He's quoted as saying it's true that you married a cannibal chief."

"How could he confirm such a thing, Sjam? He doesn't even know about it."

I wondered what it would be like for Jmy to read the slanderous things that were being said about his mother.

"In this paper," Sjam said, "Jmy says, 'My mom knows what she's doing.'"

That sounded like Jmy, like something he'd say. And no mother ever felt as proud of a son as I did in that moment.

The telephone rang. It was Jmy. No, he hadn't confirmed any marriage and yes, he thought I knew what I was doing.

Sjam was right; the telephone was bugged. I could hear the man breathing into the phone as he listened to the conversation. He even coughed at one point.

(31)

February 14, 1973. My birthday. It was also the day we were scheduled to visit Immigration in Jakarta. We called for a taxi. The newspaper reporters were outside. When the taxi arrived and the gate opened, the reporters flooded the front yard. A few of them broke into the house with cameras flashing.

The immigration officer wore a khaki uniform with braid on the shoulders and brass buttons down the front. His mustache was neatly trimmed above a mouth that never stopped smiling, not even when he smoked his gold-tipped cigarettes. He puffed on them through smiling lips.

"Miss Wyn Sargent," he said, "do you have your return airplane ticket to the United States?"

"Yes."

"You will please give me the ticket."

I gave the officer my airplane ticket.

"You will please give me your passport and your papers and your visa," he said.

I gave him my passport, my papers and my visa.

"Miss Wyn Sargent," he said, smiling, "your visa has run out. I must ask you to leave my country. You will leave on Saturday, February seventeenth, at seven o'clock in the morning on Pan American Airlines to Hong Kong. Please return here on Friday. I will give you your flight reservation and return your passport to you. Meanwhile, do not talk to the press. You piloted a Russian TU-104 in Kiev once, didn't you? Oh yes— Happy Birthday, Miss Wyn Sargent!"

I wondered how they knew I had been to Russia. Apparently

their investigation had been more than just following Sjam and me around Jayapura and Jakarta.

I also wondered why I couldn't go home right away. Immigration was purposely detaining me for seventy-two hours. This delay in my departure was the first hint that perhaps I couldn't get out of Indonesia at all.

Immigration released an interesting story for the afternoon papers. The news stated that my visa extension had been refused because Immigration did not know why I wanted to stay longer.

The following day the papers were filled with new charges. I was accused of mining uranium in the Baliem Valley and inciting warfare between the native tribes.

There were demonstrations outside the house. The people were demanding my deportment. We had to find someplace to live until Saturday. We packed our things, called a cab and sped to the outskirts of the city. The driver looked through the neighborhood for the address we'd given him. In searching, he braked the car a good deal. The car shot forward at one point and a tape recorder slipped out from under the front seat. It slid between Sjam's feet. The reels were going around. Sjam kicked the recorder back under the seat. She mouthed a word to me: "Intelligence!"

When I found a tiny microphone wired to the bedsprings in our new room, Sjam and I began to live in a state of real fear. We knew that Intelligence was trying to verify their suspicions that we'd discovered something in the Baliem Valley that would be prejudicial to the country of Indonesia.

Sjam and I began to work toward one final goal: to get me safely out of Indonesia. Everything we did was aimed at that end. When we talked to each other, we spoke Dani, and when that ran dry we spoke in whispers with lips placed against the other's ear. And we became experts at sign language.

On Friday we went to Immigration to collect my passport and flight reservation. The same official was waiting for us at his desk.

(32)

Indonesian intelligence had taped us and watched our every move in Jakarta for four days and four nights. Friday evening they finally came to interrogate us themselves.

Two burly-looking men showed up at the house, flashed their credentials and began their questioning. They didn't ask us what we did in the Baliem Valley; they wanted to know what we saw there. When they found our answers unsatisfactory, they asked me to hand over my film to them. I told them the film was not mine, it was the property of my publishers, and if they touched it, they would be in trouble with the international copyright laws. I didn't know what I was talking about, but they didn't either. Could I develop it, then, and show them the pictures? No, the rule applied to the development of the film as well. They asked to see my journal. I refused them on the same grounds.

One of the men said, "Well, I guess the truth will all come out in about one year, then?"

"What do you mean?"

"You intend to write a book, don't you?"

I told him I planned on writing a book.

"I warn you, Miss Sargent, say nothing against the Indonesian government!" he said.

An hour after the men had left, we received a reliable tip that my film and journal were to be confiscated by Intelligence at customs the next day.

Sjam and I spent the rest of the night with an underground network which dealt in smuggling. We left the exposed film and the journal with them. And we prayed that someday the material would arrive in America.

(33)

On the morning of February 17, 1973, I got ready to go to the airport to board a plane that would take me out of Indonesia.

I had no dress to wear and not even a skirt. I put on the best of my two pairs of trousers and the cleanest shirt. My boots were polished, but my hair was still dirty. There'd been no water in Jayapura to wash it. I hadn't had time in Jakarta. Well, I'd wear my hat over it.

There was a strand of blue beads around my neck. I'd worn it during our entire stay in the Baliem Valley. Mi Hijo had tied the beads there seemingly long ago. The knot was tight and I asked Sjam to untie it for me.

I'd held back nine rolls of exposed film from the smuggling team. I couldn't go home without trying every way to keep some kind of proof that this nightmare had actually happened. I dropped two rolls in one boot, three in the other and put the other rolls inside my underwear.

I broke the seals on the fresh film cartridges and scattered them around in my suitcases. They appeared to be exposed film. I placed handwritten French and German lessons in my empty journal binder and hoped the customs people couldn't read. I closed the suitcases. I was ready to go.

Sjam and I made a pact about how we would act at the airport. Certainly there would be reporters there. They would see us and hear everything we said. We promised each other we'd shake hands and say good-bye and smile. There'd be no hugging, no promises to write, and especially, no tears.

The drive to the airport was a long one. The police were ahead of us and Immigration followed.

When we arrived the press was everywhere. I was checked into the airlines and steered into customs, where my suitcases were opened. The customs official looked over the contents, took out a handful of unexposed film and closed the suitcases himself.

I passed through a metal detector device. Bleeps sounded. I remembered the concentration of metal film cartridges in my boots and underwear. I showed the attending officer my heavy metal wristwatch. He was satisfied and let me through.

Sjam went into the boarding area with me, where the press was not allowed to enter. We sat down on a bench and struggled to hold back the tears—tears of a bitter experience, tears of relief, and tears of good-bye.

A young reporter suddenly bolted through the line of pressmen and came toward us. The intelligence men grabbed him. When the reporter stopped struggling, the men released their hold.

"Miss Sargent," the reporter said, "I'm sorry we gave you a bad name. I'm really sorry. I apologize on behalf of Indonesia. It's our own fault, not yours. We want the truth now. We already know some. We know we have been wrong. Please forgive us."

I wanted to thank the reporter for his words but the intelligence officer was staring at me fiercely. I kept quiet.

A voice boomed over the loud speaker. It was time to go, time to say good-bye to Sjam, smile at Sjam and shake her hand. We stood up and walked to the door.

I turned and faced Sjam without seeing her. I smiled and shook her hand out of sheer determination. I heard her say, "Bye," and I remembered to echo the same farewell. And then I turned and walked out on the long strip of asphalt to the waiting airplane.

The sun burned the asphalt with its hot rays. The *sun!* Dani communication. I stopped walking and raised my arms toward the sun, crossed my right hand over my left and placed the palms together.

"Good-bye, Dani people. Someday I will return. I promise."

(34)

I wondered who would meet me at the Los Angeles International Airport. Besides the reporters, journalists, newsmen and photographers, there were three special people.

There was Jmy, whose words "My Mom knows what she's doing!" had brought me through my blackest hour.

There was Jeannie, my roommate at college who had unhesitatingly offered to take care of the house and cook for Jmy while I was gone.

And there was Dr. Robert Harold Schuller, pastor of the Garden Grove Community Church, who with his wife had come to the airport to extend a hand of Christian love to the controversial "cannibal queen."

(35)

Some rather unexpected things happened as a result of the stories that were released from Jakarta. One of them was that nearly everyone received the impression that I had wanted the publicity. There were some pitiful things following the unpleasant stories, too. The parents of one of Jmy's friends denied him entrance to their house because of his "mother's reputation." That act was heartbreaking to me.

I scarcely slept during the whole month it took for my film and journal to arrive. And I worried constantly about Sjam.

There was a magazine in Indonesia called *Tempo*. The editor had never published a word about me. On an impulse I mailed him a report on the brutality in the Baliem Valley and a series of photographs to support the document. A couple of months later Sjam telephoned me.

"Wyn, *Tempo* published your report and pictures! The photograph of you with the police-beaten native in Wamena is on the cover. Your name has been cleared in Indonesia and my situation is better too."

That editor earned the right to march up to the heavens one day and take his place among the stars.

I received some interesting mail. One letter arrived from Holland. It began: "Will you testify for us?" The letter was written by the Secretary-General of the High Court of Representatives of West New Guinea (West Irian.) So, West Irian had a Papuan government in exile!

Enclosed was an assortment of petitions to the United Nations protesting the way the Act of Free Choice had been carried out in West Irian in 1969. Enclosed, also, was a copy of Mr. Fernando Ortiz-Sanz's report to the Secretary-General of the United Nations (see Appendix). Mr. Ortiz-Sanz was the United Nations Representative who had been sent to Indonesia to participate in the election that would decide whether the Papuans of West Irian wanted to remain with Indonesia or sever their ties and become a Free Papuan State.

It was agreed that the United Nations would guarantee the rights and freedoms of the Papuan people during the election.

When Mr. Ortiz-Sanz was finally allowed into West Irian to begin his job, in August 1968, he found demonstrations and riots protesting the tight political control the Indonesian government held over the population. Many Papuan people were shooting at the Indonesian troops, while others were fleeing to the Australian side of the island.

Mr. Ortiz-Sanz was bombarded with petitions from the Papuans asking for the release of their political detainees. Other petitions pleaded with him to fully guarantee their rights to vote without pressure from the Indonesian government.

It wasn't long before Mr. Ortiz-Sanz learned that the Indonesian *musjawarah* was to be used in the election rather than the universally accepted "one man, one vote" system. The news was upsetting.

And then he discovered that many areas had already "voted" without the presence of the UN observers. He promptly asked for "fresh voting" in at least the most important areas. His request was granted only in part.

Mr. Ortiz-Sanz tried to guarantee the Papuan people their rights of free speech, freedom of movement and of assembly. But he couldn't do it.

On June 10, 1969, he flew to Jakarta to appeal for help from President Suharto. The President was so busy that he could not receive Mr. Ortiz-Sanz until August 12, ten days *after* the completion of the Act of Free Choice.

Indonesia obviously illegally occupied the territory of West Irian when the United Nations failed to guarantee the rights of the Papuan people.

I felt shame that such a thing could happen. I thought about Kusupia, Inyomosi and Huseroba in the Wamena jail and about the others who had been brutalized by the Indonesians. Clearly, the maltreatment of these indigenous people was a result of the Act of Free Choice.

I thought about Kelion, Kolo, Walek and Obaharok and all the people who followed them. They were a people who wanted to be free. And now they were prisoners on their own land.

While reading Mr. Ortiz-Sanz's report, I kept thinking that the people in the free world should know about the sad plight of the Papuan people. But how could their story be told? The Papuans in West Irian have no voice in the outside world. I wondered if I could tell it. Well, I could try.

I walked into my office and closed the door. I sat down at my desk, put a new ribbon in the typewriter and began to write:

"This book is written for Kelion and Kolo, for Walek and Obaharok, and for all the people who followed them. . . ."

APPENDIX

Report of the Secretary-General regarding the act of self-determination in West Irian
A/7723
6 November 1969

[excerpts]
26. I assumed my duties as the United Nations Representative on 1 April 1968 . . .
27. . . . Despite my willingness and readiness to travel to the territory immediately after my appointment, my departure was postponed until 7 August 1968 at the official request of the Indonesian Government.
11. I must state at the outset of this report that, when I arrived in the territory in August 1968, I was faced with the problem of non-compliance with the provisions of article XVI of the Agreement. Though the United Nations experts who were to have remained in the territory at the time of the transfer of full administrative responsibility to Indonesia had been designated, they had never, owing to well known circumstances, taken up their duties . . .
84. . . . The consultative assemblies would not reach a decision through voting but through *musjawarah* which, as explained at that meeting, consisted in reaching a "decision based on discussion, understanding and knowledge of a problem."
114. When . . . some elections took place without the presence of United Nations observers, I went so far as to suggest the holding of fresh elections in some of the more important places in order to stress the importance of the eligibility of all adults to participate in them.
144. . . . Many petitions requested our mission to take steps or measures clearly beyond our terms of reference, such as the withdrawal of Indonesian armed forces to be replaced by

United Nations security forces, the taking over of the administration of the territory by the United Nations, the guaranteeing
by the United Nations of proper rights and freedoms for the
population, and so on. All of them, however, advocated the
severance of ties with Indonesia and the establishment of a
Free Papuan State.

160. The leaders of the insurgents requested the withdrawal of
Indonesian troops from Paniai with the explanation that the
people wanted to exercise the right of free choice without pressure. A government plane brought reinforcements of sixteen soldiers, and on 30 April shooting started between the Indonesian
troops and the insurgents aided by the armed police deserters.

162. On 1 May the insurgents hoisted their flag at Enarotali and
on 3 May the appeal for the withdrawal of Indonesian troops
was repeated and the United Nations Representative's assist-
ance in the withdrawal requested. The answer given by the
Military Commander was that the withdrawal of troops was a
matter for the Army to decide and that the United Nations
Representative had nothing to do with it.

180. Notwithstanding the fairly negative result achieved up to
that time, I continued my efforts to have article XXII* properly
implemented. At a meeting at the Ministry of Foreign Affairs
on 24 May, I said that the problem of the full implementation
of article XXII concerning rights and freedoms had to be dealt
with because, up to that time, no concrete measures had been
adopted. I suggested that the Indonsian Government should
allow the opposition the opportunity to express its views, since
that was the moment to adopt courageous and generous measures.

181. In a conversation with the Minister for Foreign Affairs
on 30 May, I pressed for concrete measures in regard to this
and other outstanding questions.

182. In a last attempt to have article XXII of the Agreement
properly implemented, I asked, on 10 June 1969, for an audience with the President of the Republic of Indonesia, General
Suharto. Owing to his heavy schedule of work, the President
could not receive me before 12 August, ten days after the completion of the act of free choice, so that I did not have the opportunity of making my appeal regarding the implementation
of the basic rights and freedoms of the population of West
Irian to the highest office of the Republic.

249. It can be seen from my report that United Nations observers were able to attend the election of 20 per cent of the
total membership of the consultative assemblies. . . .

250. The petitions opposing annexation to Indonesia, the cases of unrest in Manokwari, Enarotali and Waghete, the flight of a number of people to the part of the island that is administered by Australia, and the existence of political detainees, more than 300 of whom were released at my request, show that without doubt certain elements of the population of West Irian held firm convictions in favour of independence. . . .

251. I regret to have to express my reservation regarding the implementation of article XXII of the Agreement, relating to "the rights, including the rights of free speech, freedom of movement and of assembly, of the inhabitants of the area."* In spite of my constant efforts, this important provision was not fully implemented and the Administration exercised at all times a tight political control over the population.

---

* Article XXII (Agreement Between The Republic of Indonesia and The Kingdom of The Netherlands Concerning West New Guinea, August 15, 1962.) "The UNTEA and Indonesia will guarantee fully the rights including the rights of free speech, freedom of movement and of assembly of the inhabitants of the area."

GLOSSARY

Dani

abarek	spear that has killed a man
abiai	women's house
anekuku	flower petals used in medicine
aniekekoen	leaves used for bandages
apelagap	leaves used in medicine
apemakelok	fork
bapaweka	vegetable
beka	leaves (medicinal)
buen	orchid fibers
cabanee	native bird found in West Irian; feathered headdress
chimo	hardwood
cuscus	opossum
Dani	indigenous people of the Baliem Valley
dipik	running circle during *etai*
egenbpuga	leaves used for bandages
el	sugar cane
etai	victory dance
haki	banana
hakiloma	compound garden
hano	all right; good
hanom	tobacco
hariken	decorations on *wesa* stones
heik	roots used in medicine
hela	spinach
helekirikare	cremation ritual
hetali	sap, burned to clear air
hipere, hiperi	sweet potato(es)
hiperica	vegetable that looks like fern
holim	tubular gourd used as penis sheath
hom	taro

honnaboen	funeral shell strands
Houtdogon!	"Wait!"
hum	leaves used for bandages
hunike	running back and forth during *etai*
hunila	kitchen
ilko	death ceremony
isatare	ritual pig cooking
jabee	buttock leaf
jawi	leaves used in medicine
kaa	leaves for bandages
kain	overlord
kanake	religious feast; also refers to religious objects
kayo	watchtower
kebee	spinach
kelok	leaves used to cure dysentery
kem	grass
kepu	poor man
kiloe	cucumber
kipie-kipie	spinach
kud	halo worn by men
Laok	"Hello," used between man and woman
Lu!	"Go!"
lukwaka	grass
malikeb	wild raspberries
maweh	marriage ritual
mikak	large cymbium shell necklace
mileh	digging stick
mokat	ghost
mokat aku	small bridge in garden (for ghost)
mol	rattan
moli-moli	wild nuts
molin	spinach
murikaka	spiderweb necklace
nagot	sister
Narak	"Hello," used between men
nassa	snail shells
Nayit	"No"
Nen	"Yes"
nibie	spinach
Nocksu	"Hello," used between women
noken	carrying net
nyawak	boar tusks used as decoration
oak	wooden cremation box
oeka	leaves used in medicine

omaken	roots used in medicine
pain	yam
pawih	leaves used in medicine
pemut	white limestone chalk
pia	funeral chair
pikkon	bamboo harp
pilai	warriors' house
poel	digging stick
pupalep	insect nest
sege	spear used by men
sigi-sigi	water gourd
sigogo wasin	"kill the hoop" game
sike	bow
silo	danger sign made of grass and sticks
sin	tree
soa	vegetable
sowa	vegetable
suap	five-pronged arrow
teboe teboe	spear used by children
tege	digging stick
tekan	wrist and upper-arm band worn by men
thali	single girl's skirt
thop	entrance to a village
thuelaga	stick filled with bird feathers
tipats	dried pig testicles worn as decorations
topo	arrow with hard wooden ball at end
towa	vegetable
Ukeemay!	"Enter!"
uma	house
umain	intertribal feudal war
urai	specie of orchid fibers
uwe namet mina	
pike	god
waganin	witch doctor
walimo	shells sewn together to form wide necklace
wamai	pigsty; pigpen
wamamo	pig fat
wamare	pigtails used as decoration
wampalin	bamboo knife
wamwariagai	ritual pig killing
wanepahut	kill song
warema	funeral ritual
warok	love, like, want
werrakkboak	colored beads

wesa	sacred; sometimes used to refer to stones
wieleh	digging stick
wietat	spinach
wim	arrow; also war
wip	wood bark used in medicine
yalie	pea-shaped berry
yen-yoko	cooperative group of men and women
yerak	funeral shell strands
yoh	tree
yokal	married woman's skirt
yoli	tree
yopo	necklace of fibers
yori	hardwood

Indonesian

Bahasa Indonesia	official language
biasa	commonplace
bupati	regent (title)
dandin	army
danres	police
Irian Barat	West Irian
koteka	penis sheath
musjawarah	consultations which lead to consensus
Selamat jalan	"Good-bye," "Good day"
Selamat pagi	"Good morning"

Village	Tribe	Chief
Hiyasi	Dogahilapok	Obaharok
Pabuma	Kosihilapok	Obaharok
Yumugima	Kosihilapok	Obaharok
Lunagima	Kosihilapok	Obaharok
Molapua	Kosihilapok	Obaharok
Mapilakma	Kosihilapok	Obaharok
Obasia	Iklai-Faluk	Kolo
Abulakma	Iklai-Faluk	Kolo
Analaga	Iklai-Faluk	Old Dialec
Jiwika	Dloko-Mabel & Dabimabel	Kurulu
Wiyagoba	Walilalua/Dloko-Mabel	Walek; Kelion
Opagima	Wililhiman	Wali
Tumagonem	Wililhiman	Asuan
Wenebuborah	Kosi	Winoco (Mi Hijo)
Punycul	Kosi	Sike
Aikima	Siepeloksa	Hulolik
Feratsilimo	Wililhiman	Wamdierick
Pumo	Witipoulua	Kusupia
Sekan	Dogahilapok	Hubi
Pikke	Siepeloksa	Kasare
Abukulmo	Wililhiman	Hanemoak
Elima	Walilalua	Milika

DISTRICTS

The territory of West Irian is divided into nine districts. Each district consists of thirty-four subdivisions and one hundred and fourteen subdistricts.

The following are the nine districts:

Jayapura
Biak
Manokwari
Sorong
Faktak
Paniay
Japenwaropen
Jayawijaya*
Merauke

---

* The Baliem Valley is located within Jayawijaya district.

ABOUT THE AUTHOR

WYN SARGENT is a photojournalist, a Quaker and head of the Sargent-Dyak Fund, which was established to help the people of Central Borneo (and about whom she wrote in *My Life with the Headhunters.*) She now lives in Huntington Beach, California, with her son, Jmy.

(continued from front flap)

trying to nationalize the Baliem Valley in much the same way as was done with the American Indian) were torturing and brutalizing the Dani.

She adopted a boy, and became a "blood brother" to one of the chiefs. She also realized that the reverence and attention the Dani gave her (they originally mistook her for a white *kain*—male overlord) could result in a coming together of the various warring tribes if she "married"—in name only—the most powerful chieftain.

But by this time she had collected a strong case against the Indonesian government. And it was then that she was ordered to leave.

People of the Valley is more than the record of a remarkable adventure. It is also the inspiring account of a humanitarian effort which revealed the kinship of people everywhere, no matter how different their way of life.

WYN SARGENT is a photo-journalist, a Quaker and head of the Sargent-Dyak Fund, which was established to help the people of Central Borneo (and about whom she wrote in *My Life with the Headhunters*). She now lives in Huntington Beach, California, with her son Jmy.

Random House, Inc., New York, N.Y. 10022
Publishers of the RANDOM HOUSE DICTIONARIES,
The Modern Library and Vintage Books
Printed in U.S.A.
11/74